Aotearoa New Zealand in the Global Theatre Marketplace

Aotearoa New Zealand in the Global Theatre Marketplace offers a case study of how the theatre of Aotearoa has toured, represented and marketed itself on the global stage. How has New Zealand work attempted to stand out, differentiate itself and get seen by audiences internationally?

This book examines the journeys of a dynamic range of culturally and theatrically innovative works created by Aotearoa New Zealand theatre makers that have toured and been performed across time, place and theatrical space: from Moana Oceania to the Edinburgh Festival Fringe, from a Māori Shakespeare adaptation to an immersive zombie theatre experience.

Drawing on postcolonialism, transnationalism, cosmopolitanism and globality to understand how Aotearoa New Zealand has imagined and conceived of itself through drama, the author investigates how these representations might be read and received by audiences around the world, variously reinforcing and complicating conceptions of New Zealand national identity. Developing concepts of theatrical mobility, portability and the market, this study engages with the whole theatrical enterprise as a play travels from concept and scripting through to funding, marketing, performance and the critical response by reviewers and commentators.

This book will be of global interest to academics, producers and theatre artists as a significant resource for the theory and practice of theatre touring and cross-cultural performance and reception.

James Wenley is a theatre academic, practitioner and critic with a passion for promoting the theatre of Aotearoa New Zealand. He was awarded a PhD from the University of Auckland and is a lecturer in the theatre programme of Te Herenga Waka—Victoria University of Wellington. James directs and produces for his company Theatre of Love. He is the editor and founder of TheatreScenes.co.nz, was a theatre critic for *Metro Magazine* and won the People's Choice Award for Best Critic at the 2015 Auckland Theatre Awards. His writing has been published in the *Journal of New Zealand Literature*, *Australasian Drama Studies*, *The Pantograph Punch* and *Playmarket Annual*.

Routledge Advances in Theatre and Performance Studies

For more information about this series, please visit: www.routledge.com/Routledge-Advances-in-Theatre--Performance-Studies/book-series/RATPS

Aotearoa New Zealand in the Global Theatre Marketplace

Travelling Theatre

James Wenley

Routledge
Taylor & Francis Group

LONDON AND NEW YORK

First published 2021
by Routledge
2 Park Square, Milton Park, Abingdon, Oxon OX14 4RN

and by Routledge
52 Vanderbilt Avenue, New York, NY 10017

Routledge is an imprint of the Taylor & Francis Group, an informa business

© 2021 James Wenley

The right of James Wenley to be identified as author of this work has been asserted by him in accordance with sections 77 and 78 of the Copyright, Designs and Patents Act 1988.

All rights reserved. No part of this book may be reprinted or reproduced or utilised in any form or by any electronic, mechanical, or other means, now known or hereafter invented, including photocopying and recording, or in any information storage or retrieval system, without permission in writing from the publishers.

Trademark notice: Product or corporate names may be trademarks or registered trademarks, and are used only for identification and explanation without intent to infringe.

British Library Cataloguing-in-Publication Data
A catalogue record for this book is available from the British Library

Library of Congress Cataloging-in-Publication Data
Names: Wenley, James, author.
Title: Aotearoa New Zealand in the global theatre
marketplace: travelling theatre / James Wenley.
Description: First edition. | Abington, Oxon; New York: Routledge, 2021. |
Series: Routledge advances in theatre and performance |
Includes bibliographical references and index.
Identifiers: LCCN 2020018859 | ISBN 9780367192020 (hardback) |
ISBN 9780429200991 (ebook)
Subjects: LCSH: Theater–New Zealand–History–20th century. |
New Zealand drama–20th century–History and criticism. |
Performing arts–Marketing.
Classification: LCC PN3014 .W46 2021 | DDC 792.0993–dc23
LC record available at https://lccn.loc.gov/2020018859

ISBN: 978-0-367-19202-0 (hbk)
ISBN: 978-0-429-20099-1 (ebk)

Typeset in Times New Roman
by Newgen Publishing UK

Contents

Illustrations

Figures

Maps

Images

Acknowledgements

Profound gratitude to my PhD supervisors, Murray Edmond and Rina Kim, and staff and colleagues from the University of Auckland's English, Drama and Writing Studies who supported me during my PhD studies, especially Tom Bishop, Emma Willis, Erin Carlston, Claudia Marquis, Selina Tusitala Marsh and Michelle Johansson.

Examiners Stuart Young and Diana Looser for their generous engagement with the thesis, whose comments have been invaluable in both clarifying and expanding the scope of my thesis for this book project.

Laura van Peer for the original proofreading assistance.

Murray Lynch, Salesi Le'ota and Playmarket staff for their continuous assistance and access to their Client Files.

Alexander Turnbull Library, Hocken Collections (University of Otago Library), Auckland Libraries, University of Auckland Special Collections and the J.C. Beaglehole Room (Victoria University) staff for their assistance with archival research.

All the practitioners who agreed to be interviewed for this research and share their knowledge: Stella Duffy, Charlie McDermott, Kip Chapman, Vela Manusaute, Justin Lewis, Deborah Hunt, Julia Croft, Sums Selvarajan, Rutene Spooner, Joel Baxendale, Tānemahuta Gray, Lydia Zanetti, Leo Gene Peters, Eleanor Congreve.

The Victoria University of Wellington Research Establishment Grant Committee for enabling me to conduct research in Edinburgh and to complete this book project.

Nina Joynson for hosting me in Edinburgh.

Research Assistant Zoë Christall for helping with the transcriptions and Amanda Grace Leo with indexing.

My Victoria University of Wellington theatre programme colleagues Sarah Thomasson and Nicola Hyland for feedback on chapters, and David O'Donnell, Lori Leigh, Megan Evans, Sean Coyle, Paul Tozer and Sam Tippett for their support.

Family, friends and students who kept me going.

Editor Laura Hussey, Swati Hindwan and the staff at Routledge and Rebecca Willford and the team at Newgen Publishing UK.

Some content in this book has been adapted from previously published material:

Wenley, James. 2019. "Playing the Edinburgh Lottery: Six Decades of New Zealand Theatre at the Edinburgh Festival Fringe". *Australasian Drama Studies*, 74: 161–188

——— 2020. "Indian Ink via New Zealand Inc.: Hybrid Exports for the Global Theatre Marketplace". *Journal of Postcolonial Writing*, 56 (2): 203–216

My thanks to Shutterstock, Carol Rosegg, Oliver Rosser, Red Leap Theatre, Indian Ink Theatre Company and Zanetti Productions for granting permission to publish their photographs.

Research approved in 2015 by the University of Auckland Human Participants Ethics Committee. Reference number 013152.

Research approved in 2019 by the Victoria University of Wellington Human Ethics Committee. Reference number 0000027863.

This is for the dream chasers, the identity shapers, the risk takers: the theatre makers.

Introduction

If someone were to ask you what you associate with the country Aotearoa New Zealand, what images, events and values would come to your mind? For people around the world, New Zealand will have particular meaning based on personal proximity and exposure, but some commonalities based on New Zealand's global image may emerge. You might identify New Zealand's geographical location in the South Pacific, at the "bottom of the world" – although the frequency of New Zealand's absence on world maps provoked a tongue-in-cheek campaign from Tourism New Zealand in 2018 to #getnzonthemap.[1] Aotearoa is the Indigenous Māori name for New Zealand, often translated as "the land of the long white cloud".[2] According to Māori mythology, the demigod Māui caught a giant fish which formed Te Ika-a-Māui (the North Island of New Zealand) and his waka (canoe) formed Te Waipounamu (the South Island). You might associate Aotearoa New Zealand with Māori culture, or the Indigenous haka famously performed at matches by national rugby team the All Blacks. You might make a connection with the colonisation of the country by the British settlers in the 19th century. There could also be associations with the country's environmentally conscious "clean and green" image and stunning natural scenery; a long-running international marketing campaign has branded New Zealand as "100% Pure", a rhetoric that overlooks the country's serious environmental challenges. There could be recognition of progressive politics, from the country's anti-nuclear stance in the 1980s through the nation's response, led by Prime Minister Jacinda Arden, to the white supremacist terror attack against two Christchurch Mosques in 2019.

In the past two decades the nation has also been indelibly tied with "Kiwi" (the name for the flightless bird that New Zealanders use as their own moniker) filmmaker Peter Jackson's *The Lord of the Rings* (2001–2003) and *The Hobbit* (2012–2014) trilogies. Visitors to the nation's capital Wellington were welcomed to "Middle of Middle-Earth" at the airport (and this Tolkien link continues with Amazon opting to film their *Lord of the Rings* television show in Auckland). Or you might associate the country with other films – *The Piano* (1993), *Once Were Warriors* (1994), *Whale Rider* (2002), even vampire-themed

What We Do in the Shadows (2014) – that have represented New Zealand culture to the globe.

This question of how Aotearoa New Zealand is perceived globally has been an acute concern for the nation's theatre makers desiring to have their plays performed overseas: would the world be interested in their work? Bruce Mason (1978), a foundational playwright in establishing a "homegrown" nationally oriented theatre in New Zealand, posed this question around what image New Zealand lights in the "world imagination"; his caustic conclusion was "sheep, probably, sunshine, dullness […]. No mythological droppings accrete to the name". Reviews of Aotearoa New Zealand theatre performed internationally provide some examples of the typical associations that have been made with the country, and how theatrical work can provide an alternative vantage point. When *Bare* (1998) by Toa Fraser toured England in 2001, the British press still evoked Mason's fears of a New Zealand perceived by the world to be a "cultural backwater, noted only for its sheep and its rugby"; however, the *Guardian Guide* went on to advise that seeing *Bare*, in which two actors portray a range of urban Auckland characters, "is liable to make you think again" about these New Zealand clichés ("Bare Touring").[3] In 2004 Massive Company was invited by London's Royal Court to present *The Sons of Charlie Paora* (2002), a collaboration between the company and English playwright Lennie James. *The Guardian* critic Michael Billington (2004) observed that "there is far more to New Zealand than a location for *Lord of the Rings*" and that the play, set in South Auckland, with a high Polynesian population, represented New Zealand's multiculturalism. These works offered a fuller perspective of Aotearoa New Zealand culture beyond the stereotypical representations.

Still, if the rest of the world were to be asked what they associate with Aotearoa New Zealand, its theatre is likely to be a long way down the list for most people, if it were to register as an association at all. There is perhaps some irony in writing a book about how theatre from Aotearoa New Zealand has attempted to gain prominence and success within the global marketplace. However, for some people, the experience of watching a particular play that originated from Aotearoa New Zealand might be precisely what they associate with the nation. The inherent live and embodied features of the artform have the potential to create a profound personal impression. Certainly, while some theatrical experiences may quickly fade, images and impressions of certain productions will be transferred to the long-term memory; regardless of whether a person has visited the said country, a memorable play – that is identifiably representing an alternative location to the audience member's own – can offer a tangible connection and association with that location. When a work is identified as a New Zealand play, it opens the possibility that it will reveal something of what life is like in New Zealand, and how similar or different it is to the non-local audience's context. And for the New Zealand artists presenting their work, theatre has become "essential to who we are and how we communicate with each other, and the world, as New Zealanders" (Mazer 2013: 110).

This book offers a case study of how work from a specific nation – Aotearoa New Zealand – has attempted to tour, represent and position itself in the global theatre marketplace. My reason for discussing Aotearoa New Zealand theatre in relationship to its overseas performance history is that a desire for international performance has been a powerful impulse in both the development of the nation's theatre and the careers of contemporary practitioners, despite New Zealand's substantial distance from international markets and the challenges of making a profitable return. Influenced by the country's colonial history and anxieties around national identity, detailed in the following section, international validation is craved; New Zealand theatre makers have sought to test the quality of their work and display their cultural identities by bringing plays and productions to various geographic theatrical marketplaces, from the Edinburgh Festival Fringe to North America to Moana Oceania.[4] This book will introduce a number of journeys taken by a wide range of plays and productions from Aotearoa New Zealand to overseas destinations across time, place and theatrical space.

What is required to enable plays and productions to travel beyond a local context to arrive in international market destinations? Jacob Rajan, co-founder of Indian Ink Theatre Company, a prolific international touring company based in New Zealand, offers one answer: "you need your entire set to fit in your suitcases" (Rajan 2017: 13). With set designer John Verryt working "miracles with sari silk, canvas, and string", to create an economically transportable set, Indian Ink has toured *Guru of Chai* (2010) to Australia, Fiji, Singapore, USA, Canada and India. But the New Zealand theatre makers' airplane luggage contains more than simply tightly packed set pieces – through performance the maker unpacks a network of representations, identity markers and ideologies. The audiences in turn bring their own baggage of expectations and associations into the performance. As Tim Creswell (2006: 265) states, "mobility is more than about just getting from A to B". We can understand mobility as "socially produced motion", revealing "contested worlds of meaning and power" and a "hierarchy based on the ways we move and the meanings these moments have been given" (3; 265). In studying mobility, we ask questions around who has privileged access to mobility, what routes may be taken, where, how and why are people and productions travelling? While mobility has often been treated as incidental to other theatrical practices that produce meaning, as Fiona Wilkie (2015: 9) contends, "circulation and production of contemporary arts practices have an intrinsic mobility that is worth conceiving as such" (9).

The ability of a theatrical work to travel across geographic contexts is powered by a combination of the work's mobility and portability. Mobility can be defined as the capability for movement; for my purposes, it refers to the material and economic conditions that make a theatrical work mobile in the global theatre marketplace. A production's ability to move between market contexts is determined by intersections of funding, programming and personnel support, overcoming barriers such as distance and cost. Portability can be defined as the capability for transportation and conveyance, which we can reframe as *what* is conveyed and *how* the production transports its audience (rather than mobility's concern with how the production is transported *to* audiences). Portability refers to the potentiality of audiences from a range of cultural contexts to make connections with non-local theatrical work. As Keren Zaiontz (2018: 80) points out, "productions like goods travel, but in order to have currency in multiple markets they have to be legible to multiple audiences". Mobility and portability are what can allow a specific work to be programmed for a specific time, place and audience, where performative meanings are transported, translated and interpreted by specific individuals within specific communal contexts. As this book will demonstrate, receptions to and meanings of a work shift and change as a production travels between various geographic and cultural contexts.

This book aims to offer a culturally specific perspective on the subject of how theatre travels, complimenting existing scholarship on national identity, theatrical commodification and globalisation. There are few comparable works that focus on the international performance history and reception of theatre from the perspective of a singular nation. *Playing Australia: Australian Theatre and the International Stage* (Elizabeth Schafer and Susan Bradley Smith 2003) considers Australian theatre that travelled abroad in the 19th and 20th centuries, but the multi-authored series of essays do not provide an overall paradigm or method of analysis. Similarly, *Irish Theatre on Tour* (Nicholas Grene and Chris Morash 2005) offers a series of collected essays on theatre toured from Ireland between the 18th and 21st centuries. I have written *Aotearoa New Zealand in the Global Theatre Marketplace* with a concern for the specific contexts of presenting and selling Aotearoa New Zealand theatre in various geographic markets and the receptions that were generated, with a wider view towards offering concepts and frameworks that can be used to analyse and understand the processes of theatrical mobility, portability and cross-cultural receptions in other contexts. Readers can use this study to find contrasts and intersections with the international performance and tours of work that originate from various other cultures and national theatres.

In this Introduction I establish the historical context and key theoretical concepts of the study. First, I outline "My journey", detailing my positionality in relation to this study and summarising my methodology. "Indigeneity, identity and colonial anxieties: The creation of New Zealand in drama" provides a concise history of the development of theatrical performance domestically within Aotearoa, from precolonial traditions to today. I explain why anxiety around national identity has been one of the defining features of the nation's drama, due to the country's colonial settler-invader context. "The overseas experience of New Zealand theatre" relates this history to the factors that have motivated theatre makers to pursue international performance of their work and why this has been such a significant impulse within the New Zealand context. In "Travelling theatre: Concepts" I offer some theoretical frameworks for investigating the processes that occur when national work is performed in an international market context and consider a number of concepts and terms relevant to this study: national, international, global, transnational, cosmopolitanism, cultural difference, universalism, the common and the global marketplace. "The journey from here" closes with a preview of the chapters to come.

My journey

When I went to London in 2015 to experience the New Zealand-originated production *The Generation of Z: Apocalypse* (2013) by David Van Horn, Simon London and Benjamin Farry, which theatrically immerses the audience in a Zombie apocalypse, a Zombie character spat fake blood all over me, which was one novel way of becoming immersed in my research. A truism of theatre is that it is an ephemeral form. Each performance offers a new re-creation of the work to win over the hearts and minds of a particular group of people gathered to watch the event. The performance exists, and then it is gone. Sometimes performances are captured on video, or photographs are taken, but our main record is usually the printed script. Reviews also offer clues as to what happened during the performative moment when play and audience met. The ephemerality of theatrical performance carries issues of access and loss. Katie Normington (2011: 86) questions how one can "retrieve a theatre history for which there are few traces". While I was able to see (and be splattered) by *The Generation of Z* live, for the majority of my cases I had to reconstruct the moment of live performance through the textual traces the productions had left behind.

The international performance story of Aotearoa New Zealand's theatre has been an overlooked component of the country's theatre history in scholarship. Critical writing about New Zealand drama has understandably focussed inwardly on the formation and consolidation of a unique national tradition. References to international productions are often brief and written in largely positivist terms – they went over there, and it was good.[5] Seeking a greater understanding of my own theatrical heritage as a Pākehā theatre practitioner and critic, from 2014 to 2017, I embarked on a PhD study of New Zealand theatre's overseas experience at the University of Auckland, charting new territory for New Zealand dramatic scholarship. This book has allowed me to revisit and update my research and share it with an international readership. In tracing the performance journeys of plays and productions that have sought to perform Aotearoa New Zealand to the world, I too am seeking to represent and promote the value of Aotearoa New Zealand theatre to the world through my writing.

I decided it would be most relevant in this book to primarily focus on examples of Aotearoa New Zealand travelling theatre over the past 30 years, a period when a broad and diverse range of theatrical works have attempted to gain performance in a globalised theatrical marketplace. Although I have aimed for a comprehensive study, it is beyond the scope of this book to present a completist history of all instances of travelling theatre from New Zealand. Deciding which productions to use as case studies comes with significant responsibility. I have selected plays and productions that resonate between one another, variously representing both typical and exceptional instances of New Zealand theatre overseas, whether this be an experience of a particular market, a complex international reception to a work or a distinct kind of New Zealand identity being performed to audiences overseas. The productions cross many genres and forms, but in the interests of maintaining a manageable scope I have limited my focus to work that can be broadly identified as *theatre*, that is, theatrical (performed live by actors) and dramatic (usually working from a script, containing elements of character, conflict and narrative), but I have not been dogmatic, recognising that some performance work may blur formal categories.[6]

This study engages with the whole theatrical enterprise as a play travels from concept through to funding, marketing, performance and reception, balancing the conceptual and theoretical with the artistic and economic realities of theatrical practice and performance. Archival records have proved a substantial aid in telling this story. Interviews were also conducted with practitioners with experiences of touring; these add further context, as their subjective testimony can join the other traces to assist the analysis of what happened and why. The most challenging task was recovering the traces of information about how the multi-faceted spectators from various cross-cultural contexts received and interpreted the performance. Reviews are used in the same way Ric Knowles (2004: 21) does in his work, "as providers of evidence of receptions and interpretations – readings – that were enabled by particular local stagings for specific local audiences". Reviews demonstrate possible meanings that were made available to, and produced by, a specific audience at a specific location, channelled through the critics' agendas and choices around what aspects of a production to emphasise to their readership. This book project has also given me the opportunity to conduct new field research at the 2019 Edinburgh Festival Fringe, collecting responses from audiences attending works touring from New Zealand, and I share my findings in Chapter 8. It is through my reading of all the available traces that I analyse how the meaning of a work might operate in a specific time, place and moment, in order to assess the wider significance of theatre from Aotearoa New Zealand theatre travelling throughout the global marketplace. But, before we can discuss travelling theatre in further detail, it is useful to have some knowledge of the development of New Zealand's domestic theatre market in relation to the country's wider colonial history.

Indigeneity, identity and colonial anxieties: the creation of New Zealand in drama

Anxiety around national identity has been one of the defining features of Aotearoa New Zealand drama, memorably articulated by the explosive challenge – "Whaddarya?" – delivered to the audience at the end of Greg McGee's *Foreskin's Lament* (1981: 46). Examining the toxic masculine culture of a provincial rugby team as a synecdoche for the nation, the play was heralded as a breakthrough for homegrown theatre upon its debut in 1980, presenting the local audience, "at last, with indigenous language" according to critic Peter Wells (1981). Wells' reference to "indigenous language" is not a reference to the language of tangata whenua (Indigenous Māori – the people of the land), but an appeal to an indigeneity of the decedents of the European settlers: *Foreskin's Lament* primarily represented a masculine-orientated Pākehā perspective. Pākehā is a Te Reo (Māori language) term adopted by some New Zealand Europeans to lend Indigenous authenticity to the white Anglo–New Zealand identity as one that has diverged from its settler antecedents. In articulating a distinct "New Zealand identity", *Foreskin's Lament* was rapidly produced by regional theatres around the country (and the play would go on to represent New Zealand in the productions staged by companies in Australia, London, and Edinburgh).

As *Foreskin's Lament* demonstrates, theatre has been an important artistic medium used to articulate and demonstrate how Anglo–New Zealand culture has developed from British settler origins, and in turn, these theatrical representations are used to reinforce this cultural divergence and difference. *Foreskin's Lament* became a key marker of the effort to create "New Zealand" in drama, reflecting the cultural uniqueness of New Zealand society. But the formation of an "indigenous" dramatic language of *Foreskin's Lament* involves the side-lining of Aotearoa's Māori language and customs. Helen Gilbert and Joanne Tompkins (1996: 3) explain that settler-invader colonies, in which settlers overwhelmed the Indigenous population, resulted in historical guilt and amnesia, as the settler-invaders were "implicated in the dispossession of Indigenous peoples from their homelands and in the (partial) destruction of their cultures". But the settler-invaders were also driven to establish "authenticity for a society dislocated from the imperial centre and, simultaneously, alienated from the local land and Indigenous culture" (133). The drama of Aotearoa New Zealand, influenced by its settler-invader colonial history, is profoundly bound with questions of authenticity and belonging, and the ongoing contestation of what kinds of identity are performed and who speaks for the nation. The reception of *Foreskin's Lament* as an "indigenous" breakthrough for New Zealand theatre reflects ongoing historical amnesia and erasure of the cultural practices of tangata whenua.

Performance is a key pou (supporting post or pole) in Māori culture. Kapa haka (dance combining action and chants) and waiata-a-ringa (action songs developed in the early 20th century) are central to contemporary Māori performance. Precolonial Māori pā (settlements) typically featured a whare tapere, a building set aside for entertainment, storytelling and amusement; whare tapere could also refer to the performance activities that would occur in other buildings or outside the pā (Royal 1998: 8). Scholar Te Ahukaramū Charles Royal summarises that "in all cases, the whare tapere stood for a collection of discrete activities whose overall description might fall under the title of 'entertainment'" (8). Whare tapere encompassed a range of activities including haka, whaikōrero (oratory and storytelling), waiata (song), playing of Taonga Pūoro (musical instruments), wrestling, darts and puppetry (101; 164). Following the British settlement of Aotearoa during the 19th century, whare tapere "fell into disuse" (14).[7]

In oral tradition, Kupe is credited as the first person to discover Aotearoa, named thus by Kupe's wife Hine Te Apārangi. One of the last significant land masses to be populated, Polynesian settlement of Aotearoa occurred circa 1250–1300 AD. Dutch explorer Abel Tasman sighted the country in 1642 but did not make landfall, and Tasman's encounter with the Ngāti Tūmatakōkiri people was marked by violence, with one Māori and four of Tasman's crew meeting their deaths.[8] Dutch cartographers provided the name Nova Zeelandia in 1645 after a Dutch province. The next European encounter took place in 1769 with English explorer James Cook, whose men killed a number of Māori over the first days of Cook's landfall (Cook made two subsequent voyages to New Zealand).[9] European expansion impacted Aotearoa in the late 18th century as European sealers and then whalers came to the country. Meanwhile, Christian missionaries arrived in 1814. In 1835 the British government recognised the sovereignty of Māori by acknowledging He Whakaputanga o te Rangatiratanga o Nu Tireni (the Declaration of Independence of the United Tribes of New Zealand), a document signed by 34 northern chiefs asserting their mana (authority) and confirming that foreigners did not have power to make their own laws.[10] This legal recognition was altered in 1840 with the introduction of Te Tiriti o Waitangi (The Treaty of Waitangi) between the British Crown and Māori. With growing numbers of British migrants, lawless behaviour and concerns about French interests, this was an arrangement offered by the British government which aimed to annex the country to protect Māori and control British subjects and commercial interests. However, translation differences between the English and Te Reo Māori versions would have profound political and social repercussions. In the reo translation of Te Tiriti o Waitangi, which was signed by the majority of signatories, the Crown had the right to govern its own citizens, but Māori retained rangatiratanga (sovereignty). The positions were reversed under the terms of the English Treaty of Waitangi: the Crown had sovereignty, while Māori held governorship of their people.[11] While the treaty was intended to secure the Crown exclusive purchase rights of Māori land, the document was further undermined by corporate power: the New Zealand Company had made dubious land purchases in Wellington which were promised to settlers who arrived in 1840, and the government bowed to pressure to validate them.[12]

The first recorded performance of Western theatre occurred at a hotel in Auckland the following year, at which time the population of Aotearoa consisted of 80,000 Māori and 2,000 Europeans (Pool and Jackson 2011). In 1843 the Royal Victoria theatre was opened in Wellington by James Marriott, and regular performances of farces, melodrama and variety programmes also became established in Auckland and Nelson under the patronage of hotels. As categorised by Howard McNaughton (1981: 15), "colonial New Zealand drama was initially a labouring-class phenomenon which often attracted wider public attention only through the court columns of the newspapers". During the New Zealand Wars, 1854–1870, during which a series of unjust land seizures and armed conflicts took place, North Island theatre was "invested" in the British regiments sent to support the colonial government, whose ranks dominated the audiences and also presented their own entertainments (16). The Otago Gold Rush in the South Island from 1861 also helped to create an audience base to support Australian, British and North American touring companies, alongside the construction of theatre and opera house infrastructure to host them (Carnegie 1998: 333). By 1871, the European population of Aotearoa was close to 300,000 while Māori had reduced to 47,000 (Pool and Jackson 2011). In 1881 the J.C. Williamson Company toured New Zealand for the first time. Australian tours to New Zealand were a major economic endeavour in the late 19th and early 20th centuries, with J.C. Williamson productions of plays, opera and ballet regularly visiting New Zealand.

The economics of theatrical touring to New Zealand by external companies were challenged in the early 20th century due to the disruption of World War I (WWI), the rise of silent pictures, and the subsequent depression (Carnegie 1998: 333). From the 1920s, amateur theatre became a widespread leisure past time in New Zealand. Following World War II (WWII), there were calls for the establishment of a professional national theatre as part of a wider cultural nationalist movement, but ministers declined to establish this. In 1962 Director Ronald H. Barker identified a lack of interest in plays written by New Zealanders:

> Really, at the moment, there is no New Zealand Theatre, because so few New Zealand plays see the light of the stage. And there will be no New Zealand theatre until New Zealand plays are the rule rather than the exception – plays that deal with the life of the people and the country.
>
> (60)

The existing theatre infrastructure, dominated by amateur societies, offered an "internationalist" foreign programme of plays "mostly copying successes on the English stage" which "catered to a small, local, middle-class audience, providing that audience with a taste of the wider world" (Edmond 1991: 186). Meanwhile, "home-produced plays in general met with indifference, distaste, and even hostility" (Thomson 1984: 26).

This phenomenon became known as the cultural cringe, a colonial hangover involving the discomfort towards and devaluing of local art in preference to the international. Bill Pearson (1952: 12) believed that the New Zealander was "afraid to recognise himself [...]. A play that presented without sentimentality the patterns of New Zealand life would possibly bore an English audience: A New Zealand small town would 'tsk-tsk' it off the stage". The

New Zealand Players was established in 1953, a professional company that toured across New Zealand with a repertoire mainly consisting of scripts from overseas. One exception was the 1959 North Island tour of *The Tree* (1957) by Stella Jones, programmed only after the play had received international validation: *The Tree* had been performed first by UK companies in Bristol and Newcastle in 1957. Proving Pearson wrong, the play enthralled English audiences, during its New Zealand tour, and small towns welcomed its slice of New Zealand life. Nevertheless, *The Tree* was exceptional, and the New Zealand Players collapsed in 1960. In 1967 actor Tim Elliott expressed the colonial anxiety that "there is no great hope for our New Zealand culture as something distinct and immediately identifiable and unique in the world [...] we have no national identity" ("Theatre Personalities No. 2 Tim Elliott").

At the forefront of a movement from the 1950s to attempt to define a national identity in drama was playwright Bruce Mason. In 1960 he observed that most theatre produced in New Zealand was spent on the "reproduction of established European and American commercial successes", but strongly advocated that "theatrical activity in New Zealand could never wholly justify itself until New Zealanders began writing, designing, dancing on themes thrown up by their own way of life" (Mason 1960). Mason's work attempted to construct a distinctive New Zealand identity, informed by the relationship between Māori and Pākehā. His 1956 play *The Pohutukawa Tree* gained a workshop production from the New Zealand Players, which was described by critic Ralph McAllister as "the true birth of indigenous theatre in New Zealand" (in Edmond 2014), a sentiment recognising the then novelty of a state-of-the-nation play, albeit problematic since Māori culture was being represented through the gaze of a Pākehā playwright. Frustrated by the lack of groups willing to produce his plays, Mason created his own solo work *The End of the Golden Weather* (1959) which he performed across New Zealand and toured to the 1963 Edinburgh Festival Fringe.

From the mid-1960s there was a growth in playwriting, influenced by the policies of the New Zealand broadcasting service which commissioned radio plays (a new income for writers), and the government's Queen Elizabeth II Arts Council of New Zealand, established in 1963, which supported the formation of professional theatres to service each of the main regions, with Downstage Theatre opening in the capital Wellington in 1964 and Mercury Theatre in Auckland (the country's biggest city) in 1968 (Carnegie 1998: 334). These were followed by the Court in Christchurch (1971), Centrepoint in Palmerston North (1973) and Fortune in Dunedin (1974). With this infrastructure in place, the period from the 1970s onwards was termed the "professional years" of New Zealand theatre by John Thomson (1984: 69): a decade which saw the establishment of national playwrights agency Playmarket and the acting training programme that would become Te Kura Toi Whakaari New Zealand Drama School. This decade also brought both commercial success for and acceptance of New Zealand plays as popularised by local playwrights Joseph Musaphia and Roger Hall. Hall's comedy-of-manners

Glide Time (1976) and *Middle Age Spread* (1977) were box office smashes, largely reflecting mainstream Anglo–New Zealand middle-class values, unconcerned with a Māori worldview. Alongside the emerging playwriting culture was an alternative collective counter-culture with groups including Living Theatre Troupe (1970–1975), Amamus (1971–1978), Theatre Action (1972–1977) and Red Mole Enterprises (1974–2006) influenced by the commedia dell'arte revival, Jacques Le Coq and Jerzy Grotowski. Artistic and financial stability proved challenging, and only Red Mole was able to sustain itself as a collective beyond the 1970s by moving to New York City (NYC).

During the 1970s and 1980s "New Zealand stages were the Pākehā's oyster" (Amery 2013: 99), or to put it more bluntly, white and mostly male. The Māori protest movement from the 1970s, exemplified by the Land March to parliament promoting Māori rights in 1975 (the same year as the Treaty of Waitangi Act was passed by the government, establishing a mechanism to hear claims of breaches of the treaty and a process of redress and reparations) and the 1977 Bastion Point occupation over disputed land, also produced Māori writers and artists who used theatrical forms to "work through significant social and political issues affecting Māori and Pākehā" (Parker 2008: 127). In 1972 Auckland Festival commissioned *Te Raukuru: The Feathers of the Albatross* by Harry Dansey, the first play by a Māori writer, based on the government's invasion of pacifist Māori settlement Parihaka in 1881. Te Ika a Maui Players debuted Rore Hapipi's *The Death of the Land* in 1976 in the Newtown Community Centre in Wellington, a courtroom drama surrounding the proposed sale of ancestral Māori land. Wellington's The Depot Theatre opened in 1983 with a mission statement of producing solely New Zealand plays, including an emphasis on work by Māori practitioners. The Depot subsequently became Taki Rua, the leading producing company for Māori theatre. Taki Rua instituted an annual Te Reo Māori season from 1995.

Although the professional regional theatres were the dominant model through the 1970s and 1980s, 40 years later, only The Court and Centrepoint survive. Auckland Theatre Company (1992–), the successor to Mercury Theatre (which closed in 1992), has bucked the trend by opening a permanent home theatre in 2017. Since the 2000s a number of boutique theatre-producing companies have been established, catering to various cultural and formal niches, including Massive Company (1991, originally Maidment Youth Theatre), Indian Ink Theatre Company (1997), The Conch (2003), Tawata Productions (2004) and Red Leap Theatre (2008). These companies are recurrently funded by Creative New Zealand, Arts Council of New Zealand Toi Aotearoa (CNZ), the government's national agency for the development of the arts, formed in 1994 through an amalgamation of the Queen Elizabeth II Arts Council and other arts bodies.[13] CNZ also supports non-recurrently funded companies and independent artists on a project-to-project basis through competitive arts round funding. With a capacity in their main spaces of fewer than 100 people, BATS Theatre (1989–) in Wellington and Basement Theatre (2009–) in Auckland have also been crucial in nurturing the arts ecology as affordable programming venues for the independent sector and supportive of new local work (there is a strong lineage of work debuted at these venues going on to tour internationally).

Works from Māori, Pasifika, Asian and feminist perspectives continue to challenge Pākehā and masculine perspectives. Playmarket's survey of work produced by theatre companies funded by Creative New Zealand for the year 2018 found that of the 241 productions staged, 84% were New Zealand works, 51% were by New Zealand women, 17% were Māori works, 11% were Pasifika works and 6% were Asian works (Playmarket 2019). For comparison, the 2018 New Zealand census recorded that 70.2% of the population identified as European, 16.5% as Māori, 15.1% Asian, 8.1% Pacific and 1.5% who identified as Middle Eastern, Latin American or African ethnicity (Stats NZ 2019).[14] While the cultural identities represented in New Zealand theatre has expanded over the past 30 years, a sense of insecurity has remained stubbornly present. Theatre makers continue to grapple with what it means to live in Aotearoa New Zealand, make theatre in Aotearoa New Zealand, and whose voices get to represent it, domestically and internationally.

The overseas experience of New Zealand theatre

The unresolved anxiety around defining Aotearoa New Zealand identity has contributed to the impulse to present drama overseas in order to articulate New Zealand identities and gain international validation for the quality of the country's theatre. The colloquial expression OE (Overseas Experience) marks the importance of a New Zealander's desire to travel. The OE has become a mythic rite of passage for New Zealanders, in which one travels and works overseas, traditionally Britain, New Zealand's colonial motherland – "it became the 'accepted thing' to go off on the 'big OE' immediately after college and before settling down" (McCarter 2001: 11). The OE is connected with New Zealand's settler-invader culture, "the result of a young colony's search for a distinctive and separate cultural identity" (Wilson, Fisher and Moore 2009: 16). Historian Michael King (2004: 178) described his personal realisation that his overseas travels made him feel "more, not less, a New Zealander":

> I became more deeply conscious of my roots in my own country because I had experienced their absence […]. I missed common perspectives with Māori and Pākehā New Zealanders: the short-cuts to communication that people from the same cultures share in accepted reference points, recognised allusions, a similar sense of comparison, contrast and incongruity, a peculiar sense of humour.

On his OE, King formed a better sense of what he saw as a unique culture in New Zealand. Paradoxically, the more New Zealanders were able to experience the outside world, the further their sense of home could be developed; it is overseas where one finds oneself.

As with the New Zealander's OE, New Zealand theatre's OE is most significant in terms of the forging, testing and consolidating of identity in the nation's dramas. Murray Edmond (1996: 359) flips the OE letters to create the EO, the Enormous Other, "everything that lay beyond the small town". In this conception, New Zealand is small, isolated and insignificant; the world beyond the island is enormous and special. While travelling on his OE, Michael King (2004: 178) began to resent "being made to feel that the centre of the universe was *there*, and what happened on the periphery, where I came from, was of little consequence". Marc Maufort (2003: 19) identifies in New Zealand drama a "struggle for self-definition hampered by an acute sense of social and intellectual inferiority towards the centre of the Empire". Acknowledgement from the Enormous Other is craved and resented. As Bruce Mason (1986: 269) sarcastically put it, "if Elsewhere says it's good, then it must be". Nationalistically motivated tours, beginning with Mason's performance of *The End of the Golden Weather* at the 1963 Edinburgh Fringe, then, can be understood as an attempt to demonstrate what makes New Zealand culture unique and gain legitimacy for this identity through international approval, akin to a Hegelian model where recognition by the other is the basis of self-consciousness. New Zealand theatre makers cannot be certain of the quality of their work until they have tested themselves in the global marketplace.

While international performances can be linked with the formation of New Zealand identities, they can also be motivated by ideas of escape. For Pearson (1952: 12), the New Zealand audience for fiction, films and plays was unwilling to "co-operate" or "speculate about themselves", and he wondered, therefore, whether it would be preferable for artists to leave the country. Pearson's sentiment has continued to echo through the decades. Bruce Mason often wrote about New Zealand as a hostile climate for the artist; for example, his conception of New Zealand as a culture of "recession and diminution" (1987: 296). In 1974 playwright Robert Lord moved to America, leaving behind a New Zealand "hampered by its smallness"; Lord expressed that "if you're stuck [in New Zealand] and can't get out, then it is hell" (McNaughton and Ioana 1986). When I interviewed Charlie McDermott, the producer of *The Generation of Z: Apocalypse*, in London in 2015 (covered in Chapter 9), he shared the view that New Zealand theatre was "a tiny, tiny speck of an industry" where the majority of New Zealanders "do not value the arts in our culture" (McDermott 2015). It is true that the relatively small population of New Zealand limits potential audience reach, and if work is to have an ongoing life, there is significant appeal in targeting audience in overseas destinations. But these comments also point to a persistent feeling that the New Zealand audience is inferior to those that can be found "Elsewhere". Little New Zealand, with its isolated industry and small audience size, is the hell to be disowned, while overseas is the paradise to be embraced. Such a view speaks less to the actual quality of New Zealand audiences, and more to the continuing manifestations of the anxieties of national identity, a recurring theme throughout this study.

Travelling theatre: concepts

Before travelling any further, it is necessary to elaborate on the key conceptual concerns that will underpin this journey through Aotearoa New Zealand theatre's attempts to enter the global marketplace.

The nation and the feedback loop

The first key concern regards the ways the Aotearoa New Zealand nation is represented, constructed and performed within theatrical works, and how this national identity can be read and received by theatre audiences around the world. Benedict Anderson (2006: 6) reminds us that the nation state is a relatively recent construct, which he defines as an "imagined political community". The "imagined" is particularly pertinent for our dramatic purposes: there is nothing inherent or natural about the national community, but repeated cultural performances of all kinds encourage its members to imagine it as if it were so. While Anderson states that the imagined nation is also "always conceived as a deep, horizontal comradeship", in practice, the monolithic signifiers of nationhood construct a fantasy of limited imagination (6). National identity absorbs and narrows, so only some forms of cultural expression come to represent the nation. Identity is often "exclusive and homogenous", and "usually represent[s] and consolidate[s] the interests of the dominant power groups within any national formation" (Ashcroft, Griffiths and Tiffin 2007: 135). However, the identity is never stable and what constitutes the "imagined community" is continually challenged. As national identities are "neither biologically or territorially given", Jen Harvie (2005: 2) argues that, instead, they are "creatively produced or staged". This recalls Stuart Hall's (1990: 234) metaphor of identity "as a 'production' which is never complete". Hall describes this production as "always constituted within, not outside representation [...]. We all write and speak from a particular place and time, from a history and a culture which is specific. What we say is always 'in context', positioned".

Theatre is an ideal experiential and communal form in which identity can be positioned, enacted and negotiated; live theatrical performances of identity draw attention to the ways identity itself is a performance and the ways various narratives surrounding identity "can compete for our attention and allegiance" (Blandford 2013: 3). Representations of specific national identity within a theatrical text may reify and conform to dominant expressions of the imagined community or deconstruct and resist them. As a "site of circulating representational forms", Helen Gilbert (2004: vii) explains how theatre's entanglement with ongoing narratives of nationhood provides a "means by which communities register, reiterate or contest modes and models of national belonging". In "small nations" such as Aotearoa New Zealand, Steve Blandford (2013: 4) argues that "the scope for meaningful proportions of the population to be involved with and affected by theatre's role in the construction of national identity is genuinely significant". As the preceding overview of Aotearoa's dramatic history conveys, the development of the nation's theatre registers the ongoing tensions generated by colonisation and concepts of national belonging.

Since New Zealand national identity itself is a broad and unstable concept, defining what constitutes a New Zealand work is not always straightforward. What, for instance, should we make of Richard O'Brien who emigrated from Britain to New Zealand aged 9 and returned to Britain aged 23 where he would write his cult classic *The Rocky Horror Show* (1973)? Can *Rocky Horror* be considered a New Zealand work? To answer this question, we might look for markers of New Zealandness within the play: distinctive elements that are perceived to represent a national character, culture or consciousness. In order to understand the processes of how national identity is produced and received through drama, we can use the concept of a feedback loop. The term implies a network of cause-and-effect where information is fed back into itself. Erika Fischer-Lichte (2008: 38) argues that live performance involves an autopoietic feedback loop in which the interaction between the audience and the performers results in constant adjustments as "spectators as well as the actors perceive and, in turn, respond" to each other's reactions. My reference to the feedback loop is specific to how national identity is imagined, identified and understood within a work. On one side of the loop is the work itself, made and interpreted by a specific creative team, and on the other side, the audience receiving the work in performance or on the page, who will have varying degrees of proximity to the place, characters and incidences represented in the work, whether that is cultural familiarity or emotional recognition.

Playwrights write (and companies make) for their own sort of imagined community a desired audience who will respond positively to the concerns of the work. Most New Zealand plays produced overseas were written initially and primarily for an ideal local and knowing audience – what Ric Knowles (2014: 116) terms the "model spectator" – who would understand the work's semiotic codes, references and meaning within the given local context. This model "Kiwi" spectator would share with the show's makers, to repurpose Michael King's (2004: 178) description of his encounters with other New Zealanders on his OE, "accepted reference points, recognised allusions, a similar sense of comparison". Jerry C. Jaffe (2009: 8), in an essay on the performance of New Zealand identity, refers to "self-referential" markers of identity that operate within a feedback loop, which Jaffe defines as "markers New Zealanders might recognise as markers of New Zealand identity". The markers are intended to resonate "in a particular way for those of a particularly sympathetic cultural background" (8). Similarly, Catherine Rees

(2017: 3) discusses how productions "may embed nationality into the text, suggesting location through accent, dialect and oblique reference to place", but cautions that such images of national identity may not be shared with all, with the potential to be "troubling or stereotypical".

The feedback loop process is not simply a case of a theatre maker embedding a text with markers of national identity; I use the term feedback loop precisely because the markers can become markers of national identity only if the audience perceives them to be so. In *The Rocky Horror Show*, Brad, the young American, exclaims, "I thought it was the real thing", when he realises he has been seduced by his host, Dr Frank-n-Furter, rather than his fiancée (O'Brien 1983: 18). To pose the question "Is *Rocky Horror* the real thing – a New Zealand play?" opens critical possibilities and meanings that may not exist in performance.[15] *Rocky Horror*'s New Zealand consciousness exists under the surface as an alternative narrative and reading; the thing itself can be said to be "in drag". Applying Judith Butler's discussion of gender performativity to national identity complicates the search for the "real thing" and provides further nuance to the feedback loop concept. As Butler famously argues, "gender parody reveals that the original identity after which gender fashions itself is an imitation without an origin" (Butler 1999: 175), and *Rocky Horror*'s cultural parody can be viewed as an imitation without a national origin. Like gender identity, we can perceive national identity to "be neither true nor false, neither real nor apparent, neither original nor derived" (180). Butler's gender paradigm is analogical to New Zealand's colonial situation, in which the identities of both tangata whenua and colonisers are changed post-contact, and everyone is a simulacrum. Therefore, there is no "real" New Zealand identity, because there can be no "real" national identity, but just a set of assumptions and a "stylised repetition of acts" that become naturalised by their very repetition (179). This is one way the theatrical feedback loop operates in relation to national identity: New Zealanders read a work in a particular way and recognise markers of New Zealandness within a work, which reinforces their own sense of New Zealandness. The identified New Zealandness is a fantasy, but the recognition of what constitutes national identity is perpetuated by the feedback loop process. (I have contextualised the process in terms of dramatic texts, but this feedback loop can also be applied to the wider sociological phenomenon of the construction of and belief in mythologies of nationality.)

The feedback loop is a useful strategy for considering how New Zealand identity can be read and received in a work overseas. How does the feedback loop operate when plays are transported outside of their national boundaries and received by a non-local, non-knowing audience? Non-local audiences might identify markers that reinforce their conception of New Zealand identity, but some markers may not travel or might be read differently, or other markers might only become apparent when a work is placed outside of its local context. The constant modifications and changes implied in the feedback loop process can become especially pronounced when engaging with a non-local theatrical work, the loop drawing attention to and disrupting the naturalising fantasy of a stable national identity as a play moves across different international locations.

International and global

Having established the national as a theoretical concept, we move out to the international. Benedict Anderson's (2006: 7) nation is limited, because of the "finite, if elastic boundaries", beyond which lie other imagined communities. Glenda Sluga (2013: 3) argues the "twinned liberal ideologies internationalism and nationalism inspired a wide range of imagined communities". When a national imagined community is placed against another, the identities can be made stronger in opposition: our imagined community is not like theirs. Internationalism advocates for greater co-operation between nations for their mutual interest. Sluga (2013: 7) sees the relationship between nationalism and internationalism as "neither antagonistic nor even analytically separate principles". The international, therefore, is not the same as the global. Where the international sees co-operation between many, for the global, "what was many becomes one" (Daly 1999). This conceptual difference between internationalism and globalism allows us to identify two general periods in the story of New Zealand theatre overseas: the international world (1941–1989) and the global world (1990–present). Internationalism, of which WWII was its "apogee", defines the first historical period (Sluga 2013: 79). The nation remains the "basic unit" in international relations of trade and treaties (Daly 1999). As will be detailed in the first chapter of this book, the internationalist perspective is reflected in the New Zealand theatre produced overseas during this period, which is largely concerned with constructing a coherently defined and distinct image of the New Zealand nation.

Whereas internationalism describes the interactions between nation states and, in doing so, consolidates the sense of the homogenous national state, globalisation brings the "effective erasure of national boundaries for economic purposes" (Daly). Darren O'Byrne and Alexander Hensby (2011: 20) identify the current epoch, beginning with the collapse of the Soviet Union, as a "global age". David Capie (2009: 594; 596) situates 1990 as a "turning point" for New Zealand's foreign relations due to the end of the Cold War, alongside the country's integration into a "new worldwide empire" of global capital. New Zealand's economic and political ties shifted, with an increased focus on the ascendant Asia-Pacific region, culminating in the 2008 New Zealand–China Free Trade Agreement. Roland Robertson's (1992: 8) definition of globalisation is that it "refers both to the compression of the world and the intensification of consciousness of the world as a whole". This is not to claim that globalisation is unique to this era, and indeed, the case can be made for versions of globalisation throughout history. What is important is how globalising pressures "increasingly undermine much of the discourse on the peculiarities of the nation and render it partly redundant" (Kennedy 2010: 3). The national is also challenged by the transnational, in which "the relationship between culture, people and place is reconfigured as national territories no longer automatically provide the main locus of identification and belonging" (Rogers 2015: 7). The global period is one of "increasing diversification, of new hybrids forms emerging from the continuous interplay of difference" (O'Byrne and Hensby: 3). This is reflected in the range of work discussed in Chapters 2–9 which examine cases of Aotearoa New Zealand theatre performed globally over the past 30 years.

Theatre as mirror and cosmopolitanism

Hamlet's speech to the players in William Shakespeare's play, written between 1599 and 1602, has often been used as the basis for defining the purpose of theatre, to hold "the mirror up to nature, to show virtue her own feature, scorn her own image, and the very age and body of the time his form and pressure" (3.2, 22–24). Hamlet's ideal is a theatre that can reflect back the audience's own society, revealing aspects of themselves: their desires, fears, hypocrisies and the time and place that they live. Crucially, *Hamlet* is set in Elsinore, not England, but presumably, if Shakespeare followed the view of his protagonist, he believed a play about the Denmark court could hold his audience's attention and entertain, and also speak to something of their own age and body of time. *Hamlet* the play has proven endlessly malleable in its revivals over the past four centuries. Modern revivals are often eager to prove how "relevant" the play is for audiences. In 2014 *Hamlet* was selected by Shakespeare's Globe to embark on a Globe-to-Globe tour, aiming to visit every country in the world over two years. The tour's central principle was that "Shakespeare can entertain and speak to anyone, no matter where they are on earth" (The Shakespeare Globe Trust 2014). Hamlet's mirror is remarkably versatile, but it begs the question of exactly what reflection the audiences see. Are people much the same everywhere, or do cultural distinctions create very different reflections, meanings and uses for this play, speaking in very different ways to people around the globe?

In *Theatre and Postcolonial Desire*, Awam Amkpa (2004: 2) tweaks Hamlet's mirror, situating the role of theatre as "reflecting a desiring process through which we imagine and live alternative universes". While people consume stories, and enter alternative worlds through a range of mediums on the screen and on the page, what makes theatrical performance unique is the embodied liveness of the medium. The physical presence of the performers within the same space as the audience gives this confrontation an immediate corporeal reality. Marianne Schultz emphasises that "a live performance can never be repeated or received the same way twice" as "each performance constitutes new expressions, understandings, and interactions from both performers and audience members" (2016: 19). The mirror is influenced by these real bodies, marked out and othered as actors and characters. For this study, what is at stake is how the mirror operates when a New Zealand play is placed in an overseas context, and what happens in the moment of theatrical exchange between two cultural others – the performers and the audience. How are the cultural identities of each disrupted, transformed or reinforced by the passage of live performance? Do audiences see the other in the performance mirror – exotic and different to themselves – or do they ultimately see themselves reflected back?

To examine this question, I adapt and apply the concept of cosmopolitanism, which involves a "receptive and open attitude towards the other" and attempts "to work towards the possibility of connection and dialogue with the other" (Kendall, Woodward and Skrbiš 2009: 1). As a philosophical framework it promotes a shared ethics of global citizenship whilst simultaneously promoting an openness towards difference and "identities more locally specific to geographical placement or individual subjectivities" (Holdsworth 2010: 67). Cosmopolitanism has been criticised as being an ideal rather than a practice. However, as Gilbert and Lo (2007: 113) discuss, cosmopolitanism offers a useful theoretical model for performance analysis because of "its provocation to examine the political and aesthetic aspects of cross-cultural exchange, positioned within the broader transnational flows of people and commodities associated with globalisation". Applying this concept provides another layer to the feedback loop process in order to explain and analyse what happens when drama is performed to a non-local "away" audience who may not have the same frame of reference for the text's identity markers that a local "home" audience may bring.

Exoticism and alterity can attract an audience to a foreign work because of the novelty of difference as a commodity. Nevertheless, a self-selected audience, who have opted to attend a theatre show that has travelled from New Zealand (assuming the show's country of origin is identifiably marketed), could be said to display "a conscious attempt to be familiar with people, objects and places that sit outside one's local or national settings" (Kendall, Woodward and Skrbiš 2009: 113). Gilbert and Lo (2007: 113) distinguish between an audience of "consumers" of difference versus a cosmopolitan audience of "cultural negotiators". Homi K. Bhabha (2014: 260) argues that the value of perceiving the human condition from a cosmopolitan perspective is that "the complex intersections of our diverse histories – our regional, historical, or cultural differences – seem to be, at one and the same time, both strange and familiar". The strange *and* familiar quality is essential for Bhabha, holding both connection and difference without one superseding the other. Whilst choosing to attend theatrical production originating from a foreign nation can be seen to involve such cosmopolitan attentiveness and engagement, there is also the possibility that it can reinforce existing cultural assumptions and power structures, fostering "further inequitable exchange between cultures" (Singleton 2014: 84). This study takes up Margaret Werry's (2014: 97) call for scholars to pay close attention to the "inequities that attend performance encounters across geographical difference" and analyse "the aesthetics, ethics, and significance, the politics and economics, of such encounters".

According to Susan Bennett's (1990: 149) influential framework for the study of theatre audiences, spectators arrive to a performance event as an "already-constituted interpretive community", bringing with them a "horizon of expectations shaped by the pre-performance elements". Crucially for this study, Bennett emphasises that "cultural assumptions affect performances, and performances rewrite cultural assumptions" (2), the feedback loop oscillating between an outer frame of expectations and associations the audience brings to the work and an inner frame of the moment-to-moment experience of the live performance, reading and reinterpreting a multitude of potential markers of identity that "signify on a number of possible levels" (149). Catherine Rees (2017: 177) suggests that "the way in which one nation is regarded by another is not a fixed picture but rather a series of negotiated narratives, whereby easily translatable images are favoured over more complex, nuanced realities". Whilst a cosmopolitan engagement with performance can add nuance to pre-existing cultural and national associations, many of the case studies in this book suggest that audiences broadly seek markers of similarity and cultural equivalence: generally, what is familiar becomes favoured over the strange.

Audience, culture and nation are flattening terms, reducing complex phenomena to comprehensible units. Helen Freshwater warns that a focus on the singularity of audience "risks obscuring the multiple contingencies of subjective response, context and environment which condition an individual's interpretation of a particular performance event" (2009: 5). Ric Knowles (2014: 116) modifies Bennett's conception of audience, arguing it is "made up of intersections of different, pluralistic interpretive communities with different competencies, reading strategies, and even languages". Touring a New Zealand work can place it in front of an audience that is different to the "model spectator" the show might have been intended for at home, but Knowles makes clear that *any* audience is unlikely "to be filled with model spectators who know all the codes, get all the references, and are able or willing to respond to the show's imperatives" (115). Whilst this study necessarily uses broad geographic and communal categories – investigating what happens when a play that originates from one nation is placed in front of an audience within another nation – the individual constituents will always belie these categories: audiences, like nations, resist generalisations. It is also vital, therefore, to acknowledge that cultures are not "hermetically sealed, homogenous entities", but, as Erika Fischer-Lichte (2014: 11) reminds us, "constantly undergo processes of change and exchange, which can become difficult to entangle". The travelling theatrical work discussed in this book is part of this change and exchange process; as audience and performer become interweaved and entangled within the performance event, culture is defined and redefined, producing and manifesting "cultural adjustments, ambiguities, and misalignments" (Alzate 2014: 42).

The particular, universal and the common

The markers of cultural equivalence that audience members may locate and produce within the feedback loop are features that tend to be identified as "universal" in a work. However, this universality is often Anglo-centric (belonging to a wider worldview of the English-speaking world) and misleading. Ric Knowles (2004: 9–10) argues that traditional dramatic analysis assumes:

> scripts and productions "have" universal meaning that is available for interpretation by audiences anywhere [, speaking] across various kinds of difference to our common humanity. In doing so, however, such work tends in the interests of what is understood to be universal truth to police the norms of common-sense understandings of dominant cultures, and to efface significant cultural and material differences based on such things as national, political, cultural and geographical location, together with class, race, ethnicity, gender and sexuality.

This is the binary of cultural difference (or particularism) versus universalism. Knowles notes that cultural difference in theatre tends to either be "packaged for consumption as exotic or charming", or, "to be treated as interesting and energising but fundamentally incidental local variants on a (therefore more important) universal or transcendent humanism" (187). Fischer-Lichte (2014: 8) also critiques the hypocrisy where claims are made of plays holding universal truths and values, with universalism "accorded to Western cultures and particularism to the rest".

To complicate the binary, I employ and adapt philosopher Francois Jullien's concept of the common. Jullien (2014: 16) defines the common as "what we are a part of or in which we take part, which is shared out and in which we participate". The common is not a neutral space; it is highly charged and political, where different cultural practices, histories and power structures meet. For the purposes of this study, I define the common as what peoples believe they share, or hold in common, with one another. The common does not reveal universal themes or actual cultural similarities, but is a subjective space of flux through which bodies of cultural knowledge connect. It is when an audience member in Edinburgh, Singapore or India can watch a performance from New Zealand's Indian Ink Theatre Company and can see something of their own lives in the dramatic mirror. I find it useful to consider a particular kind of theatrical resonance that audiences can receive from a work; specific resonators might include embodied action, image and gesture, certain lines of dialogue, the general dramatic situation represented, or identification with character choices, feelings, and predicaments. These create the theatrical resonance within the common space, associations and personal connections with the represented material that, through the feedback loop process, can stimulate individual and group identity in relation to the performance, lubricating a show's perceived portability outside of its home context. I am also interested in what falls outside the common, what does and does not translate, what does and does not resonate. As such, the chapters to follow will oscillate around these questions of cultural similarity and difference, and the space in common between the drama and potential audiences.

The global marketplace

I have titled this book *Aotearoa New Zealand in the Global Theatre Marketplace* as a statement of purpose, delineating the difference between performing within a local New Zealand domestic market versus attempting to access theatre markets around the globe. Of course, what I am referring to as a global marketplace is a series of local constitutive markets, formed by the interaction of consumers and producers, and marked by place. As Gay McAuley (2013: 81) states, "theatre is always and necessarily local, performance is always and necessarily emplaced". Touring companies have to renegotiate their approach for each local market that they arrive in; each market is influenced by a myriad of factors including size, population demographics, venue infrastructure, marketing distribution channels and so on.

In economic theory, the operation and development of markets has been conceptualised using the metaphors of drama. John Deighton (1991: 371) analyses the market as a series of staged events, where market actors seek to create an impression for the consumer audience. Markus Giesler (2008: 752) reiterates that "conceptualising markets as systems of monetary transactions is useful but distancing fiction", and instead advocates for centring "our cultural embeddedness in, and social responsibility for, the action in the market theatre". Primed then with dramatic metaphor, we can view the global theatre marketplace itself as a theatrical event: a series of dramatic interactions and adjustments between actors and (potential) audiences, driven at times by competing motivations and agendas, where narratives of comedy, tragedy and romance are played out – a cyclical drama of dramas arriving to a venue (or performance site), attempting to attract and connect to an audience. Thus, the global theatre marketplace can be situated in economic terms as a container for the production and circulation of capital and cultural capital, but it can also be conceived as a network of individual movements and actions, centred around the dramatic question of "do I go?" (for the prospective audience: do I go to this play?; for the prospective producer/theatremaker: do I go to this place?). While the blunt and dehumanising language of the market may view a theatre production as a product to be sold, and the audience as a consumer to be sold to, Deighton (1991: 362) reframes this to state that whilst "consumers may be said to choose products", what they actually do is "consume performances".

The potential mobility of a play from Aotearoa New Zealand which enables it to be produced in an overseas market is influenced by various funding, touring and venue models. Most theatrical organisations in the English-speaking world can be categorised as either commercial or not-for-profit

(Knowles 2004: 54). Not-for-profit venues and presenting organisations are subsidised by public funding and private donors. In theory, the not-for-profit sector can take more risks, programming work on perceived artistic merit over box office considerations and may, therefore, be receptive to, even positively interested in, Aotearoa New Zealand work if it aligns with their organisational priorities. However, presenters remain accountable and tied to funding bodies, and are liable to become more risk-averse within climates of policy changes and funding cuts. Touring theatre makers may attempt to position their works artistically and financially for the international Festival and Fringe circuit. For open access Fringe Festivals like Edinburgh's, companies need only to secure a venue and pay a registration fee to enter the Fringe marketplace. In contrast, curated International Festivals demand a particular type of artistically and conceptually high-end theatrical product that "tend to be admired for virtuosity, innovation, or skill" (90). Pertinent to this study, Ric Knowles argues that "remounting productions at international festivals that emerged from particular cultural contexts or were designed for specific local audiences changes the cultural work that they perform and the ways in which they are read" (181). As for commercial theatre, such as New York's Broadway and London's West End, where the theatre district is valued as a signifier of status and for the ancillary benefits that it contributes to the city's economy (spending on dining, transport, accommodation and so on) (Bennett 2005: 412), Knowles advises that

> the theatrical production is understood to be a "property" (hot or not), a commodity whose value is primarily, if not exclusively, economic, and whose participation in dominant models of commercial production is virtually prohibitive of extensive or radical social critique.
>
> (54)

In a commercial context the perceived saleability and profitability of a New Zealand work are likely to be valued over artistic considerations. While artists may have high-minded ideals about the artistic worth of their work, generally the programming comes back to two key questions: Who will fund this? Will this sell?

The global theatre marketplace needs to be acknowledged as a precarious one for industry professionals; even in mega-markets like New York's Broadway and London's West End, making a living through the theatre alone can be fraught for practitioners. While international touring has been a source of financial sustainability for some companies, in turn helping to fund domestic projects, overseas touring can be exorbitantly cost prohibitive for a New Zealand company. A fee-paying model, where host programmers buy in a work for a set fee, mitigates risk, although it does not always cover the full company expense. Under a box office model (such as the one that operates in Fringe Festival contexts), ticket sales alone rarely cover the costs of travel and freight, accommodation, venue fees, personal fees, marketing and other associated costs. To enter the global marketplace, companies must apply for grants, court sponsorship and hold fundraisers. From the mid-2010s, local crowdfunding websites, such as *Boosted*, have become a ubiquitous way of eliciting donations from theatre makers' networks, which often results in an unsustainable practice of industry colleagues subsidising each other.

Most contemporary tours from Aotearoa rely on government subsidy from Creative New Zealand to enable mobility in the global marketplace (just as the majority of professional theatre produced in New Zealand in general relies on some funding from CNZ). In 2009 CNZ implemented a pan-artform International Strategy which promoted international exposure as priority for the artistic and economic sustainability of New Zealand artists. This was renewed as part of CNZ's 2018–2023 Investment Strategy Te Ara Whakamua, which articulated the goals of the international investment programme thus: to "increase artists' income, develop their practice and networks in relation to the international arts environment, support artistic and cultural exchange, and promote New Zealand arts to international audiences" (Creative New Zealand 2018: 19). Eleanor Congreve, senior adviser in CNZ's International Services and Initiatives department, expressed that "at the very core" of CNZ's international support was the belief that

> New Zealand arts are of an international standard and we are a long way from everywhere else […], it's important to feel part of the world and for our artists to tell their stories outside of New Zealand and not just to ourselves.
>
> (Congreve 2019)

CNZ's International Services and Initiatives team run the Te Manu Ka Tau: Flying Friends programme, which funds international festival directors, venue programmers and producers to visit New Zealand and meet artists and see work, in recognition that presenters will rarely programme a work without having been able to view it themselves. CNZ also supports New Zealand producers and artists to attend international performing arts markets such as Australian Performing Arts Market (APAM) and Association of Performing Arts Professionals (APAP) in New York. If a company receives a fee-paying tour invitation as a result of CNZ's international initiatives, it is eligible to apply to the international market development fund, and CNZ may subsidise costs associated with international travel and freight. Companies can also apply for funding to support international touring through CNZ's general arts funds. Funding rounds are competitive, and CNZ ultimately has the power to deem if a company is "international ready" or not.[16] In this way, the funding body acts as an arbiter of what *kind* of New Zealand theatre gains representation overseas. Of course, companies may choose to bypass CNZ funding, but rarely do professional touring productions have the financial means to support overseas mobility without some form of support from CNZ.

In *Performance and the Global City*, D.H. Hopkins and Kim Solga (2013: 9) identify cities (potential markets), as "geographic nodes" that provide "material access to, and serve as economic concentrators for, the uneven flow of the global". The "uneven flow of the global" is pertinent here; in considering the concept of a "global theatre marketplace" we can consider both what is going where, and what is *not* going where (or, where we are unable to access). Varney et al. (2013: 143) have observed that Australian touring companies, for example, typically bypass locations in the Asia-Pacific region "and take productions straight to European-American cities". Regarding the performance routes of New Zealand plays, the British centre has held considerable sway; a trip to the UK, as Diana Looser (2014: 144) states, remains "the customary benchmark for successful New Zealand dramatic works". North America has also been a privileged destination for New Zealand theatre makers. However, companies such as Indian Ink Theatre Company, Red Leap Theatre, Modern Māori Quartet and Little Dog Barking have pursued touring in Asia, and, as will be detailed in Chapter 5, work from Aotearoa has regularly travelled across Moana Oceania. The chapters ahead will catalogue visits by Aotearoa New Zealand theatre to a range of marketplaces and contexts around the globe.

The journey from here

The chapters that follow will introduce a diverse range of theatrical enterprises that have attempted to get Aotearoa New Zealand seen on the world stage.

The first chapter, "National travels in an international world: overseas performances 1940–1990", essentially provides the backstory for the cases which will be explored in the rest of the book. Tracking instances of New Zealand theatre overseas from WWII to the end of the Cold War reveals a considerable anxiety regarding the formation of a distinct regionalist identity in New Zealand drama. At the start of the 1940s New Zealand performance was represented overseas by the Kiwi Concert Party, an entertainment unit that provided performances for allied troops throughout WWII and continued to tour Australia and New Zealand until 1954. The chapter also discusses the emergence of the cultural nationalist strain in theatre and the attempts to perform identifiably New Zealand work overseas, including Bruce Mason's *The End of the Golden Weather* and Amamus' tour of *Gallipoli* to London and Poland in 1974. This movement is contrasted with the long exile of Red Mole Enterprises overseas from 1979 to 1988, a collective which challenged emerging nationalist narratives in their attempt to find their own place within New York City's avant-garde. I end Chapter 1 with three examples of New Zealand playwrights "writing New Zealand away": Richard O'Brien writing *The Rocky Horror Show* in London, Roger Hall's rewriting of *Middle Age Spread* (1977) for a 1979 performance in London's West End and Robert Lord's attempts to have his work produced in the American market from 1974 through to the 1980s.

Moving forward to 1990, Chapter 2 – "A kiwi *Hedda Gabler*: Downstage on the festival stage" – analyses in detail the touring experience of a localised production of Henrik Ibsen's *Hedda Gabler* as it moved between multiple markets. Debuting at Wellington's Downstage in February 1990, director Colin McColl transposed Ibsen's classic 1891 text to 1950s Wellington. The production was invited to play at the inaugural Ibsen Festival in Oslo in September that same year and was also toured to the Edinburgh, London and Sydney. I use this production to test Ric Knowles' (2004: 181) contention that remounting productions at international festivals designed for specific local audiences changes the ways in which they are read.

In Chapter 3, "Performing mana: taking Māori theatre to the globe", I examine how Māori identity has been articulated on international stages. Touring work overseas from a Māori cultural perspective has been a way to enhance artist's mana (a concept relating to extraordinary prestige, power and influence), gain acknowledgement and educate overseas audiences about Māori culture and history. The chapter contains an extended focus on John Broughton's play *Michael James Manaia,* toured to the Edinburgh Festival Fringe in 1991, which explores the Vietnam War, cyclical family violence and a traumatic colonial legacy. *Toroihi rāua ko Kāhira* (*The Māori Troilus and Cressida*, 2012), directed by Rachel House, which opened London's Globe to Globe Festival in 2012, is then used as a major case study examining receptions to Māori identity within the global theatre marketplace.

In Chapter 4, "*Skin Tight*'s world flight: the production of New Zealand plays by international companies", I turn my attention to performances of New Zealand scripts performed by non-New Zealand companies. I contrast two of the most licensed New Zealand plays to international companies: *Ladies Night* (1987) by Stephen Sinclair and Anthony McCarten, in which the play's setting is relocated for each country it is produced in, and *Skin Tight* (1994) by Gary Henderson, which has been performed by companies in South Africa, UK, USA and Australia with its originating New Zealand setting intact. Another of Gary Henderson's plays, *Mo & Jess Kill Susie* (1996) also provides a further contrast, as the play's Māori context was adapted for an Indigenous Canadian one when produced by companies in Canada.

Globalising forces, changing migration patterns and a promotion of multiculturalism influenced the construction of broader identities for New Zealand theatre toured in the global world beyond the bicultural paradigm. Transnationalism further complicates the representation and reception of cultural identities. This becomes the focus for Chapter 5, "Beyond biculturalism: touring Pasifika and transnational theatre". I analyse a range of internationally performed plays representing transnational immigration narratives: Oscar Kightley and Simon Small's *Fresh Off the Boat* (1993), Makerita Urale's *Frangipani Perfume* (1997), Jacob Rajan's *Krishnan's Dairy* (1997), Toa Fraser's *No. 2* (1999), Dianna Fuemana's *Falemalama* (2006*)*, Red Leap's *The Arrival* (2010) and Vela Manusuate's *The Factory* musical (2011).

As an extended case study of *The Factory*'s international touring experience demonstrates, works representing experiences of cultural displacement raise further questions of emplacement and displacement when toured outside of a New Zealand context.

As a prolific international touring company based in New Zealand, Indian Ink Theatre Company is the focus of Chapter 6, "Exporting culture: Indian Ink Theatre Company". The chapter details Indian Ink's evolution as an international touring company: from a change in market destinations for its work, pursuing Singapore, India and the North America markets, to how the identities expressed in the company's work have shifted from a transnational New Zealand–Indian focus towards a global orientation, as demonstrated by three of Indian Ink's touring works: *Guru of Chai* (2010), *Kiss the Fish* (2013) and *Mrs Krishnan's Party* (2017).

Registering the contemporary importance of the Edinburgh Festival Fringe as a destination for New Zealand theatre seeking to enter the global marketplace, Chapters 7 and 8 both focus on New Zealand's relationship with this specific market. In "Selling the nation at the Edinburgh Festival Fringe", I explore why touring to the Edinburgh Fringe has become a significant rite-of-passage for New Zealand theatre makers, encouraged by Creative New Zealand's substantial investment in this market. I consider how Creative New Zealand's Edinburgh strategy has developed following the first branded "NZ at Edinburgh" country showcase season at the 2014 Fringe. In "Making meaning: responses to Aotearoa New Zealand at the Edinburgh Festival Fringe 2019", I present my findings from a survey of audiences attending five New Zealand touring shows performing at the 2019 Fringe: *Two Worlds* (2018) by the Modern Māori Quartet, *Super Hugh-Man* (2017) by Rutene Spooner, *My Best Dead Friend* (2016) by Anya Tate-Manning and Isobel Mackinnon, *Aunty* (2017) by Johanna Cosgrove and *Working on My Night Moves* (2019) by Julia Croft and Nisha Madhan.

The final chapter, "Cultural apocalypse: *The Generation of Z: Apocalypse* in London", focuses on the three-month London performance in 2015 of this immersive theatre work, which invites participants to imagine themselves as survivors of a Zombie apocalypse. New Zealand identity is placed at the margin in the hopes of gaining lucrative access to the overseas market by engaging with globally popular entertainment forms and stories. I consider the possibility that this work signals a kind of *cultural* apocalypse, in which Aotearoa New Zealand identity in theatre is increasingly homogenised or devalued as productions pursue globality as a means to enter the global marketplace.

What follows is a story of how New Zealand has imagined and conceived of itself through theatre and performance, how national identities have been represented and performed on global stages, and how these identities have been read and received by audiences around the world; in other words, how New Zealanders perceive themselves and how the world, in turn, perceives Aotearoa New Zealand.

Notes

1 See *Guardian News*. 2018. "Off the Map: New Zealand Tourism Ad Takes On 'Conspiracy'". Last modified May 1, 2018. https://www.youtube.com/watch?v=HynsTvRVLiI

2 I refer to the country as Aotearoa, New Zealand and Aotearoa New Zealand interchangeably throughout this book.

3 When a year in brackets appears after the title of the play this indicates the year of first performance.

4 This region was named the Pacific by Portuguese explorer Ferdinand Magellan in the 16th century, and Oceania is a common alternative suggesting a connected sea of islands; where possible, I am preferencing the Indigenous term Moana (ocean or vast space) in using Moana Oceania to describe this region.

5 Three general histories of New Zealand theatre – *A Dramatic Appearance* by Peter Harcourt (1978), *New Zealand Drama* by Howard McNaughton (1981) and *New Zealand Drama 1930–1980: An Illustrated History* by John Thomson (1984) – were published during a period concerned with the legitimisation of theatre in New Zealand, but there remains a significant gap in the historiography as there have been no comprehensive general performance histories since. Acknowledging this absence, *Performing Aotearoa*, edited by Marc Maufort and David O'Donnell, was published in 2007 and features essays and interviews documenting developments in Aotearoa theatre. More recently, Lisa Warrington and David O'Donnell have contributed *Floating Islanders: Pasifika Theatre in Aotearoa* (2017).

6 I have endeavoured to be mindful of issues of representation in choosing my case studies, but I was unable to resolve the gender imbalance in the final selection. This reflects a systematic bias, not only in the work produced in and toured from New Zealand, but theatre worldwide, of gendered hegemony in which male playwrights are overwhelmingly produced on stages compared to female or non-binary playwrights. These issues are especially pertinent when showcasing a selection of New Zealand work in an international market, such as at the 2014 and 2017 Edinburgh Festivals (see Chapter 7).

7 Ōrotokare Trust, founded by Charles Royal, held its first contemporary whare tapere revival in 2010.

8 See "Abel Tasman". *NZ History*. Last modified January 4, 2020. http://nzhistory.govt.nz/people/abel-tasman

9 See Wilson, John. 2005. "European Discovery of New Zealand – Cook's Three Voyages". *Te Ara*. Last modified May 1, 2016. www.TeAra.govt.nz/en/european-discovery-of-new-zealand/page-5

10 See "He Whakaputanga – Declaration of Independence, 1835". *NZ History*. Last modified January 4, 2020. http://nzhistory.govt.nz/media/interactive/the-declaration-of-independence

11 See Reynolds, Ted. 1990. "The Treaty Today – What Went Wrong and What Are We Doing about It?" *New Zealand Geographic*. Last modified January 4, 2020. www.nzgeo.com/stories/the-treaty-today-what-went-wrong-and-what-are-we-doing-about-it/

12 See Orange, Claudia. 2012. "Treaty of Waitangi". *Te Ara*. Last modified June 20, 2012. http://teara.govt.nz/en/treaty-of-waitangi/print

13 Creative New Zealand and its abbreviation CNZ are used interchangeably throughout this study.

14 In March 2020 New Zealand's total population reached the milestone of 5 million.

15 This question of whether we can read *The Rocky Horror Show* for markers of New Zealandness is explored in more detail in Chapter 1.
16 Funding applications are initially externally peer assessed, with recommendations for funding moderated by CNZ.

References

Alzate, Gastón A. 2014. "Cultural Interweaving in Mexican Political Cabaret" in *The Politics of Interweaving Performance Cultures: Beyond Postcolonialism*, edited by Erika Fischer-Lichte, Torsten Jost and Saskya Iris Jain. New York; London: Routledge: 42–59.

Amery, Mark. 2013. "Pakeha and Palagi: New Zealand European Playwriting 1998–2012" in *Playmarket 40*, edited by Laurie Atkinson. Wellington: Playmarket: 99–103.

Amkpa, Awam. 2004. *Theatre and Postcolonial Desires.* London; New York: Routledge.

Anderson, Benedict. 2006. *Imagined Communities: Reflections on the Origin and Spread of Nationalism.* London; New York: Verso.

Ashcroft, Bill, Gareth Griffiths and Helen Tiffin. 2007. *Post-Colonial Studies: The Key Concepts* (Second Edition). London; New York: Routledge.

"Bare Touring". 2001. *Guardian Guide.* May 5 in Client File: Toa Fraser, Playmarket, Wellington.

Barker, Ronald H. 1962. "Reflections on the New Zealand Theatre". *Theatre* 60 (6): 15–17.

Bennett, Susan. 1990. *Theatre Audiences: A Theory of Production and Reception.* London: Routledge.

——— 2005. "Theatre/Tourism". *Theatre Journal,* 57 (3): 407–428.

Bhabha, Homi K. 2014. "Epilogue: Global Pathways" in *The Politics of Interweaving Performance Cultures: Beyond Postcolonialism,* edited by Erika Fischer-Lichte, Torsten Jost and Saskya Iris Jain. New York; London: Routledge: 259–275.

Billington, Michael. 2004. "The Sons of Charlie Paora". *The Guardian.* Last modified February 27, 2004. https://www.theguardian.com/stage/2004/feb/27/theatre1

Blandford, Steve. 2013. *Theatre and Performance in Small Nations.* Bristol; Chicago: Intellect.

Butler, Judith. 1999. *Gender Trouble: Feminism and the Subversion of Identity.* New York: Routledge.

Capie, David. 2009. "New Zealand and the World: Imperial, International and Global Relations" in *The New Oxford History of New Zealand,* edited by Giselle Byrnes. South Melbourne: Oxford University Press: 573–598.

Carnegie, David. 1998. "New Zealand" in *The World Encyclopaedia of Contemporary Theatre Asia/Pacific,* edited by Don Rubin, Chua Soo Pong, Ravi Chaturvedi, Ramendu Majumdar, Minoru Tanokura and Katharine Brisbane. London: Routledge: 333–353.

Congreve, Eleanor. 2019. Interviewed by James Wenley. Video Conference (Auckland/Wellington). December 19.

Creative New Zealand. 2018. "Investment Strategy Te Ara Whakamua". April. Last modified January 4, 2020. https://www.creativenz.govt.nz/assets/paperclip/publication_documents/documents/547/original/investment_strategy_2018final.pdf?1526248718

Creswell, Tim. 2006. *On the Move: Mobility in the Modern Western World.* New York: Routledge.

Daly, Herman E. 1999. "Globalization vs Internationalization". *Global Policy Forum.* Last modified January 2, 2020. www.globalpolicy.org/component/content/article/162/27995.html

Deighton, John. 1991. "The Consumption of Performance". *Journal of Consumer Research*, 19 (3): 362–372.

Edmond, Murray. 1991. "Lighting Out for Paradise: New Zealand Theatre and the 'Other' Tradition". *Australasian Drama Studies*, 18: 183–206.

—— 1996. "Old Comrades of the Future: A History of Experimental Theatre in New Zealand, 1962–1982". PhD Thesis, University of Auckland.

—— 2014. "Plays and Playwrights – Plays of the Mid- and Later 20th Century". *Te Ara.* Last modified October 22, 2014. www.TeAra.govt.nz/en/video/43951/the-pohutukawa-tree-1956

Fischer-Lichte, Erika. 2008. *The Transformative Power of Performance: A New Aesthetics.* London; New York: Routledge.

—— 2014. "Introduction: Interweaving Performance Cultures – Rethinking 'Intercultural Theatre': Toward an Experience and Theory of Performance beyond Postcolonialism" in *The Politics of Interweaving Performance Cultures: Beyond Postcolonialism*, edited by Fischer-Lichte, Torsten Jost and Saskya Iris Jain. New York; London: Routledge: 1–21.

Freshwater, Helen. 2009. *Theatre & Audience.* London: Red Globe Press.

Giesler, Markus. 2008. "Conflict and Compromise: Drama in Marketplace Evolution". *Journal of Consumer Research*, 34 (6): 739–753.

Gilbert, Helen. 2004. "Foreword" by Jacqueline Lo in *Staging Nation: English Language Theatre in Malaysia and Singapore.* Hong Kong: Hong Kong University Press: vii–viii.

Gilbert, Helen and Jacqueline Lo. 2007. *Performance and Cosmopolitics: Cross-Cultural Transactions in Australasia.* Hampshire: Palgrave Macmillan.

Gilbert, Helen and Joanne Tompkins. 1996. *Post-Colonial Drama: Theory, Practice, Politics.* London; New York: Routledge.

Grene, Nicholas and Chris Morash. 2005. *Irish Theatre on Tour.* Dublin: Carysfort Press.

Hall, Stuart. 1990. "Cultural Identity and Diaspora" in *Theorizing Diaspora: A Reader*, edited by Jana Evans Braziel and Anita Mannur. Oxford and Maiden, MA: Blackwell. 2003: 233–246.

Harcourt, Peter. 1978. *A Dramatic Appearance: New Zealand Theatre, 1920–1970.* Wellington: Methuen.

Harvie, Jen. 2005. *Staging the UK.* Manchester: Manchester University Press.

Holdsworth, Nadine. 2010. *Theatre & Nation.* Hampshire: Palgrave Macmillan.

Hopkins, D.H. and Kim Solga. 2013. *Performance and the Global City.* Hampshire: Palgrave Macmillan.

Jaffe, Jerry C. 2009. "Loop/I/-ness in the New Zealand Performance of Identity (or, Id Entity)". *Australasian Drama Studies*, 55: 4–9.

Jullien, François. 2014. *On the Universal: The Uniform, the Common and Dialogue between Cultures.* Cambridge: Polity Press.

Kendall, Gavin, Ian Woodward and Zlatko Skrbiš. 2009. *The Sociology of Cosmopolitanism: Globalization, Identity, Culture and Government.* Hampshire: Palgrave Macmillan.

Kennedy, Paul T. 2010. *Local Lives and Global Transformations: Towards World Society.* Hampshire; New York: Palgrave Macmillan.

King, Michael. 2004. *Being Pakeha Now: Reflections and Recollections of a White Native*. Auckland: Penguin.

Knowles, Ric. 2004. *Reading the Material Theatre*. Cambridge: Cambridge University Press.

——— 2014. *How Theatre Means*. Hampshire: Palgrave Macmillan.

Looser, Diana. 2014. *Remaking Pacific Pasts: History, Memory, and Identity in Contemporary Theater from Oceania*. Honolulu: University of Hawai'i Press.

Mason, Bruce. 1960. "The Māori as Artist". *Te Ao Hou*, 8 (31): 1.

——— c.1966–1977. "Kiwi Abroad". Undated manuscript in Carton 5, Box 2, Folder 1, Bruce Mason Papers, J.C. Beaglehole Room, Victoria University, Wellington.

——— 1978. *Letter to Colin H. Wright*. March 7 in Carton 7 Box 4, Bruce Mason Papers.

——— 1986. *Every Kind of Weather*. Auckland: Reed Methuen.

——— 1987. "Awatea: Note to the Second Edition" in *The Healing Arch: Five Plays on Maori Themes*. Wellington: Victoria University Press: 296–299.

Maufort, Marc. 2003. *Transgressive Itineraries: Postcolonial Hybridizations of Dramatic Realism*. Bruxelles; New York: PIE Peter Lang.

——— 2007. "Performing Aotearoa in an Age of Transition" in *Performing Aotearoa: New Zealand Theatre and Drama in an Age of Transition*, edited by Marc Maufort and David O'Donnell. Bruxelles; New York: PIE Peter Lang: 13–16.

Mazer, Sharon. 2013. "A National Theatre in New Zealand? Why/Not?" in *Theatre and Performance in Small Nations*, edited by Steve Blandford. Bristol; Chicago: Intellect: 106–121.

McAuley, Gay. 2013. "What Is Sydney about Sydney Theatre? Performance Space and the Creation of a 'Matrix of Sensibility'" in *Performance and the Politics of Space: Theatre and Topology*, edited by Erika Fischer-Lichte and Benjamin Wihstutz. New York: Routledge: 81–99.

McCarter, Nigel. 2001. *The Big OE: Tales from New Zealand Travelers*. Auckland: Tandem Press.

McDermott, Charlie. 2015. Interviewed by James Wenley. London. July 14.

McGee, Greg. 1981. *Foreskin's Lament*. Wellington: Price Milburn and Victoria University Press.

McNaughton, Howard. 1981. *New Zealand Drama*. Boston: Twayne.

McNaughton, Ioana. 1986. "Lord Home from the Big Apple". *Sunday Star Times*. December 28.

Normington, Katie. 2011. "Case Study 1: Tracing Medieval English Convent Drama" in *Research Methods in Theatre and Performance*, edited by Baz Kershaw and Helen Nicholson. Edinburgh: University Press.

O'Brien, Richard. 1983. *The Rocky Horror Show*. London: Samuel French.

O' Byrne, Darren and Alexander Hensby. 2011. *Theorizing Global Studies*. Hampshire; New York: Palgrave Macmillan.

Parker, George. 2008. "Actor Alone: Solo Performance in New Zealand". PhD Thesis. University of Canterbury, Christchurch.

Pearson, Bill. 1952. "Fretful Sleepers – A Sketch of New Zealand Behaviour and Its Implications for the Artist". Republished in *Fretful Sleepers and Other Essays*. Auckland: Heinemann Educational Books, 1974: 1–30.

Playmarket. 2019. "More NZ Work from Our Professional Companies". *Theatreview*. Last Modified May 24, 2019. https://www.theatreview.org.nz/news/news.php?id= 1671

Pool, Ian and Natalie Jackson. 2011. "Population Change – Key Population Trends". *Te Ara*. Last modified August 23, 2018. www.TeAra.govt.nz/en/graph/28720/new-zealand-population-by-ethnicity-1840-20

Rajan, Jacob. 2017. "Still Pioneers" in *Playmarket Annual*. Wellington: Playmarket: 12–13.

Rees, Catherine. 2017. *Adaptation and Nation: Theatrical Contexts for Contemporary English and Irish Drama*. London: Palgrave Macmillan.

Robertson, Roland. 1992. *Globalization: Social Theory and Global Culture*. London: Sage.

Rogers, Amanda. 2015. *Performing Asian Transnationalisms: Theatre, Identity and the Geographies of Performance*. New York: Routledge.

Royal, Te Ahukaramū Charles. 1998. "Te Whare Tapere: Towards a Model for Māori Performance Art". PhD Thesis. Victoria University. Wellington.

Schafer, Elizabeth and Susan Bradley Smith. 2003. *Playing Australia: Australian Theatre and the International Stage*. Amsterdam: Rodopi.

Schultz, Marianne. 2016. *Performing Indigenous Culture on Stage and Screen: A Harmony of Frenzy*. Hampshire; New York: Palgrave Macmillan.

Shakespeare, William. c. 1599–1602. "Hamlet" in *The Complete Works* (Second Edition), edited by Stanley Wells and Gary Taylor. Oxford: Clarendon Press. 2005: 681–718.

The Shakespeare Globe Trust. 2014. "Hamlet the Play: About the Project". Last modified January 4, 2020. http://globetoglobe.shakespearesglobe.com/hamlet/about-the-project

Singleton, Brian. 2014. "Performing Orientalist, Intercultural, and Globalized Modernities" in *The Politics of Interweaving Performance Cultures: Beyond Postcolonialism*, edited by Erika Fischer-Lichte, Torsten Jost and Saskya Iris Jain, New York; London: Routledge: 77–94.

Sluga, Glenda. 2013. *Internationalism in the Age of Nationalism*. Philadelphia: University of Pennsylvania Press.

Stats NZ. 2019. "2018 Census Population and Dwelling Counts". Last modified September 23, 2019. www.stats.govt.nz/information-releases/2018-census-population-and-dwelling-counts

"Theatre Personalities No. 2 Tim Elliott". 1967. *NZ Stage*. April 8–9.

Thomson, John. 1984. *New Zealand Drama, 1930–1980: An Illustrated History*. Auckland: Oxford University Press.

Varney, Denise, Peter Eckersall, Chris Hudson and Barbara Hatley. 2013. *Theatre and Performance in the Asia-Pacific: Regional Modernities in the Global Era*. Hampshire: Palgrave Macmillan.

Warrington, Lisa and David O'Donnell. 2017. *Floating Islanders: Pasifika Theatre in Aotearoa*. Otago: Otago University Press.

Wells, Peter. 1981. "Putting the Boot In". *NZ Listener*. January 10.

Werry, Margaret. 2014. "Oceanic Imagination, Intercultural Performance, Pacific Historiography" in *The Politics of Interweaving Performance Cultures: Beyond Postcolonialism*, edited by Erika Fischer-Lichte, Torsten Jost and Saskya Iris Jain. New York; London: Routledge: 97–118.

Wilkie, Fiona. 2015. *Performance, Transport and Mobility: Making Passage*. London: Palgrave Macmillan.

Wilson, Jude, David Fisher and Kevin Moore. 2009. "Reverse Diaspora and the Evolution of a Cultural Tradition: The Case of the New Zealand 'Overseas Experience'". *Mobilities*, 4 (1): 159–175.

Zaiontz, Keren. 2018. *Theatre & Festivals*. London: Palgrave Macmillan.

1   National travels in an international world

Overseas performances 1940–1990

At the close of WWII, the New Zealand nation state faced existential questions about the country's place in the world. Although New Zealand still had absolute loyalty to the old Empire (now the Commonwealth) following the war, Britain's influence had been weakened, and New Zealand began to be "more active in dealing with states outside the Empire" (Capie 2009: 586). The nation needed to negotiate an internationalised world in which the United Nations represented new hope for cooperation between nation states, and "find its way in a global political and economic system dominated by the USA and constrained by the exigencies of the Cold War" (576). As the New Zealand state reoriented its place in the world under these post-war internationalist conditions, a cultural nationalist strand of New Zealand's drama became concerned with representing the local and the distinctive elements of life in New Zealand. The New Zealand theatre performed internationally during this period is bound with issues of national self-definition and New Zealand's place in the shifting geopolitical landscape. It was a question of what particular kind of New Zealand national would be represented internationally – on the political stage, as well as the theatrical.

The New Zealand theatre performed overseas during this international world period (from WWII to the end of the Cold War) revealed a considerable anxiety regarding the formation and display of a distinct regionalist identity to international audiences. This was an issue New Zealand playwright Bruce Mason highlighted during an address at the first International Drama Conference held in Edinburgh in 1963 coincident with the Edinburgh International Festival and Fringe Festival (Mason had toured with his own play, *The End of the Golden Weather*, to the Fringe that year). Such was the status of the attendees at this conference (which included British luminaries Joan Littlewood, Bernard Levan and John Arden) that critic and conference chairperson Kenneth Tynan remarked that "if a bomb were to drop on this room, world drama might never recover" (Cryer 1964). Mason addressed the state of New Zealand's emerging national theatre, what it could offer the world and "provincial and regional problems" (I.E. 1963). Mason critiqued comments made by art historian Sir Kenneth Clark in support of Britain joining the European Common Market. Clark (1963: 56) argued that "an innocent, authentic local culture is impossible", pointing out that the belief that "art must be national" was a relatively recent construction from the German Romantic Movement, and that the greatest periods of European art were international. Clark continued:

> All that the Artist can do is to master the international language and, if he speaks it involuntarily with his own native accent – Australian, Mexican, or whatever – that may add to his charm. But if he tries to trade on his accent he becomes a provincial nuisance.
>
> (56)

Clark's position, although highly Eurocentric, was that national difference was an artificial separation between peoples. Mason's counter-argument was that establishing distinctive national/regional identities was of vital importance, especially for countries on the margin like New Zealand. This debate was articulated via the terms regionalism and provincialism, which is the particularism versus universalism debate (as outlined in the Introduction) in another guise. The extremes of the regional and provincial poles are "equally sterile", leading either to "universal sameness" or "the incommensurability of cultures (cultural relativism)" (Kendall, Woodward and Skrbiš 2009: 57).

The provincialism versus regionalism debate featured in New Zealand's literary scene in the 1960s. Cultural nationalists like Mason were concerned with establishing what made life in New Zealand unique compared to the rest of the world, which led poet Kendrick Smithyman (1965: 12) to warn that New Zealanders' "understandable interest in how different we may be from others sometimes persuades us not to see how like others we are". Like Clark, Smithyman believed that "the discovery of continuity and simultaneous order" was the truer aim compared to "the searching and teasing of distinctiveness" (26). For New Zealand theatre, provincialism emphasised continuity with the shared colonial culture. Regionalism emphasised discontinuity and difference and the unique locational pressures that can be located in an artistic work. Regionalism is generally identified with segmentations within countries, notably the Southern Agrarian movement espoused by Allen Tate and others in the USA, but if New Zealand is considered a hinterland to an Anglo metropolis, regionalism and nationalism can generally be interchangeable as terms. Although there may be regional differences within New Zealand, when set against the world, the entire country can contain distinct "influences that can be found in this country and nowhere else" (39).

Mason was a passionate advocate for this regionalist view, described as the "first New Zealand playwright to consistently insist on the affirmation of his own culture and so challenge the hegemony of colonising power" (Williams 2006: 88). In his speech at the International Drama Conference, Mason argued for the importance of regional locality. Echoing lines from *The End of the Golden Weather*, Mason told delegates:

When your ancestors and mine put all their chattels on to ships and went half-way across the world to transplant the Scottish and British way of life, they took with them not only pots and pans and thousands of years of history, but also a whole system of totem and taboo and a British and Scottish puritan background, which they unleashed on the unsuspecting population.

(I.E. 1963)

Though early settlers attempted to transplant and replicate these cultural systems, Mason argued that a divergent culture and worldview had developed in New Zealand, and was continuing to transition: "New Zealanders with British and Scottish ancestry were slowly turning Polynesian" (I.E.). Mason predicted that "the effect of this is going to be our special contribution to art and theatre in particular" (I.E.). The newspaper report quoting Mason's speech recorded that these comments "caused a clash among the delegates, particularly among the coloured delegates who were extremely touchy, Mr Mason said" (I.E.). For Mason, the confluence of cultures at the bottom of the world would result in something unique, but the identity process that he described betrayed a settler-invader impulse, a unique contribution to art established through both appropriation and erasure of indigenous expression. In the 1970s, the Amamus company, which toured *Gallipoli* (1974) to England and Poland, was also committed to representing a regional identity forming in New Zealand. Amamus argued that "there are specific experiences, specific cultural patterns which are in essence New Zealand; and if local theatre is to truly interpret the culture in which it exists, it should be concerned with these patterns" (Edmond 1996: 177). Mason's comments, together with Amamus' position, reveal a considerable colonial anxiety about establishing what was unique about the nation and that it was more than just a provincial echo of the British motherland. The cases in this chapter explore how New Zealand's search for an elusive authentic regional identity manifested in productions performed overseas to the international world over this period.

Colonial mimicry

New Zealand entertainment in the immediate post-war period was dominated by the Kiwis, a group that originated during WWII as an entertainment division of the New Zealand army under their original name, the Kiwi Concert Party. The Kiwis are one of New Zealand's most successful theatrical touring companies: from 1946 to 1954 the Concert Party toured Australia and New Zealand, including a two-year occupation of Melbourne's Comedy Theatre. While nominally linked with the New Zealand national, the Kiwis epitomise provincialism in New Zealand performance, largely mimicking popular colonial entertainment from the pre-war period.

The Kiwi Concert Party was assembled in early 1941 from soldiers within the New Zealand division as a permanent entertainment unit and required to maintain their own weaponry with a regular infantry drill. They debuted their first revue in Crete on May 1, 1941, and their final war-time revue outside Siena on November 6, 1945, for an audience of the Divisional Artillery. The Party was unique during the war; while there were frequent performances for the allied troops, these conventionally comprised non-combat performers who toured to army bases. Each Kiwi Concert Party performance was approximately two-and-a-half hours. Sketches were interspersed with vocal and instrumental items, and their revues included clowning and female impersonators. Terry Vaughan (1995: 23), who was the musical director and producer for the majority of the company's existence, explained that:

> The Kiwis were not the popular idea of a soldier show [...]. There were no uniforms on stage, no jokes about the cook or the colonel. [...]. The idea was to simply give the boys a break from what they heard all day, to give them a reminder of civvy street – something they might have taken the girlfriend to back home and, with luck, would again.

The shows performed during the campaign attempted to transport audiences back to civvy street and provide a nostalgic re-creation of the popular entertainment they had enjoyed at home. According to historian Christopher Burns (2012: 143), "the most popular routines were those, such as Red Moore's impersonations of American celebrities, which drew on the audience's familiarity and fascination with a wider culture of entertainment". One aspect that more clearly identified the company as New Zealanders was the inclusion of Māori songs, a "sure-fire hit" (Vaughan 1995: 21). When the all-Pākehā unit played to the Māori battalion, the Māori songs resulted in an "almost continuous barrage of laughter, cheers and applause" according to Vaughan, who expressed that the occasion of "Pākehā singing [to Māori] their own songs and getting away with it" was "pretty funny" (21). The tokenistic acknowledgement of New Zealand's indigenous culture contrasts with the lack of the Anglo–New Zealander's own distinctive regionalist culture; instead, they borrowed from the Māori, English and Americans.

The Kiwi Concert Party reformed as the Kiwis under Vaughan's leadership after the war, and continued to tour New Zealand and Australia for almost a decade. The Kiwis opened in Melbourne in the Comedy Theatre on December 21, 1946, and played 857 performances before transferring to Sydney's Empire Theatre on February 2, 1949. The Kiwis named their postwar revues after significant campaigns during the war: Alamein, Benghazi and Tripoli. The company appeared in battledress in the first half of the show, and despite not having any Māori company members, performed the item "Songs of the Māori Battalion" in uniform during the second half (71). This shifted the focus from pre-war civvy street towards a romanticised nostalgia for the war period itself. The only other overseas tour in this period also followed the Kiwi Concert Party by boat to Australia. The Canterbury Student Players, directed by Ngaio Marsh, visited Sydney, Melbourne and Canberra in

1949, with productions of Shakespeare's *Othello* (1603) and Pirandello's *Six Characters in Search of an Author* (1921), an "unprecedented undertaking for a student company" (Simpson 2016: 289). Both the students, who attracted "good crowds and excellent reviews" (290), and the Kiwi Concert Party were in Melbourne at the same time and demonstrated the extreme ends of colonial theatrical performance: the high-art of Shakespeare and European "modern" drama, and the popular entertainment of the concert party.

During the Kiwis' 1953 tour of New Zealand, a reviewer for the *NZ Truth* criticised the company for being "content to imitate all the overseas patterns", stating that "even their policeman is a burlesque London 'bobby'" and was disappointed about the show's "lack of New Zealand character", suggesting that the company "could go so much further if they had a script writer who could give these young New Zealanders the material to put their country on the stage" ("Kiwis Home Again" 1953). The *NZ Truth* reviewer was the minority view; Burns (2012: 21) argues that the Kiwis' "popularity implies that a large body of New Zealanders saw no contradiction in presenting a troupe that drew their material from 'overseas patterns' as a source of national pride". Indeed, many New Zealanders would have seen the Kiwis as representing a national character precisely because the shows imitated these overseas, especially British, patterns. The Kiwi Concert Party demonstrated a desired continuity with the colonial past, but the anonymous *NZ Truth* reviewer's cultural nationalist call to see their "country on the stage" became a passionate project for dramatists Stella Jones, Bruce Mason and Paul Maunder of Amamus.

Towards cultural maturity

Michael King (2004: 413; 415) notes that "the immediate effect of WWII and its aftermath was to turn New Zealanders in on themselves"; returning to pre-war social patterns, society's focus was the nuclear family, the house and garden, and Britain was still invoked as "home". This retreat to insularity began to plant the seeds for a reorientation of where "home" might be located, setting into motion a shift away from the expression of a "fondness for the imagined English past", towards a search "for domestic sources from which its nostalgic imagination could be (re)assembled" (Moon 2013: 297). Thus, playwrights began writing plays featuring New Zealand characters and settings, and some sought production overseas. *The Tree*, by Stella Jones, in fact premiered in Bristol for the Rapier Players in 1957, and was also performed by the Newcastle Repertory later that year, before it was produced locally by the NZ Players in 1959. The play revolves around the Willis family grouping of ageing father Herbert and – in a Chekhovian nod – three sisters: Lucy and Daisy (who still live with their father) and Hilda who left New Zealand 15 years earlier, aged 19. *The Tree's* dramatic conflict is whether it is better to leave for overseas opportunities like Hilda, or to stay and make a life on the "tame, safe little" New Zealand back porch like her sisters (Jones, Stella 1960: 83). During the play's Bristol season it was reported that it was "exciting to see on the English stage a play about a group of recognisable New Zealanders and their troubles" (Bell 1957). The Newcastle producers claimed their audiences could appreciate the play's universal themes, while also being given a "glimpse of life in New Zealand" (Playhouse Newcastle 1957). The New Zealand context is maintained while simultaneously offering the possibility of more generalised meanings for English audiences to discover.

Bruce Mason, often claimed as a pioneering dramatist in the New Zealand canon, enthusiastically pursued overseas production of his work. In 1958 he sought commercial West End performance of his play *Birds in the Wilderness* (1958), in a Sunday night try-out at the Lyric Theatre, Shaftesbury Avenue. The play "failed to run" and it "was difficult for managers to know in quite what milieu the play was set and how to make it viable to audiences" (Mason 1967). Mason received interest from a theatre manager who wanted the setting transposed to Northern Ireland, but Mason refused as it would "make mincemeat, not to say nonsense of my theme" (Mason 1981: 9). Mason's most notable British success came when a BBC Television version of his play *The Pohutukawa Tree* (1956) was screened in Britain in October 1959 as part of Sunday Night Theatre, giving Mason a larger audience than any live theatre production would have done. In a fascinating instance of New Zealand theatre overseas, *The Pohutukawa Tree* was also produced by Theatr Fach Llangefini in 1960, a Welsh company attempting to find cultural renewal through a play from New Zealand which deals with the decline of Māori culture. Another significant production during this period was James K. Baxter's *The Wide Open Cage* (1959), which became the first New Zealand play (with a New Zealand setting) to be produced in New York City at the off-Broadway Washington Square Theatre venue in 1962.

Following the circulation of these New Zealand scripts, Bruce Mason became the first to tour the emerging regionalist (Anglo/Pākehā) New Zealand identity with his play *The End of the Golden Weather* (1959) to the Edinburgh Festival Fringe in 1963. Described as "a voyage into a New Zealand childhood", Mason's "Boy" narrator gains a burgeoning sense of maturity over a 1930s New Zealand summer (Mason 1994). Helen Gilbert and Joanne Thompkins (1996: 113) argue that post-colonial dramas in settler societies "are often concerned with establishing authenticity for a society dislocated from the imperial centre and, simultaneously, alienated from the local land and indigenous culture". Mason's *Golden Weather* was intended to suggest that the country had moved out of its colonial phase and now had a culture unique to itself, if still tentative and maturing, like the young protagonist of Mason's play. Mason had conceived *Golden Weather* as a solo work, utilising the British convention of the literary recital popularised by Emlyn Williams (who had toured New Zealand), out of frustration that his large-cast plays went unprogrammed by New Zealand theatres. When Mason reached 150 performances of *Golden Weather*, it was deemed "the most performed theatrical work in New Zealand history, with the exception of *My Fair Lady*", the reference to the 1956 musical indicating popular imported theatrical tastes ("The 'Golden Weather' Marathon" 1962).

Mason was one of 16 shows at the 1963 Edinburgh Fringe which played during an 11 p.m. performance slot (after buses had stopped and street lights were out), which meant that he could perform only the first half of *Golden Weather*. Nevertheless, he received positive critical notices and was compared favourably to British figures Dylan Thomas and Emlyn Williams. Mason had been concerned that the play's "provincial locale would have only a parochial appeal", but found "that, like some wines, my work 'travels'" (Mason 1963). Mason also performed a short season at London's Mayfair Theatre. As the first tour to the Fringe by a New Zealander, and taken in the context of Mason's larger efforts to gain overseas validity and visibility, *Golden Weather*'s initial overseas showcase was an important stage in the theatre's maturity.

With the internal production of New Zealand theatre still relatively rare through the 1960s, excepting a tour by the New Zealand Opera company to Australia of Gershwin's *Porgy and Bess* in 1966, featuring an all-Māori cast, the next notable international tour was not till a decade later in 1972, when Theatre Action became the first of New Zealand's emerging experimental companies to travel overseas, taking *Once Upon a Planet* (1972) to Suva, Fiji, as part of NZ Trade Week. Founder Francis Batten had spent two years training under Jacques Lecoq in Paris, and Theatre Action's work demonstrated that not all New Zealand theatre artists were interested in the regionalist debate; Theatre Action was more concerned with an internationalist theatre practice. It would take until 1975 for Mason's overseas regionalist legacy to be matched when Amamus toured to Poland and London with *Gallipoli* (1974), a play about New Zealand's involvement in the ill-fated 1915 WWI campaign, a site which has become mythically associated with New Zealand's history as the crucible through which a distinct national identity was formed as a result of the conflict and sacrifice in war.

Amamus was formed in 1971 by Paul Maunder and several young actors as part of a nationalistic search for identity, opting to create plays based on New Zealand society and history (Maunder 2013: 50). Maunder stated to the British press that "most New Zealanders of artistic talent have pursued their careers in Europe", but recently, "a stirring of cultural nationalism has been felt and many artists now prefer to work and live in New Zealand to attempt to discover their own identity" (Amamus 1975). Maunder echoed Mason's comments at the International Drama Conference, arguing for the distinctiveness of New Zealand's national identity, as the "elements that have infiltrated the New Zealand version of Western culture give it vitality not found in the mainstream European tradition" (Amamus 1975). *Gallipoli* sought to emulate Polish director Jerzy Grotowski's theories of poor theatre, which advocated stripping away all that is non-essential in theatre to focus on the relationship between the actor and the audience. Once again, we see the borrowing of overseas forms in order to display the New Zealand identity, but unlike

Mason's literary recital, Amamus was searching beyond the traditional forms of its colonial heritage.[1]

Amamus was invited to perform at Fifth International Student Festival of the Open Theatre in Wrocław, Poland. In his letter to the Arts Council requesting funding for the tour, Maunder made the case that the invitation was a unique opportunity for New Zealand experimental theatre to "perform an indigenous play in an international environment", as the opportunity to "see and meet other groups would be a stimulation not often gained in this corner of the world". He argued that "to be able to present a contemporary piece of NZ drama in this setting would be a small but perhaps significant step towards cultural maturity" (Maunder 1975). The Arts Council and Ministry of Foreign Affairs jointly funded the cost of the group's return airfares, a significant political development in recognising the value of international performance. During October and November 1975 Amamus toured to the Institute of Contemporary Arts, London, the International Student Festival in Wrocław, and subsequently to the Polish University and cities of Szczeczin, Gdańsk and Łódź. Through the tour the New Zealanders were searching for their place within a larger international experimental community. There were 20 companies involved in the International Student festival, mostly from Eastern and Western Europe, featuring several well-known experimental companies, including Poland's Theatre of the Eighth Day (Edmond 1996: 206). Amamus played to capacity houses, suggesting curiosity from the Polish audiences towards the New Zealanders. Maunder (1976: 2), however, reported a "certain lack of understanding from the Poles of the nature of New Zealand's cultural problems – I think we seemed a little naïve to them to be worrying about whether we exist as a nation". The overall effect of this tour was to make notions of a regionalist New Zealand identity less, not more, secure.

The tours of *The End of the Golden Weather* and *Gallipoli* were attempts by very different theatre makers to prove a regionalist identity for New Zealand, and to gain validation for this identity through recognition by overseas audiences. Both Mason and Amamus bought into a nationalist paradigm, where "being a New Zealander" was a defining aspect of their work. Their plays sought to showcase New Zealand reaching towards cultural maturity through coming-of-age narratives (implicitly linking the attainment of manhood with nationhood). The next significant touring story would fundamentally challenge the importance of touring national identities.

Alternative internationalism

On an initial glance, Red Mole Enterprises lived the Overseas Experience dream. The experimental collective relocated to New York City in December 1978 and toured to London and throughout the USA. At their high point, in Easter 1979, the Red Mole community had expanded to include 25 Kiwis connected with the company, all living together in the twelfth floor of the Consulate Hotel in New York (Edmond 1996: 346). When Red Mole's founders Alan Brunton and Sally Rodwell finally decided to return to New Zealand, they purchased their plane tickets while resident in Amsterdam. Red Mole was generally uninterested in displaying and dramatising New Zealand during its overseas adventures. Red Mole's work looked beyond the nation, towards the international. Red Mole's first work in New York City, *Goin' to Djibouti* (1979), had a geopolitical focus on American and Cuban revolutionary interventions in Africa, and had, as one puzzled New York critic stated, "nothing to do with life in the far Pacific" (Fox 1979). Exemplified by their decade of mostly permanent exile from their home country, the Moles removed themselves from the nationalist New Zealand theatre project of the 1960s–1980s. Red Mole chased another deceptive nostalgia: the bohemian dream of the travelling theatre troupe forever on the move, the anarchic American avant-garde a world away from New Zealand in both geography and attitude.

Red Mole Enterprises was founded in 1974 to produce radical and alternative performance, initially touring political satire, cabaret and experimental drama throughout New Zealand. "Someday all theatre will be like this" was a slogan often used by Red Mole, an ironical brag that highlighted how far removed they were from mainstream and commercial theatrical fare and the fervent belief in its mission. Brunton situated the desire to leave New Zealand in terms of overseas travel being a rite of passage for most New Zealanders, and told a reporter that "we came to the United States because in New Zealand you run into ocean wherever you go [...], we felt we needed to try a bigger scene" (Jones, Don 1993). Deborah Hunt (2017), a core Red Mole member, told me that the lack of "institutional support" in New Zealand was a motivating factor for the group's move, as well as the notion that in New York City there "were more of our own kind of restless creatives. We were right".

Red Mole's first work for New York City, *Goin' to Djibouti,* was created in two weeks. The Moles used the then current Ethiopian civil war for their subject matter, claiming that, in Red Mole's version of the dramatic mirror, "watching the present confrontations in Africa will tell us a great deal about ourselves" (Patterson 1979). Playing at the Westbeth Theatre, a cavernous off-off-Broadway space that had once been a film studio, the show featured "masks, puppets, erotic dance, music, stilt walkers, and magic" (Ginsberg 1979). A large audience of New Zealanders living in New York came to see *Goin' to Djibouti*, but the Moles reported that the American audience members were the most enthusiastic and "came back again and again, sitting in the front row" (Hunt, Barbara 1979).

New York's critics tried to understand Red Mole by comparing them with American avant-garde groups Bread and Puppet Theatre and the San Francisco Mime Troupe, but reviewers drew opposing conclusions. For a radio reviewer, Red Mole combined the best elements of these companies with a "sparkle and sauciness of their own. They are hardly N[ew] Zealand lambs!" ("SY SYNA Drama Critic WNYC" 1979). However, *Other Stages*' Tish Dace (1979) argued that the Moles were less savvy than their US counterparts, concluding that, since Moles are blind, the company's name was well chosen, as "their lack of artistic sophistication suggests they have developed without seeing other fine avant-garde groups or without benefitting from the chance to observe others' experiments [...]. The day that all theatre becomes like this is the day I get myself Home Box Office". The *Village Voice*'s Terry Curtis Fox (1979) was the only critic to question the ethnic representation of African and Cuban characters being portrayed by New Zealanders, and argued that "use by a colonial society of European forms of radical thought to discuss a Third World problem is cultural imperialism of a very refined degree". Murray Edmond (1996: 358) argues that "in New York being from New Zealand had more currency than being from New York" and, though the Moles had been "alienated at home, they became ethnic overseas, but without losing their alienation" and, therefore, "doubled their value". Conversely, their New Zealand origins could also be seen as a problem because they had not been exposed to what Americans perceived as their more sophisticated avant-garde.

Red Mole's first year abroad was marked by ambitious productivity, achieving three new works produced in New York City, a three-month tour of the UK, and had embarked on the start of the 1979/1980 "An American Tour", which saw the Moles tour across to a number of states including New Jersey, Texas, New Mexico and California.[2] The Moles returned to New Zealand for most of 1980, but in February 1981 they were back in New York City, with a "a determination to dig in, to put down roots, almost to swap one home for another" (Edmond 1996: 381). The Mole's leased and renovated the Pyramid venue in Times Square, a 70-seat former burlesque club, where they premiered *The Early Show* and *The Late Show* (Murphy 1981). Times Square was considered a "no-no" area, but Red Mole would "stand out on Broadway with our music and masks and drag people down to see us" (Vandenberg 1988). Three months after moving in, the venue was sold and Red Mole's operations ground to a halt.

While the Moles were never able to match the output of their first year as the financial realities of living in New York City took their toll and the collective reduced in numbers, Red Mole continued to make and tour work around the USA until 1986. With the company finally reduced to just Brunton and Rodwell, Red Mole left for Amsterdam in 1987 on an invitation to help create a new venue for the English-speaking Theatre of Amsterdam (ESTA), where the Moles performed *Playtime* (1986) and premiered *Hour of Justice* (1988). Rodwell felt the "pull to come back to our own country", and the Moles returned to New Zealand in February, 1988 (Vandenberg 1988). Deborah Hunt (2017) told me that the Moles "never forgot where we came from", although they "were also fascinated by events in the rest of the world". The Moles displaced anxieties about national identity by drawing from other international identities and conflicts. They employed their country of origin where it could enhance their outsider-narrative and attract curious audiences, but their political and aesthetic aims did not include an interest in New Zealand nationality in their overseas works. Instead, the company embraced the international world and was invigorated by their contact with the "Enormous Other".

Writing New Zealand away

Having examined the case of a collective company creating an internationalist body of work for an overseas market, I turn now to examples of individual playwrights who have attempted to directly write for British and American markets. The stories of these playwrights – Richard O'Brien, Roger Hall and Robert Lord – reveal varying processes of cultural adaptation to work within the pressures of commercial theatre markets.

Richard O'Brien

The first, Richard O'Brien, is not conventionally claimed as a New Zealand playwright because his major works were written outside of New Zealand. In 1964, aged 23, Richard O'Brien, whose family had moved to New Zealand from England when he was 9, returned to live and work in London. O'Brien's *The Rocky Horror Show* opened at London's Royal Court in 1973, with its creator in the role of servant Riff-Raff. Set in Midwest USA in the 1950s, clean-cut couple Brad and Janet are initiated into the home of mad transvestite scientist Dr Frank-N-Furter, who introduces them to the pleasures of the flesh. The cult film followed in 1975, and the show has continued to be produced worldwide. O'Brien gained his New Zealand citizenship only in 2010, which is perhaps one reason why the New Zealand relationship has not conventionally been emphasised in theatre historiography. The show's high-camp yet low-brow alternative cultural status may be another.

Scott Michaels and David Evans (2002: 25) contend that *Rocky Horror* "could never have been created and developed from anyone from the British theatrical tradition", noting that "those most intimately involved with the nascent *Rocky* [...] were all children of the colonies". Amongst the fishnet stockings and heels, can we find O'Brien's coming-of-age in New Zealand hidden within the show? Murray Edmond (2004: 117) reads *Rocky Horror* as the "psychic experience of growing up in New Zealand in the 1950s and 1960s". Such a reading is productive for *Rocky Horror*, and accords with O'Brien's own reminiscences. When I interviewed O'Brien ahead of a 2010 New Zealand tour of the show, he confirmed that "Eddie's Song" was written using "lots of images" from his "teenage youth" in Hamilton, New Zealand (Wenley 2011). It was also in Hamilton that O'Brien saw his first female impersonator act Noel McKay – "Frank-N-Furter [...] came out of [Hamilton's] Embassy Theatre", O'Brien recalled. Edmond (2004: 116) argues that *Rocky* "turns out to be uncannily autobiographical and can be read as a text which dramatises Kiwi dreams of 'overseas experience'". The protagonists Brad and Janet are analogues of small-town New Zealanders who venture overseas, where they can give themselves "over to absolute pleasure" and experience "erotic nightmares beyond any measure/and sensual daydreams to treasure forever" (O'Brien 1983: 28–29).

Rocky Horror is a rock-and-roll pastiche, but it is also a cultural pastiche, incorporating a range of influences in such a way that nationalistic borders are blurred. Reflecting the globalised B-movies screened at Hamilton's Embassy Theatre, *Rocky Horror* at first glance seems to hold a greater allegiance to American popular culture than New Zealand culture, let alone British culture. O'Brien said that "a lot of my teenage angst, and small-town New Zealand [experience] is not dissimilar to the Midwest of America" (Wenley 2011). New Zealand and America's Midwest are psychically linked by the colonial heritage of British settlement. O'Brien's teenage experience is allegorised, displacing Hamilton with a larger, generalised Midwest American location. The show's focus on otherness and championing of non-mainstream sexuality reflects O'Brien rejecting New Zealand provincialism to embrace the "absolute pleasure" of his overseas London life. *The Rocky Horror Show* has a place in the New Zealand theatre canon, but pushed to the edge, as its cultural identities are hybrid and unfixed. It is of New Zealand, but also of other places, an imitation of national identities without an origin (to borrow from Judith Butler).

Roger Hall

As evidenced with O'Brien, New Zealand and Britain's colonial legacy has meant that, for many New Zealand playwrights, production in London has been viewed as the pinnacle of international theatrical success. This was also the case for Roger Hall, who emigrated to New Zealand from England when he was 19, and is recognised as New Zealand's most commercially successful playwright, although unfairly disregarded with disdain by advocates of "serious" writing. Hall's play *Middle Age Spread* (1977) made it to the West End in 1979 and ran for 18 months. The trade-off for commercial production was the request by the UK director Robert Kidd to change the play's setting to England. This meant that it was not a visible example of a play from New Zealand in its content, but passed as a British one. The reason Kidd offered for the transposition request was casting pragmatism: he did not feel the British public could accept actor Richard Briers, known as the quintessentially English TV star of *Marriage Lines* (1961–1966) and *The Good Life* (1975–1978) as any other nationality. The request "made sense" to Hall, as "it happens to many plays, especially those from either side of the Atlantic [...], if I wanted a play on the West End this would be the compromise I'd have to make" (Hall 1998: 148). Hall had also allowed his plays *Glide Time* (1976) and *Footrot Flats* (1983) to be adapted for Australian productions, but the difference here was Hall undertook to rewrite *Spread* himself. The West End as institution demands product; therefore, a British context is privileged over what is perceived to be a commercially and culturally inferior New Zealand. The newly adapted *Middle Age Spread* began an out-of-town try-out in

Brighton and was subsequently booked for the Lyric Theatre in the West End in 1979.[3] *Middle Age Spread* won Comedy of the Year at the Society of West End Theatres Awards (now known as the Olivier Awards).

The Financial Times' critic Michael Coveney (1979) found echoes of British playwright Alan Ayckbourn and suspected that "Mr Hall's extremely adroit examination of middle-aged mores chimes exactly with Thatcherite expectations in the stalls". *The Guardian's* Michael Billington (1979), however, identified the play's "topographical vagueness" as a weakness. He perceptively argued that:

> written for a New Zealand audience, it has clearly been doctored for an English one and I wasn't entirely convinced [...]. I couldn't work out what the once idealistic Colin was doing hitched to a hard-faced Thatcher-loving wife: I felt the Thatcher references had been bunged in to replace something that was once local and plausible.

Billington's review reveals a potential dissonance within the British audience's feedback loop. Provincialism valued the British adaptation and allowed the majority of the play to be transferred intact from New Zealand to Britain, but the ability to distinguish a New Zealand version of the play, and New Zealand's absence in the British, no longer "local and plausible" as Billington put it, upheld regionalist differentiation.[4]

Robert Lord

The final playwright in this section is Robert Lord, who, eschewing the colonial route, was pulled towards New York City as a theatre centre. Encouraged by attendance at the 1974 Eugene O'Neill playwrights conference and a production of his play *Well Hung* (1974) by Providence's Repertory Company, Lord decided, as he put it, to become "a New Zealander living in New York, coming from a little wee place to great big country, a farm boy come to town" ("New Zealand Writer Brings Comedy to the Globe" 1985).[5] Hilary Halba (2012: 34) notes that 1970s New York City was "a city bigger, more exciting and more dangerous by far than any in New Zealand [...], it featured peepshows, adult cinemas and pickpockets", conditions that would later attract Red Mole. Lord left New Zealand just prior to that moment when Roger Hall's *Glide Time* in 1976 demonstrated a commercial demand for populist New Zealand plays. Nonnita Rees has said that when she co-founded the NZ playwright's agency Playmarket in 1973 with Lord, Judy Russell and Ian Fraser, there was "still a widespread belief that [...] audiences would not come to see New Zealand plays" (Rees 1984: 23). Lord, about to turn 30, did not see any continuing prospects in New Zealand. Lord explained that "opportunity is scarce for playwrights in a land of 3 million people and four theaters" ("New Zealand Writer Brings Comedy to the Globe" 1985) and that if he "wanted to make a living from writing I had to go overseas"

(Coke 1985). Lord, however, discovered that opportunity was scarce even in a city of millions and an entire theatre district. Lord began to write plays set in America, the first of which, *I'll Scream If I Want To* (later retitled *High as a Kite*), was produced by the Provincetown Playhouse in 1976. The play's poor critical reception made Lord realise he was "not really familiar with the American psyche" ("Small Town Enzed" 1983).

An important step for Lord finding belonging as a playwright in New York City was the invitation in 1978 to become a member of the New Dramatists, whose main activity was to workshop members' plays. Each year there were roughly 400 applications for memberships, of which eight to ten playwrights were selected and offered a seven-year membership term. Membership was capped at 45 writers at a time. A 1983 reading of his new play *Bert and Maisy*, which Lord set in New Zealand, was observed by a journalist profiling the New Dramatists. The article explained:

> You've probably never heard of the playwright, unless you hail from his native New Zealand or happen to be hunting for a Manhattan apartment (Lord is also a licensed real estate agent). His play may one day light up a Broadway marquee; tonight, however, it is being presented to the public for free.
>
> (Mann 1983)

The audience was a who's who of Broadway. Lord even had one degree of separation with a young Kevin Bacon – the American film star was part of the cast reading *Bert and Maisy*. These public readings were an opportunity "to see the cream of America's playwrights show their wares", and for producers to "find hot new properties in which to invest" (Mann). Executive director Tom Dunn explained that New Dramatists' scripts had been picked up by regional theatres, Broadway, and turned into television and feature films (Mann). Unfortunately, Lord's script was not to be granted that fate in America, although the play was subsequently produced by San Diego's Old Globe Theatre in 1986.

Lord's next American milestone was the 1986 American tour of *Country Cops*, a revised version of *Well Hung*. *Country Cops* was toured around the Summer Stock Circuit with Conrad Bain, of television's *Diff'rent Strokes* (1978–1986) as the headlining star.[6] Meanwhile, Lord struggled to get his American plays programmed. *China Wars* (a satire of American suburbia) had workshop presentations in New York City and San Diego in 1987, and finally a full production at Primary Stages in New York City opening March 1, 1989, a venue Lord described as "one of the smallest theatres in creation" (Lord 1988). A year later, *The Travelling Squirrel* (a semi-autobiographical play about a writer in New York) made its New York City debut at the Primary Stages, opening February 23, 1990, with Lord himself directing. Lord had found it ironical that his most successful plays in America – *Well Hung* and *Bert and Maisy* – were the "most New Zealand" (Lord 1987). While

Lord had perceived that writing about America would lead to him being pro-grammed in the market, his experience demonstrates programming and audi-ence curiosity in the regionalist New Zealand identity represented in these plays as a point of difference within the US marketplace. Tragically, after 15 years living and writing in New York, *The Travelling Squirrel* would be Lord's final production in America; Lord died in Dunedin, New Zealand, in June 1991 aged 46.

Regional or provincial?

The plays and productions tracked in this chapter span half a century of sig-nificant changes in New Zealand theatre and society. While the Kiwi Concert Party was content to play within a provincial colonial paradigm, subsequent theatre sought to articulate an alternative postcolonial identity and then to further consolidate this identity through performance overseas. As we have seen, a recurring question in the period is whether New Zealand theatre might represent a provincial or regional identity to overseas audiences, or in the case of Red Mole, something else entirely.

The circulation of play scripts was a key means of gaining international per-formance of New Zealand work within this period. Whilst Amamus and Red Mole collectives embarked on overseas tours, motivated by New Zealand's perceived isolation from European and American centres of experimental the-atrical activity (with the Red Mole collective permanently basing themselves in America), there were few other international tours by companies through the 1970s and 1980s, primarily because the activity was rarely supported by the government's Arts Council. In 1977 Bruce Mason had sought support from the Ministry of Foreign Affairs to present New Zealand drama at either the Edinburgh International Festival or the Fringe. Mason argued that a devoted showcase of New Zealand works "would attempt to redeem [New Zealand drama] from a purely provincial status", but the proposition was rejected by the government ministers (Mason 1977). While Amamus was funded for its London and Poland tour, Red Mole was entirely self-funded and resented the lack of institutional New Zealand support. In 1979 both Red Mole and Heartache and Sorrow, a New Zealand company based in London, applied to represent New Zealand at that year's Edinburgh Fringe, but only Heartache and Sorrow was eventually successful with government funding.[7]

In 1981 Christchurch's Court Theatre's production of Bruce Mason's final play, *Blood of the Lamb* (1980), toured for two months in Australia. Mason was proud that his play was travelling "true to label", meaning the script had not been rewritten for Australian audiences; Mason perceived the "trans-position of [a play's] theme or setting into another country", such as had occurred to *Middle Age Spread* in London, to be a "baneful practice [that] must now cease" (Mason 1981). Mason, who died on December 31, 1982, was preoccupied throughout his career with representing New Zealand region-alism and would not compromise regarding this, even if it meant turning down international productions. Others have been willing to adapt their dramaturgy, exchanging the New Zealand setting with the cultural context of the production's intended market. Acquiescing to the cultural centre status of the USA or UK, such adaptation is intended to meet the perceived needs of the new audience, bypassing cosmopolitan engagement by presenting a localised production featuring ready-made markers of the audience's own society. Playwrights Roger Hall and Robert Lord pursued contrasting strategies of such adaptation. Hall's *Middle Age Spread* represents an explicit colonially orientated cultural adaptation, writing the original identity out of the play and reverting to a British identity. Robert Lord struggled to fit either New Zealand or American identities. Though he attempted to adapt his writing for American society, it was the novelty of his plays representing New Zealand identity that gained the most programming interest from American companies. Whereas Hall's case demonstrated how easily New Zealand culture could be exchanged for the British, challenging the regionalist argument, Lord's failed attempts at identity-transfer when writing "American" plays demonstrate a distinction between New Zealand and American cultures that he was unable to completely assimilate.

This chapter has covered examples of New Zealand theatre that travelled to Poland and Australia; yet the United Kingdom and North America presented a powerful pull. There is some irony that, in attempting to move beyond a provincial colonial identity, Mason, Amamus and even Red Mole all arrived in London, eager to show the motherland how different they now were. Felicity Barnes (2012: 2–3) argues that London was historically claimed under "cultural co-ownership" as New Zealand's cultural capital. Britain has been the traditional destination for New Zealanders on their OE; as Nigel McCarter (2001: 11) states, "almost all travellers headed for Britain", especially London, with its "sense of familiarity" acting as a "powerful magnet". While Red Mole and Robert Lord's arrival in New York attempted to bypass the colonial journey, little New Zealand was still disowned in favour of the Big Apple as a powerful cultural centre. Recognition is sought from overseas audiences and institutions of the quality and distinct identity represented in Aotearoa New Zealand theatre, but this need for recognition implicitly values the prestige offered by the international over the local, maintaining a colonial bind.

The final observation to make as we leave the international world and travel to the global world is the evident anxiety revealed in the cases surveyed in this chapter around what constitutes a national New Zealand identity. What sort of "imagined community" were these productions constructing and displaying to the international audience? In the examples of the Kiwis continuing to replicate British and American entertainment as they toured Australia following the war, or Roger Hall pragmatically agreeing to rewrite *Middle Age Spread*, the concept of a distinct regionalist expression is devalued in favour of provincial continuity. In the case of Red Mole Enterprises, the company's work in America displaced anxieties about national identity by drawing from other international identities and conflicts, such as the Cubans in Africa in *Goin' to*

Djoubiti. The Moles employed their country of origin where it could enhance their outsider-narrative and attract curious audiences, but their political and aesthetic aims did not extend to an interest in presenting New Zealand national narratives in their overseas works.

Of the cases that privilege a distinct regionalist identity, this identity was constructed in part through a troubling absence. These dramas reveal an anxiety by Pākehā to demonstrate they belong to their New Zealand home, thus the attempt to establish their naturalised national identity and the utilisation of self-referential markers of belonging. The relationship between Pākehā and Māori identities is a challenging aspect of the New Zealand fantasy being projected to overseas audiences in these works. For the Kiwi Concert Party, Māori waiata was one of the few explicit acknowledgements that they were the *New Zealand* entertainment division, though the songs were performed by Pākehā company members. The young protagonist of Mason's *The End of the Golden Weather* is barely aware of Māori culture (a metaphorically apt situation). Other works by Bruce Mason, like *The Pohutukawa Tree*, are intensely anxious about the interaction between Māori and Pākehā, but as with the waiata of the Kiwis, the Māori voices are represented from a Pākehā perspective. In choosing *Gallipoli* as the moment New Zealand broke away from its colonial identity, Amamus' insistence on regional identity is connected with an absence of the indigenous. *Gallipoli* cast the colonial conflict as the settler versus the emasculating British Mother, which was resolved once the settler had forged his own distinct identity through an international war. Red Mole, meanwhile, repressed the colonial situation and this anxiety by leaving New Zealand entirely.

These troubling currents continue to manifest in varied ways in Chapters 2–8, which follows Aotearoa New Zealand theatre performed overseas in the global world from 1990 onwards. If the major feature of New Zealand theatre overseas throughout the international world period was the struggle to define a distinct regionalist identity (while also acknowledging the counter-narrative of Red Mole), in the global world these identities fragment and national boundaries are complicated (so Red Mole would appear to have been ahead of its time). As we shall see in the chapters to come, there is a renewed challenge around what constitutes New Zealand identity, with a range of voices emerging with a stake in what kind of Aotearoa New Zealand identity is represented to global audiences.

Notes

1 Maunder met Grotowski during the director's visit to New Zealand in 1973, and Amamus went to Sydney in May 1974 to view Grotowski's touring production of *Apocalypsis cum Figuris* (1968), a production which influenced the development of *Gallipoli*.

2 In NYC, *Goin' to Djibouti* was followed by *The Last Days of Mankind* and *Dead Fingers Walk*, performed at the Theatre for the New City. In the UK the Moles performed *Mankind* and premiered *Blood in the Cracks*. During their 1979/1980

USA tour the Moles characteristically created a new work for the road, *Numbered Days in Paradise.*

3 This was the same venue that Bruce Mason's *Birds in the Wilderness* had been showcased in 1958.

4 *Middle Age Spread* closed at the end of 1980 and toured the English provinces for a year. Hall next targeted a Broadway run of the play, and this time actively rewrote it with an American setting for the market, but it proved difficult to raise the required capital. The play had a six-week run in a small venue in Washington DC in 1983. A negative critical response ended any further hopes of a Broadway production.

5 Lord's *Meeting Place* (1972) was subsequently produced by the New Phoenix Repertory Company in 1975.

6 In its heyday, the circuit consisted of a ring of 30 venues, but in 1986 *Country Cops* toured to 4 venues.

7 Heartache and Sorrow and Red Mole defined a contrast in representing and performing values of national identity. Heartache and Sorrow's flagship work, *The Case of Katherine Mansfield* (1978) by Catherine Downes, used the writing of New Zealand's preeminent expat literary figure to reflect on Mansfield's life and also featured her stories of New Zealand life. Heartache and Sorrow went on to present five works at the 1979 Edinburgh Fringe, including *The Case of Katherine Mansfield,* with a more visible nationalistic flavour favoured by the government than which Red Mole would have offered.

References

Note: "BMP" indicates the source was accessed through Bruce Mason Papers, J.C. Beaglehole Room, Victoria University, Wellington. "BRP" indicates the source was accessed through Alan Brunton and Sally Rodwell Papers, 1950s–2007, Special Collections, Libraries and Learning Services, University of Auckland, Auckland. "PMP" indicates the source was accessed through Maunder, Paul Alan, 1945–: Papers Relating to Theatre, Alexander Turnbull Library, Wellington. "RHP" indicates the source was accessed through Roger Hall Papers, Hocken Collections, University of Otago Library, Dunedin. "RLP" indicates the source was accessed through Robert Lord Papers, Hocken Collections, University of Otago Library, Dunedin. "SJP" indicates the source was accessed through Jones, Stella Marjorie (nee Claridge), 1904–1991 Miscellaneous Papers, Auckland Libraries, Auckland.

Amamus. 1975. I.C.A. Arts Centre Theatre Press Notice. (98-166-2/05, PMP)

Barnes, Felicity. 2012. *New Zealand's London: A Colony and Its Metropolis.* Auckland: University of Auckland Press.

Bell, Brian. 1957. "Play Premiere". Unidentified newspaper. (NZMS 1525, SJP)

Billington, Michael. 1979. "Middle Age Spread". *The Guardian.* October 17. (MS-1614/012, RHP)

Burns, Christopher. 2012. "Parading Kiwis: New Zealand Soldier Concert Parties, 1916–1954". MA Thesis. University of Auckland.

Capie, David. 2009. "New Zealand and the World: Imperial, International and Global Relations" in *The New Oxford History of New Zealand,* edited by Giselle Byrnes. South Melbourne: Oxford University Press: 573–598.

Clark, Kenneth. 1963. "Contribution to 'Going into Europe'". *Encounter,* (112): 56.

Coke, Merrill. 1985. "Ten Years on, Playwright Lord Returns". *Evening Post,* December 14. (MS-2438/157, RLP)

Coveney, Michael. 1979. "Middle Age Spread". *Financial Times*. October 21. (MS-1614/012, RHP)

Cryer, Max. 1964. "N. Zealander Took Part in Edinburgh Festival". *Auckland Star*. April 16. (1959–1965 Scrapbook, Carton 5, Box 2, BMP)

Dace, Tish. 1979. "Yankee Stay Home!" *Other Stages*. January 11. (8/11/2, BRP)

Edmond, Murray. 1996. "Old Comrades of the Future: A History of Experimental Theatre in New Zealand, 1962–1982". PhD Thesis. University of Auckland.

———— 2004. "How Gothic Is S/he?: Three New Zealand Dramas". *Australasian Drama Studies*, (44): 113–129.

Fox, Terry Cutis. 1979. "Tunnelling Under". *Village Voice*. January 15. (8/3, BRP)

Gilbert, Helen and Joanne Thompkins. 1996. *Post-Colonial Drama: Theory, Practice, Politics*. London; New York: Routledge.

Ginsberg, Merle. 1979. "Red Mole Enterprises Wants to Change the World". *The Villager*, January 22. (1/16, BRP)

"The 'Golden Weather' Marathon". 1962. Unidentified newspaper. (1959–65 Scrapbook, Carton 5, Box 2, BMP)

Halba, Hilary. 2012. "Robert Lord's New York: Big and Small, Notes on Life and Art". *Australasian Drama Studies*, 60: 33–41.

Hall, Roger. 1998. *Bums on Seats: The Backstage Story*. Auckland: Viking.

Hunt, Barbara. 1979. "Red Mole Surfaces for London Performances". *New Zealand News UK*. July 19. (1/16, BRP)

Hunt, Deborah. 2017. Interviewed by James Wenley. Email. February 2.

I.E. 1963. "Bruce Mason Reviews Trip". *The Dominion*. December 28. (1959–1965 Scrapbook, Carton 5, Box 2, BMP)

Jones, Don. 1993. "Spirit of Comedy Only Survivor for New Zealand Theatre Group". *Passatiempo*. December (8/3, BRP).

Jones, Stella. 1960. *The Tree*. Christchurch: Whitcombe and Tombs.

Kendall, Gavin, Ian Woodward and Zlatko Skrbiš. 2009. *The Sociology of Cosmopolitanism: Globalization, Identity, Culture and Government*. Hampshire: Palgrave Macmillan.

King, Michael. 2004. *The Penguin History of New Zealand*. Auckland: Penguin Group.

"Kiwis Home Again". 1953. *NZ Truth*. July 8.

Lord, Robert. 1987. "A Dramatic Distance". *NZ Listener*. July 11. (MS-2438/157, RLP)

———— 1988. Letter to Swoozie Kurtz. December 20. (MS-2439/004, RLP)

Mann, Paula. 1983. "Broadway's Best-Kept Secret". *FYI*. September. (MS-2438/157, RLP)

Mason, Bruce. 1963. "Edinburgh 1963". *NZ Listener*. November 1. (Edinburgh 1959–65 Scrapbook, Carton 5, Box 2, BMP)

———— 1967. "Jottings on the Character and Spirit of Downstage". Unpublished manuscript. (Carton 5, Box 1, Folder 5, BMP)

———— 1977. Letter to Lance Adams-Schneider, Acting Minister of Foreign Affairs. November 11 (Carton 7, Box 4, BMP)

———— 1981. "Preface" in *Blood of the Lamb*. Wellington: Price Milburn and Victoria University Press: 7–9.

———— 1994. *The End of the Golden Weather*. Wellington: Victoria University Press.

Maunder, Paul. 1975. Letter to the Director of QE2 Arts Council. (98-166-1/14, PMP)

———— 1976. "Amamus in Poland". *Act*, 1 (1): 2–3.

———— 2013. *Rebellious Mirrors: Community-Based Theatre in Aotearoa/New Zealand*. Canterbury: Canterbury University Press.

McCarter, Nigel. 2001. *The Big OE: Tales from New Zealand Travelers*. Auckland: Tandem Press.

Michaels, Scott and David Evans. 2002. *Rocky Horror: From Concept to Cult*. London: Sanctuary.

Moon, Paul. 2013. *Encounters: The Creation of New Zealand a History*. Auckland: Penguin Books.

Murphy, Roy. 1981. "Red Mole Burrows into Broadway". Article reproduced at *Roy Murphy*. Last modified January 5, 2020. www.murphyroy.com/artists/redMole.html

"New Zealand Writer Brings Comedy to the Globe". 1985. Unidentified newspaper. November 24. (1907/024, RLP)

O'Brien, Richard. 1983. *The Rocky Horror Show*. London: Samuel French.

Patterson, John S. 1979. "Africa Revisited". Unidentified newspaper. (8/3, BRP)

Playhouse Newcastle. 1957. *The Tree* Programme. (NZMS 1525, SJP)

Rees, Nonnita. 1984. "'Getting New Zealand Writing into Theatres': The Story of Playmarket". *Australasian Drama Studies*, 3 (1): 23–30.

Simpson, Peter. 2016. *Bloomsbury South: The Arts in Christchurch 1933–1953*. Auckland: University of Auckland Press.

"Small Town Enzed". 1983. *Christchurch Press*. July 13. (MS-2438/018, RLP)

Smithyman, Kendrick. 1965. *A Way of Saying: A Study of New Zealand Poetry*. Auckland: Collins.

"SY SYNA Drama Critic WNYC". 1979. Radio transcript. (8/3, BRP)

"Theatre Guide". 1986. *The Austin Chronicle*. (2/40, BRP)

Vandenberg, Marita. 1988. "Mole Resurfaces Here". *NZ Listener*. July 30. (8/3, BRP)

Vaughan, Terry. 1995. *Whistle as You Go: The Story of the Kiwi Concert Party*. Auckland: Random House.

Wenley, James. 2011. "Extended Interview: Rocky Horror's Richard O'Brien". *Theatre Scenes*. Last modified January 30, 2011. www.theatrescenes.co.nz/extended-interview-rocky-horror%e2%80%99s-richard-o%e2%80%99brien/

Williams, Susan Lilian. 2006. "Metamorphosis at 'The Margin': Bruce Mason, James K. Baxter, Mervyn Thompson, Renée and Robert Lord, Five Playwrights Who Have Helped Change the Face of New Zealand Drama". PhD Thesis. Massey University. Palmerston North.

2   A Kiwi *Hedda Gabler*

Downstage on the festival stage

"Ibsen is Universal!" declared the programme of the inaugural Ibsenfestivalen (Ibsen Festival), held by the Nationaltheatret (National Theatre) in Oslo in September 1990. The programme immediately contradicted its own sentiment by including a quotation from Henrik Ibsen: "anyone who wishes to understand me fully must know Norway" (Ibsenfestivalen 1990). These statements express the tension between particularism and universalism in the cultural transmission and reception of dramatic works as they circulate around the world. The universal interpretation of Ibsen is demonstrated by the following view, expressed on the occasion of a season of three Ibsen plays performed at London's Barbican Centre in 2014: "such is the universality and timelessness of Ibsen's drama, and the themes he addresses, that directors are constantly drawn to reinvent his plays in the same way Shakespeare has been reinvented by successive generations of theatremakers" (Smurthwaite 2014). Any knowledge of specifically contextual markers of late 19th-century Norwegian society represented within Ibsen's oeuvre are secondary to the wider truth Ibsen's plays reveal about the human condition – truths that are accessible to anyone at any time. What is particular and culturally specific becomes an access route into foundational themes that can be universally applied to all people and cultures: the more specific, the greater the universality. Ibsen's quotation, however, implies that any universalist interpretation is based on the reduction of a culturally specific text – understanding of Victorian Norwegian culture is required to "fully know" Ibsen.

This tension between particularism versus universalism plays out in the production and touring history of Downstage Theatre Company's version of *Hedda Gabler* (1891), which was one of the international productions featured at the 1990 Ibsen Festival. Directed by Downstage's artistic director Colin McColl, *Hedda Gabler* was localised, transposing 1890s Norway for a 1950s Wellington setting, so the production might resonate within a New Zealand cultural context. As Catherine Rees (2017: 21) suggests, transporting and transposing the action of a play to a different nation can "expose tensions between audiences' understanding and preconceptions of those nations". However, the potential New Zealand cultural resonance that could be generated within the local feedback loop was complicated as the production travelled on a circuit of International Festivals from Wellington to Edinburgh, London, Oslo and Sydney.

McColl's production of *Hedda Gabler* continued the regionalist impulse of New Zealand theatre to display a unique national culture that had diverged from British antecedents (see Chapter 1). Echoes of Red Mole and Amamus' isolation as a motivation for travel repeat in McColl's assessment of New Zealand theatre as it entered the 1990s:

> The range of theatre, the new writing, what's happening in Māori and South Pacific theatre, the whole spectrum of it in New Zealand is very exciting. But we are a tiny country, so far away from the rest of the world, and just miss out on the stimulus of the international connection.
>
> (Martin 1990)

Downstage's tour was an attempt to gain this international connection and showcase the type and quality of theatre produced in New Zealand, goals that were institutionally supported by the government's Ministry of Arts and Culture, the Queen Elizabeth II Arts Council and the Wellington City Council. The decision to tour *Hedda Gabler* was reported by Elizabeth Dickson (1990) in the *NZ Listener* as "controversial", with questions raised around the relevance of sending a "Norwegian play to a Scottish Festival". Dickson framed the debate thus: "Shouldn't a New Zealand theatre have sent a New Zealand play, or does the strongly New Zealand thrust of this production make it an exciting cultural expedition in its own right?" This debate represented ongoing anxieties around the national image being represented to international audiences in New Zealand dramatic work.

Using an Ibsen play effectively provided Downstage with a passport to enter an international festival circuit: as a seminal text of modernist realism in the Western canon, Ibsen's *Hedda Gabler* possesses name recognition. Ric Knowles (2004: 183) advises that festival performances "tend to be based on classics or other sources that already have transcultural authority or resonance, and then to be similarly received and celebrated in most festival contexts". After debuting in Wellington, February 1990 for the NZ International Festival of the Arts, Downstage's *Hedda Gabler* toured by invitation to the Edinburgh International Festival (August/September, 1990), the inaugural Ibsen Festival in Oslo (September, 1990), the inaugural Covent Garden International Festival in London (September, 1990) and subsequently the Festival of Sydney (January, 1991). International performance festivals are premised on exclusivity and difference, offering an opportunity to consume cultural product that may not be produced outside of the specially constituted Festival time. This novelty, however, is coupled with the marketer's anxiety of how to make the unknown known and enticing. Murray Edmond (2007: 320–321) identifies a structural tension between common humanness and cultural difference in such festivals: "it is to see and experience cultural difference that we go as audience to modern arts festivals, but unless our common humanness gives us access in some way to understanding this, then the whole audience experience will be meaningless". The international mobility and portability of Downstage's *Hedda Gabler* is enhanced by its New Zealand origin within the international festival market: a known, familiar and canonically sanctioned cultural text with a hint of difference and newness provided by the New Zealand localisation.

Henrik Ibsen is "one of the most valued and frequently staged playwrights worldwide" (Hyldig 2011: 21). The first recorded production of Ibsen in New Zealand was in 1890 with *A Doll's House* (1879), starring English actor Janet Achurch, that played in Auckland, Wellington, Christchurch and Dunedin. Achurch's company was following the "trade and cultural routes of the British Empire", touring the British production across Australia, New Zealand, Sri Lanka, India and Egypt as part of the play's first wave of globalisation – by the early 20th century *A Doll's House* had been performed in 46 countries (Holledge et al. 2016: 29). *Hedda Gabler* (1891) followed *A Doll's House* to New Zealand 11 years later in 1901, touring from Australia to Auckland and Christchurch as a J.C. Williamson company production. A moralistic review of the Christchurch engagement deemed it to be "probably the most extraordinary play which has ever been staged in Christchurch", as it was "immoral, unwholesome, intensely ugly, utterly unreal and absurdly inconsequential"; the reviewer reported that it was not received with any enthusiasm by the audience ("Theatre Royal Hedda Gabler" 1901). During New Zealand's amateur era, *Hedda Gabler* was performed by the Wellington Repertory Theatre in 1936, and Unity Theatre also staged the play in Wellington in 1956. *Hedda Gabler* reappeared in New Zealand during the transition to professional regional theatre, selected for Downstage's inaugural season in 1965, and was also performed by Downstage in 1974. Downstage's third production of the play in 1990 was the first to transpose the play to a New Zealand context, identifying resonant similarities between 1890s Oslo and 1950s Wellington (the period when Unity Theatre performed its production of Hedda Gabler).

Funded by the Queen Elizabeth II Arts Council, Downstage was established in Wellington in 1964, pioneering the regional venue model following the closure of national touring company the New Zealand Players in 1960. Downstage presented eight to ten plays a year in its 250-seat venue Hannah Playhouse and in 1990 had a yearly audience of 65,000. Colin McColl was appointed artistic director in 1985, and under his leadership Downstage "concentrated on new interpretations of classic scripts and newly commissioned New Zealand plays" (Downstage 1990). McColl's decision to adapt and direct *Hedda Gabler* had been inspired by an expressionist interpretation of *The Wild Duck* directed by Lucian Pintilie at Washington DC's Arena Stage theatre in 1986, which changed McColl's perception of Ibsen's drama: "The only Ibsen's I'd ever seen in New Zealand, Australia or the UK up to that point were very naturalistic [...] all 'gloom, gloom, I sit in my room'" (Smythe 2004: 314). The premiere of McColl's production as part of Wellington's International Festival of the Arts in February 1990 reached a 62.2% venue capacity; Smythe

(2004: 314) speculates that festival goers prioritised imported shows over the local Downstage production. Critics approved of the localisation. Susan Budd (1990) recognised that Wellington in the 1950s was "as much a time and place of provincial mediocrity, bourgeois materialism and sexual repression as was a Norwegian town in 1890". For Denis Welch (1990), the choice of local setting made sense for a play about repression and the total dramatic effect of the play "out-Ibsenises Ibsen".

In McColl's transposed production, the relationship of New Zealand regionality and the feminine is considered by examining Gabler's actions within the context of a stifling provincial and patriarchal 1950s New Zealand society. McColl noted that 1950s Wellington was the same size as Oslo when Ibsen wrote *Hedda Gabler*, and drew a connection between "a society and an era as provincial, conservative and suffocating as Ibsen's nineteenth century Norway", using the example of New Zealand women in the 1950s being "confined to the home and encouraged to be good wives and mothers" (Downstage 1990).[1] In an interview to British media, McColl said that he found "Ibsen's plays speak to us in New Zealand perhaps even more than they speak to people in Britain because we live in small, relatively isolated communities" (Smith 1990). McColl also provided the anecdote that New Zealanders, who had grown up in the 1950s and who saw the Wellington production, told him, "I knew that Woman!" McColl himself remembered "seeing women just like [Hedda] at the Heretaunga Golf Club" (Martin 1990) – a specific point of reference potentially inaccessible outside of the New Zealand context.

McColl assembled the script from various English translations, assisted by a Norwegian-speaking staff member working at Downstage, with some limited additions of New Zealand colloquialisms (personal email, November 26, 2019). Welch (1990) found it remarkable how adequately Ibsen's text could correspond with the transposed setting: "no name-changes or tricks of speech; just the odd downunderism like "jack-up" or "beaut" (and one startling exchange in Māori)". The most notable aspect of the localisation, as referenced by Welch, was the Māori identity of writer Lovborg, played by Jim Moriarty, with some of his lines given in Te Reo. It was Moriarty's request to play the character as Māori, which became a comment on Māori writers in the 1950s not being expected by Pākehā-dominated society to succeed in literature (Martin 1990).[2] McColl's adaptation would prompt Wellington reviewer Laurie Atkinson to coin the term "McCollonise", defined as "to transpose a European dramatic masterpiece to a New Zealand setting with flair, wit, intelligence and without distorting the play's essential spirit and thrust" (Smythe 2004: 314). More radical than the localisation and periodisation of the play, however, were McColl's directorial interventions in its temporality and determinism. McColl's opening sequence makes a clear statement of intention:

> Director Colin McColl set an ironic tone in the first few moments: Hedda entered alone to the sound of a jazz recording of "Tea for Two". On the

line "Can't you see how happy we will be?" She knelt down before her father's portrait and shot herself.

(Shafer 1992: 107)

By beginning with Hedda's suicide, McColl focusses the audience's attention on the causalities of her action and continues throughout the production to replay selected sequences with different inflections and actions.

In touring the global marketplace, Downstage presented audiences with a version of *Hedda Gabler* which offered an alternative interpretative experience from an alternative cultural perspective. The considerable critical discussion surrounding the *Hedda Gabler* tour allows us to test Ric Knowles' (2004: 181) contention that "remounting productions at international festivals that emerged from particular cultural contexts or were designed for specific local audiences changes the cultural work that they perform and the ways in which they are read". How did the cosmopolitan process of audiences reflexively observing and interpreting work from a non-local company function in relation to *Hedda Gabler's* overseas performance contexts? The first section of this chapter, "Festival markets", provides an overview of the tour as the production moved across the Edinburgh, Oslo, London and Sydney marketplaces. "Travelling meanings" analyses how *Hedda Gabler* was read and resonated within each location. The chapter concludes with "After the tour", considering the production's historical legacy and significance.

Festival markets

Edinburgh International Festival

Downstage's international tour of *Hedda Gabler* began at St Bride's Theatre with six evening performances and two matinees from August 27 to September 1, 1990, the first New Zealand work to be invited to perform as part of the Edinburgh International Festival. The Festival was established in 1947; the debut programme "of high cultural performances codified cultural alliances and affinities of taste that symbolically transcended the geographies of war" and epitomised internationalism, attempting to promote harmonious foreign relations and cultural cooperation between nations (Jamieson 2004: 66). Downstage's *Hedda Gabler* was programmed at the 1990 Festival in the context of a curational focus "on the arts and culture of the countries of the Pacific Rim" (Edinburgh International Festival 1990). This reflected the shifting geopolitics immediately following the end of the Cold War and the economic and cultural ascension of the Asia-Pacific region: the Festival was offering audiences a gateway for cultural experiences in a changing world. Japan was represented in the Festival by three theatre companies, highlighted in the programme as the "most fascinating season of contemporary Japanese theatre ever seen in the West". In addition to New Zealand, the Republic of Korea was also invited for the first time. Australia was represented by Belvoir Street

Theatre with *Greek Tragedy*, devised by British director Mike Leigh and a Greek-Australian cast. Kenneth Branagh's productions of *The Dream* (from Shakespeare's *A Midsummer Night's Dream*) and *King Lear* were the UK headliners, but the Festival also included an Indian Kathakali version of *King Lear*.

The Daily Telegraph's Charles Osborne (1990) questioned the Festival's decision to programme a New Zealand *Hedda Gabler*: "there seems little point in bringing [...] a production of so familiar a play as Ibsen's *Hedda Gabler* unless, as Hedda herself would say, one can 'do it beautifully'" (Osborne deemed the production to be "decidedly pedestrian"). Critic John Peter (1990) expressed a counter view that *Hedda Gabler* was just the sort of performance that the festival needed: "unusual but authentic, confirming your interests and enlarging your horizons". However, Peter was uncertain if that alone justi-fied the wider programme's "eccentric designation as Theatre of the Pacific". A conspicuous absence for a 'Pacific Festival' was any performers from Moana Oceania (the Pacific Islands). Overall the 1990 programme was decidedly conservative. While the Japanese companies toured their own contemporary theatre, Downstage and the Kathakali company entered with adaptations of Western canonical work – known and familiar properties.

This proved appealing in the Edinburgh International Festival context. In contrast to the slow-to-sell Wellington season, Downstage's *Hedda Gabler* entirely sold out in Edinburgh five weeks prior to opening. Downstage was promoted in marketing as "New Zealand's leading theatre" (Edinburgh International Festival 1990), but the company was unknown in Edinburgh, so the classic status and name recognition of Ibsen's text, amplified by the validating power of Edinburgh International Festival selection, was likely to have been the decisive factor for encouraging ticket sales rather than the company's reputation or national origin. *Hedda Gabler*'s cast and crew arrived in Edinburgh five days before the performance on the back foot: they had dealt with a cast member's family bereavement, had to replace their injured stage manager and were suffering from "a virulent flu bug which had people collapsing in rehearsal" (McColl 1991). *The Guardian*'s Joyce McMillan (1990) described the opening night reception:

> There was restlessness, snorting and some loud tut-tutting from well-fed citizens who like their classics safe, sanitised [...], but the muttering was overwhelmed by a huge final roar of approval from an audience who stayed with Colin McColl's brave, dangerous production every inch of the way, and recognised that in Catherine Wilkin, they were watching a Hedda of a lifetime, the most exciting, challenging and courageous to appear in Britain for years.

Ibsenfestivalen

From Edinburgh the company travelled to Oslo, where *Hedda* played for two performances during the Ibsen Festival (September 4–5). The inaugural Festival was a major turning point in Norwegian theatre, capitalising on Ibsen's status as an international theatrical commodity in order to place "Oslo and Norway on the world cultural map" (Ibsenfestivalen 1990). The Festival was centred around the National Theatre in Oslo, which opened in 1899 with a season featuring Ibsen's An *Enemy of the People*. Writing in the Ibsen Festival programme, artistic director and Festival instigator Stien Winge characterised the venue's original purpose as being to "house contemporary Norwegian playwrights" (Ibsenfestivalen). Describing Ibsen as an "established classic" and his plays as Norway's "cultural heritage", Winge explained that the "the need and desire for a special Ibsen Festival has been obvious for a long time – a festival in which the National Theatre is a focus for the best Ibsen performances from producers and directors the world over" (Ibsenfestivalen). This was supported by Oslo critic Jan E. Hansen, who wrote in the lead-up to the Festival that "each nation should insist that its national theatre stand in the forefront of the performance and scholarship of that nation's most important playwright" and that "the National Theatre should always play Ibsen" (Samuelson and Carlson 1990: 31). The inherent contradiction in pedestalling a playwright who had emerged as part of a movement towards staging contemporary Norwegian plays does not register in the ideology expressed by Winge and Hansen, but the festival has been the subject of debate regarding whether the platform "has contributed to promote, or rather has hindered, the development of contemporary theatre and new drama" within Norway (Hyldig 2011: 46). The National Theatre was in a financially precarious position when it conceived of the Festival as an avenue for financially reviving the institution as part of a larger project of economic culture building, representing "a massive vitamin injection for the city of Oslo, with a spin-off effect for the tourist trade, hotels and restaurants, museums and libraries, concerts, exhibitions" (Ibsenfestivalen 1990). The first Festival was a box office success, "with sold out houses for every night of nearly every production" (Samuelson and Carlson 1990: 31). The Ibsen Festival went biennial from 1994, growing to become Norway's largest theatre festival and heralding "a new wave of renewal" for interest in Ibsen within Norway and beyond (Hyldig 2011: 22). The year 2018 set a new attendance record with more international spectators than any previous Ibsen Festival (Nationaltheatret 2020).

The Festival has contributed to the continued internationalisation of Ibsen. Stein Winge said that one purpose of the festival was to tear down what he referred to as a stagnant Norwegian Ibsen tradition:

> We keep walling him in! [...] We are not best at performing Ibsen! We want to organize an international festival and show the audience how well Ibsen can be performed–and that we need to see him not just from our own vantage point–that we actually could get some punches thrown from abroad.
>
> (Hyldig 2011: 22)

The final programme of the 1990 Festival was the result of "a somewhat random international search for interesting Ibsen productions to invite to the festival" (23). The Lyric Players Theatre of Belfast toured with a production of *Ghosts*. In contrast to Downstage, Lyric's marketing emphasised that "no attempt has been made to change the location, era or names featured in Ibsen's play, but where appropriate characters speak with the idiom and dialect of the Northern Irish people" (Ibsenfestivalen 1990). Other international companies were London's ARC Dance company with a version of *Peer Gynt*, and Swedish City Theatre Kalmar with a children's theatre version of *The Fairytale of Peer Gynt* (in all, the Festival featured three versions of *Peer Gynt*, with Royal Shakespeare Company's John Barton directing a third Norwegian production). The National Theatre made its own productions of *Brand*, *The Lady from the Sea*, and Ingmar Bergman directed a Royal Dramatic Theatre of Sweden production of *A Doll's House*.

McColl (1991) described Downstage's performance in Oslo as entering the "lion's den" and wondered "how would the reserved Norwegians accept this interpretation of one of their favourite plays?" The company found the Oslo audience to be highly literate in Ibsen: they "knew the play backwards" and "understood every nuance – every twist and turn of the interpretation – things that had been dismissed as tricky or downright irritating by critics here delighted them [...] we had won them over with our interpretation" (McColl 1991). It was reported that audiences "stamped their feet, shouted and went mad at the end of both the performances" and the Festival believed that "they could have played here for another week and still sold out every night", but neither Downstage nor the Festival had anticipated such a strong response to the work (Brittenden 1990).

International Covent Garden Festival

Downstage's next engagement was at the inaugural International Covent Garden Festival in London. The Festival instigators had deemed the City of London itself to be "too big, too amorphous to have a Festival of its own", but the Covent Garden area, featuring 160 food and wine outlets, 23 theatres and a number of art galleries made it "the natural place" to "focus the artistic and cultural life of London" and host a Festival (Phillips 1990). Focussed around the piazza designed by Inigo Jones in the 17th century, Covent Garden emerged as a theatrical centre during the 18th century, alongside the brothels and gambling dens in the area. In 1990 the piazza area catered to a large tourist trade, with regular busking street performances as a prominent attraction. The "normal, run-of-mill buskers", however, would be side-lined during the 12 days of the Festival; instead, the piazza would have a "more cosmopolitan mix than ever" with daily ice-carving competitions, street performance from the Natural Theatre Company and avant-garde performance artists Bobby Baker and Sivia Ziarenek programmed alongside Opera star Hildegard Behrens (Reinhold 1990). In this context, a New Zealand production of an Ibsen play was an odd fit for the

Festival. Downstage had a connection with the Covent Garden Festival's artistic director Di Robson, who had organised regional tours and PR for Downstage in New Zealand early in her career.[3] Robson's intention was to create a Festival "that is of the area and not just a programme overlanded on it" ("Kiwi Plots Covent Garden's Festival" 1990), but it is difficult to reconcile this with the selection of a New Zealand *Hedda Gabler*, which does not have an obvious association with the Covent Garden area. Despite Robson's intentions, the Convent Garden Festival lacked a coherent identity, reflecting the problems of imposing a Festival framework on top of an area that was already the site of considerable performance activity. By its final year in 2000 the Festival had stabilised with a curation largely featuring operatic work, but the Festival closed following the withdrawal of the headline sponsorship (Archive-Rw-Deutsch 2000).

While London has historically been perceived as a pinnacle centre for theatrical performance by New Zealanders, McColl (1991) found the reality to be "something on an anti-climax" compared to the "highs of Norway". National newspaper coverage of the new festival had been minimal, and, fatally for Downstage's box office, the telephone booking number at their venue, the Jeanetta Cochrane theatre, had been out of order for a week ("Growing Pains" 1990). Downstage's production initially struggled with small houses, but by the end of the two-week season (September 10–23) positive word of mouth ensured the company played to capacity numbers. Since "London does not have much opportunity to see New Zealand theatre", as stated by one London journalist, there was some curiosity about Downstage's country-of-origin (Kaye 1990). More decisively, Downstage was able to capitalise on the prestige of bringing a production to London that was "already acclaimed at the Edinburgh Festival" ("Arts and Entertainment Guide" 1990).

Sydney Festival

This validation also proved crucial when marketing *Hedda Gabler* at the 1991 Sydney Festival as "A Hedda of a life-time – according to Britain's *The Guardian*", with UK (but not Norwegian) reviews perceived as an important marker of quality. Downstage itself had been invited to perform by the Festival of Sydney programmers due to the successful Edinburgh season. The invitation to Sydney was received after the company had arrived back in Wellington, which posed one issue: Downstage had sold their props and set in London as it was not financially viable for these to be shipped back to New Zealand, so an appeal was made to Downstage patrons to help restock for the Sydney season (McColl 1991). Catherine Wilkin's casting as Hedda Gabler was considered a draw-card for the Sydney audience as she was well known for her role in Australian television show *The Flying Doctors* (1986–1992), which marketing also capitalised on. *Hedda Gabler* played a three-week season at Sydney's Seymour Centre from January 3–19, 1991.

Travelling meanings

Hedda Gabler's portability in the global festival marketplace was based on the cultural capital associated with Ibsen. While the production had been transposed to a Wellington setting in order to resonate within a local New Zealand context, this cultural resonance had the potential to be re-routed when the production was placed within various geographic and festival contexts, in which the cultural context is secondary to the primacy of Ibsen's text. The critical responses to *Hedda Gabler* provide an archive of meanings that were produced and made accessible as the production travelled from market to market.

At the Edinburgh International Festival, Colin McColl's postmodern directorial interventions were the subject of considerable critical debate. *Financial Times* reviewer Andrew Hill (1990) argued that McColl's direction "stripped" Ibsen's text of any subtextual subtlety, resulting in an "increasingly irritating and over-imaginative reading of Ibsen's play". Despite Greg Ward (1990) noting that McColl "seems to think Ibsen's brilliant play could not stand on its own with his intervention", Ward declared that *Hedda Gabler* was the most surprising production of the International Festival and the riskiest version of the play he had seen. The critical discourse generally revered the timelessness and universality of Ibsen's text, downplaying any significance of the New Zealand setting. "In the process very little changes", wrote *The Glasgow Herald*'s Julie Morrice (1990), "the updating of the setting does not pigeonhole *Hedda Gabler* in the 50s but upholds and enhances the play's ageless and universal struggle". Farrell (1990) deemed the change in setting to be "neither enhancing nor particularly intrusive", and noted that "the only very noticeable New Zealand influence is a prominent portrait of the general who is obviously in a New Zealand outfit" (a uniform from New Zealand's WWII campaign). Andrew Hill (1990) commented that without direct experiences, audiences in Edinburgh would "probably have to take it on trust" that Wellington in the 1950s was an "era as provincial, conservative and suffocating as 19th century Norway". Charles Osborne (1990) argued that "other than to justify the accents of the New Zealand cast", and the occasional colloquialism, "very little advantage has been taken of the change of locale". Nor did he believe that the production revealed a specific New Zealand identity, as "there is little sense that these people are living and existing in any particular society" and "could just as easily be in Perth, Western Australia, or Pocatello, Idaho" (Osborne 1990). On Downstage's *Hedda Gabler's* journey from Wellington to Edinburgh, some of the potential cultural resonance of the 1950s Wellington transposition appears to have been lost on the way.

Contrasting with the divided Edinburgh response, McColl's expressionist directorial approach was largely accepted in London and Sydney. Lyn Gardner (1990) in London heralded the production as "the most successful updating of 'Hedda Gabler' that London has seen for many years". Responding to the Sydney season, Hugo Williams (1991) also posited that "one thing is for sure: anyone attempting *Hedda Gabler* from now on is going to have to reckon with Downstage Theatre's revolutionary new version". The Australian discourse was especially pronounced regarding *Hedda Gabler* representing a treatment of Ibsen that the country had not seen before, with "new life pulsing through an old classic" (Evans 1991). Ken Healy (1991) expressed that "not enough of our theatre is wild as this is wild. When classics are reinterpreted by clever directors they almost never combine the extremes of this production with such an obvious justification for being extreme". Downstage's production was seen as the new definitive version of the text which future British and Australian productions could be compared to. The focus on the formal aspects of the interpretation again superseded, as in Edinburgh, specific cultural resonance. The New Zealand setting was "a masterstroke that lends immediacy and familiarity to the action, underscores the universality of the play and detracts from it not one iota" (Gauntlet 1991). Notably, the critical archive does not register any reflection around the applicability of the play's setting to Australia of the 1950s.

The uncritical engagement with the production's New Zealand transposition across Edinburgh, London and Sydney contrasted with the reception in Oslo. Here the cosmopolitan process was complicated through the dissonance of a non-local culture being represented through a canonical Norwegian play. Norwegian critic Halvor Tjermos (1990) recycled the language of universalism – the New Zealand adaptation revealed what was "universal in the Ibsen play [...], a study in increasing madness hidden by a cultural facade" – but more acute was the expression of a feeling of difference that the production had provoked, with Downstage having "turned the whole play upside down compared with the usual Norwegian version". The humour in the Downstage production was a particular revelation. Catherine Wilkin was told by Oslo audiences that she had "freed Hedda" for them by giving them permission to "laugh at her grotesque elements and to see in more complexity the personal devils that drive her to destroy the people around her and then herself" (Whelan 1990). Reviewing the Olso season, Shafer (1992: 109) observed that the production "emphasised the comedy in this play [...] which is commonly ignored [...] too often interpretations of Ibsen's plays are reverential, earnest, and dull".

Some critics argued that the New Zealanders presented a better production than the "culturally authentic" productions from the Norwegians, emphasising the revelatory nature of the production in the Norwegian market; a reimagining that can come only through the position of a cultural outsider. Norwegian Ibsen productions through the 1980s were focused around the "traditional style of psychological realism", with few productions "based on innovative and substantial concepts of direction" (Hyldig 2011: 36). According to Norwegian critic Tron Øgrim (1990), Downstage's production was "the most original Ibsen performance" he had ever seen. Whereas the Festival programme stated, "Ibsen was able – like the Greek tragedians – to elevate his characters to universal validity", as they "belonged at once to the past, the present, and the future" (Ibsenfestivalen 1990), in Oslo the New Zealanders made the Norwegian's own play foreign. As one critic stated, the effect of the production would be "something that will linger long after the doors of the Festival are closed – how new Ibsen can be" (Bratelli 1990).

The decision to cast Māori actor Jim Moriarty in the role of Lovborg, and to emphasise this identity by translating some of his lines into Te Reo, created a particular resonance within the feedback loop for New Zealand audiences, but this resonance was largely absent from the international critical discourse surrounding the play and the character's Māori identity was rarely referenced. Osborne (1990) made the problematically worded statement that Lovborg was "given a little Māori blood and a phrase or two of the language as well", but then went on to argue, as previously noted, that the production conveyed little sense that the characters were living in a particular New Zealand society. J.O. (1990) was the sole commentator from the Edinburgh season to recognise the implications of representing the character as Māori: "addressing his first words to Hedda in Māori, the figure of Lovborg links racial and sexual taboo and makes the sub-text of his ostracism genuine dynamite". Only two Sydney reviewers mentioned Moriarty's casting. Bob Evans (1991) found "casting Māori actor Jim Moriarty as the passionate and doomed Lovborg was an interesting and broadly successful move", but does not interrogate this further. Rosemary Neill (1991) wrote perceptively that the casting "adds a potent dimension to the fact that Hedda's society appropriates Lovborg as an outsider" and it "helps us understand why a 50s Hedda might suppress her strong feelings for Lovborg, and marry Tesman, whose touch she cannot bear". In reviews where critics were perhaps not as familiar with the New Zealand Māori context, the casting did not receive comment or analysis. In the cosmopolitan encounter between performance and audience, the potential resonance of a Māori Lovborg mostly remained outside the common space. Even in Oslo where the play was admired as an exoticised version of their familiar cultural product, the cultural difference *within* the work remained obscure and unremarked upon.

After the tour

While audience numbers were limited for *Hedda Gabler* in Oslo due to the two performance season, the ecstatic reception to the production contributed to the internationalism of subsequent Festivals, establishing international interpretations of Ibsen as a key anchor of the Festival. As Winge explained in the programme for the 1991 season, "the world's first Ibsen festival showed that our great playwright is international" (Hyldig 2011: 27). In the first years of the Festival, international productions were mostly sourced from Sweden and English-speaking countries, but over the course of the Festival's history it has broadened to host work from a wide range of countries and languages (23). Interest in Ibsen has increased globally from the 1990s, and the Festival itself has contributed to a revival of Ibsen within Norway and encouraged a wider range of directorial approaches to his canon. Hyldig (2011: 31) identifies the 2004 Festival as a "breakthrough for post-modern director's theatre in Norway", but the example of *Hedda Gabler* demonstrates that this approach was present from the beginning of the Festival via McColl. Indeed, McColl became a key figure in the Ibsen Festival's early trajectory, setting a record of directing three productions in a row at the Festival, each production representing a company from a different country. For the 1991 Festival, McColl was invited by Nationaltheatret to direct its company for *The Vikings at Helgeland*, which had not been performed in Oslo for 67 years (Smythe 2004: 327). McColl reduced the cast to a company of eight and the play was performed in traverse in the theatre's paint shop (315). In 1992 McColl directed *The Master Builder* for the Dutch National Theatre in Den Haag, which was also toured to the 1992 Ibsen Festival.[4]

The international tour and response to *Hedda Gabler* can also be seen as prototypical of the international journey of Australian director Simon Stone's 2011 adaptation of *The Wild Duck* in the 2010s. Like McColl, Stone and co-writer Chris Ryan rerouted Ibsen's text "temporally and geographically", setting the play in contemporary Australia with the characters speaking in broad Australian accents (D'Cruz 2017: 68).[5] Stone's directorial flourish was to set the action within a glass box, which heightened the voyeuristic naturalism of the original (Smurthwaite 2014). *The Wild Duck* became Stone's international calling card, touring to Norway (as part of the 2012 Ibsen Festival), Austria, the Netherlands and England. In London, the play was viewed as bringing a "completely new perspective to the Ibsen original" (Smurthwaite 2014) and commentary described how it was "not that often that Ibsen has felt more relevant or heart breaking than this" (Bayes 2014). While the focus was on how the production was reinventing Ibsen, as with the British response to Downstage's *Hedda Gabler*, reviews did not linger on the specific representation of Australian culture. There are distinct parallels between McColl and Stone being received as antipodean auteur directors disrupting the conventional treatment of Ibsen's plays, allowing them to be seen anew. Commenting on Stone, but equally applicable to McColl's *Hedda Gabler*, Smurthwaite (2014) wrote that "our own reinventions of Ibsen and Chekhov – the two foreign playwrights most frequently produced in the UK – tend to be less extreme, relying more on textual nuances, variations in interpretation and design innovations". Localisations like *Hedda Gabler* and *The Wild Duck* offer an appealing known narrative that assists their circulation within an international Festival context: a version of a recognised canonical text that the audiences have never seen before, perfectly balancing Edmond's identification of the tension in Festivals between common humanness and cultural difference.

The dominant narrative around *Hedda Gabler*'s overseas tour was the way the production was recognised for offering a fresh directorial approach to a play which is "performed frequently with a predictable sameness" (Shafer 1992: 109). Writing in *Theatre Journal*, Yvonne Shafer argued that Downstage's production "made a significant contribution to the current re-interpretation of Ibsen's plays" and called for "American directors to reappraise Ibsen" in light of McColl's work (109). In contrast, the specific regionalist 1950s New Zealand setting that stimulated a local feedback loop barely registered in the critical archive. McColl's adaptation replaced Norwegian cultural markers with a specific New Zealand context, simultaneously a production that had something to say about Ibsen's text, and something to say about the insular New Zealand identity in the 1950s and the legacy of this at the beginning of the 1990s, but, when toured to overseas markets, the New Zealand cultural markers were themselves displaced. The production was instead interpreted within each location's own culturally specific traditions of Ibsen performance. The shifting response to *Hedda Gabler* as it travelled across geographic markets dislocates any "Ibsen is Universal!" claim.

One of the outcomes McColl (1991) reported from the tour was an increase in the actors' sense of self-worth and credibility: "it was a particular thrill seeing our New Zealand actors pitch themselves against some of the best in the world and come to realise just how good their own work is". Downstage's *Hedda Gabler* acted as a cultural ambassador for New Zealand theatre with the values of both quality and directorial risk-taking. Having toured a New Zealand interpretation of a European classic, McColl (1991) believed that "taking a New Zealand play, unknown by European audiences, must be the second step" for Downstage in order to secure global recognition of Aotearoa theatre. Downstage's tour of *Michael James Manaia* (1991) by John Broughton to the 1991 Edinburgh Festival Fringe is one of the case studies in Chapter 3, which investigates the circulation of Māori theatre in the global marketplace.

Notes

1 This was the same territory that Stella Jones had explored in her 1957 play *The Tree*, which spoke to the contemporary situation that McColl describes (see Chapter 1).
2 From 1955 the magazine *Te Ao Hou* published short stories from Māori writers, but it was not until 1973 that Witi Ihimaera became the first published Māori novelist.
3 Robson had left New Zealand to live in London, where she had also worked as a producer for the UK-based New Zealand company Heartache and Sorrow.
4 McColl has gone on to lead a local cottage industry of Ibsen productions and adaptations. In 1994 McColl directed *Nga Tangata Toa* for Taki Rua theatre, an adaptation by Hone Kouka of *The Vikings at Helgeland*, transposing Ibsen's setting to an East Coast New Zealand marae in 1919. McColl continued his interest in Ibsen with productions of *The Master Builder* (ca. 1995) and *Ghosts* (Court Theatre Christchurch, 2003). As the artistic director of Auckland Theatre Company, McColl has commissioned localised adaptations of Ibsen from playwrights Emily Perkins (*A Doll's House*, 2015) and Eli Kent (*Peer Gynt*, 2017) and is directing his own digital adaptation of *The Master Builder* for the company's 2020 season.
5 Stone's rewriting of the Ibsen text was far more extensive than for McColl's production.

References

Note: "DTCR" indicates the source was accessed through Downstage Theatre Company (Wellington): Records. 1964–2013 (MS-Papers-8874-09:12), Alexander Turnbull Library, Wellington.

Archive-Rw-Deutsch. 2000. "10th Covent Garden Festival Opens in London". Last modified May 15, 2000. www.mtv.com/news/872635/10th-covent-garden-festival-opens-in-london/

"Arts and Entertainment Guide". 1990. *The Guardian.* September 13. (DTCR)

Bayes, Honour. 2014. "The Wild Duck". *The Stage.* October 30. (Proquest Database)

Bratelli, Tone. 1990. "Hedda". English translation by Erling Sliper of Norwegian review from unidentified publication. (DTCR)

Brittenden, Wayne. 1990. "Norwegians Wild for Downstage's Ibsen". *The Dominion.* September. (DTCR)

Budd, Susan. 1990. "Hedda the Sun around Which Rest of Cast Orbit". *The Dominion.* February 19. (DTCR)

D'Cruz, Glenn. 2017. "Re-Routing Ibsen: Adaptation as Tenancy/Occupation in Simon Stone's *The Wild Duck* and Thomas Ostermeier's *An Enemy of the People*" in *Ethical Exchanges in Translation, Adaptation and Dramaturgy*, edited by Emer O'Toole, Pelegrí Kristić and Stuart Young. Leiden, Boston: Brill/Rodopi: 65–79.

Dickson, Elizabeth. 1990. "Acting Journey". *NZ Listener.* September 3.

Downstage. 1990. Hedda Gabler Programme (Edinburgh International Festival). (DTCR)

Edinburgh International Festival. 1990. Edinburgh International Festival Programme. (DTCR)

Edmond, Murray. 2008. "A Saturated Time: Three Festivals in Poland, 2007". *New Theatre Quarterly*, 24 (4): 307–321.

Evans, Bob. 1991. "Brave Direction Sees New Life Pulsing through an Old Classic". *The Sydney Morning Herald.* January 5. (DTCR)

Farrell, Joe. 1990. Transcript of Festival View. *BBC Radio Scotland.* August 28. (DTCR)

"Fun in the Garden". 1990. *West End Theatre News.* June/July. (DTCR)

Gardner, Lyn. 1990. "Hedda Gabler". *City Limits Magazine.* September 6–13. (DTCR)

Gauntlet, Frank. 1991. "Hedda 'bove the Rest". *Sydney Daily Telegraph.* January 5. (DTCR)

"Growing Pains". 1990. *The Times.* September 12. (DTCR)

Healy, Ken. 1991. "Powerfully Stimulating, Wild Theatre". *The Sun-Herald.* January 6. (DTCR)

Hill, Andrew. 1990. "Hedda Gabler". *Financial Times.* August 31. (DTCR)

Holledge, Julie, Jonathan Bollen, Frode Helland and Joanne Thompkins. 2016. *A Global Doll's House: Ibsen and Distant Visions.* London: Palgrave Macmillan.

Hyldig, Keld. 2011. "Twenty Years with the International Ibsen Festival". *Ibsen Studies*, 11 (1): 21–50.

Ibsenfestivalen. 1990. Festival Programme. (DTCR)

Jamieson, Kirstie. 2004. "Edinburgh: The Festival Gaze and Its Boundaries". *Space & Culture*, 7 (1): 64–75.

J.O. 1990. "In Edinburgh, Hedda's Norway Becomes New Zealand". *Euromaske European Theatre Quarterly*, Winter. (DTCR)

Kaye, Nina-Anne. 1990. "Theatre". *City Limits Magazine*. September 6–13. (DTCR)

"Kiwi Plots Covent Garden's Festival". 1990. *New Zealand News UK*. July 18. (DTCR)

Knowles, Ric. 2004. *Reading the Material Theatre*. Cambridge: Cambridge University Press.

Martin, Frances. 1990. "From Norway to New Zealand... via Edinburgh". *TNT*, 366. (DTCR)

McColl, Colin. 1991. Report prepared for Downstage Theatre Company. (DTCR)

McMillan, Joyce. 1990. "Pursued by Demons". *The Guardian*. August 29. (DTCR)

Morrice, Julie. 1990. "Hedda Gabler". *The Glasgow Herald*. August 28. (DTCR)

Nationaltheatret. 2020. "The Ibsen Festival: A Celebration of Norway's Greatest Playwright". *Nationaltheatret*. Last modified January 10, 2020. www.nationaltheatret. no/hva-skjer/ibsenfestivalen/om-ibsenfestivalen/about-the-ibsen-festival/

Neil, Rosemary. 1991. "Just Why Did Hedda Die?" Unidentified Sydney newspaper. (DTCR)

Øgrim, Tron. 1990. "Ibsen's Festival 1990". English translation by Erling Sliper of Norwegian review from unidentified publication. (DTCR)

Osborne, Charles. 1990. "A Kiwi Hedda Gabler". *The Daily Telegraph*. August 29. (DTCR)

Peter, John. 1990. "Hits in a Scattershot Approach". *The Sunday Times*. September 2. (DTCR)

Phillips, Caroline. 1990. "Catering from Every Taste from Low to High-Brow". *High Life*. September. (DTCR)

Rees, Catherine. 2017. *Adaptation and Nation: Theatrical Contexts for Contemporary English and Irish Drama*. London: Palgrave Macmillan.

Reinhold. 1990. "Everything in the Garden's Lovely!" *Mirror Xtra*. September 13. (DTCR)

Samuelson, Eric and Marvin Carlson. 1990. "The First International Ibsen Festival". *Western European Stages*, 2 (2): 31–36.

"Scene on the Sydney Stage". 1990. *The Daily Telegraph Mirror*. December 3. (DTCR)

Shafer, Yvonne. 1992. "Hedda Gabler". *Theatre Journal*, 44 (1): 107–109.

Smith, Alison. 1990. Transcript of Tuesday Review. *BBC Radio Scotland*. August 28. (DTCR)

Smurthwaite, Nick. 2014. "Ibsen, Our Contemporary". *The Stage*. October 2. (Proquest Database)

Smythe, John. 2004. *Downstage Upfront*. Wellington: Victoria University Press.

"Theatre Royal Hedda Gabler". 1901. *Lyttleton Times*. February 16. (Papers Past)

Tjermos, Halvor. 1990. "New and Old Ibsen". English translation by Erling Sliper of Norwegian review published in *Klassekampen*. (DTCR)

Ward, Greg. 1990. "Sifting for the Gems in Lacklustre Season". Unidentified UK newspaper. (DTCR)

Welch, Denis. 1990. "That's Acting". *NZ Listener*. April 9.

Whelan, Judith. 1990. "A Hedda on the Edge". *Sydney Morning Herald*. December 29. (DTCR)

Williams, Hugo. 1991. "Down-Under Hedda Is Beautifully Done". Unidentified Australian newspaper. (DTCR)

3   Performing mana

Taking Māori theatre to the globe

At the curtain call of Ngākau Toa's performance of *Toroihi rāua ko Kāhira* (*The Māori Troilus and Cressida*) at London's Shakespeare's Globe in 2012, Māori audience members in attendance responded with their own mihi (tribute) and haka (dance) to honour the performers. Dominic Dromgoole (2013: xxiii), the artistic director of the Globe, described the moment: 60 Māori in the audience pounded "out a combative rhythm straight at the stage [...], the audience was thrilled and terrified, caught in the no man's land between two groups of mammoth Māori rehearsing an old tribal war rite". This ritual was an affirmation of mana, a shared display of cultural pride between the performers and Māori in the audience, and a moment of theatrical spectacle for the wider Globe audience that extended beyond Shakespeare's text. Mana is a concept in Māori culture associated with extraordinary prestige, power, charisma and influence that flows within people, places and objects as a supernatural force. Mana can be heightened through successful ventures, and almost every activity a person does can be linked to the maintenance or enhancement of their mana (Royal 2007). The mana of a performance can be measured by the depth of the reciprocal response provoked in the audience by the energies of ihi, wehi and wana (combinations of the psychic power and emotional response, reaction to the power of the performance and the aura connecting performers and audience) (Hyland 2015: 68). The spontaneous haka recognised the significant mana of the Māori group performing a Shakespearean text, translated into their own language and performed in the land of their historic colonisers. Ngākau Toa had claimed the Globe as a Māori space – an early modern Whare Whakairo (carved meeting house) – and Shakespeare was speaking Te Reo (Hyland and Conkie 2017: 159).

Ngākau Toa was a company of Māori practitioners led by Rawiri Paratene (Ngāpuhi) and Rachel House (Ngāti Mutunga; Ngāi Tahu) that formed for the project.[1] They had come to London by invitation of Shakespeare's Globe, and had been given the honour of opening the 2012 Globe to Globe Festival (part of the UK's Cultural Olympiad) on the anniversary of Shakespeare's birthday. This invitation acknowledged Ngākau Toa's mana, which was further enhanced by the success of the performance season in sharing their mahi (work and practice) and culture with Globe audiences in London. Like Downstage's production of *Hedda Gabler*, Ngākau Toa's adaptation of a text from the Western canon allowed them to display their culture back to an audience overseas. Touring Māori-centred theatre globally, such as *Toroihi rāua ko Kāhira*, has been a way for Māori theatre makers to enhance their mana, gain acknowledgement and educate overseas audiences about Māori culture and history.

Marianne Schultz (2016) highlights instances of international performance by Māori in the 19th and early 20th century. In 1863 two separate groups of "Māori Chiefs" were toured to Britain, presenting dramatised representations of Māori culture (some performers swapped groups during the tour). Led respectively by Australian and English producers, Schultz argues the tours could be categorised as colonial propaganda (especially within the context of the New Zealand wars being fought between the Crown and iwi within New Zealand during this period), but the performances were "first and foremost, popular entertainments that featured Māori performers" designed to appeal to exotic interest in the Māori culture (26). It is likely that the opportunities provided by employment and travel, as well as the mana associated with taking their culture overseas, may have motivated the performers' involvement in these tours (38). In the early 20th century, tourism entrepreneur Mākereti (Maggie) Papakura negotiated for 40 Māori performers to travel to New York in 1909 where they performed a Māori village scene as part of a Hippodrome spectacular *Inside the Earth,* presenting "a race and place virtually unknown" to North Americans in the period (12). In 1911 Papakura's Te Awara Warriors troupe was invited to set up a village at London's Festival of Empire exhibition at the Crystal Palace, presenting a programme which included tableaus of "living pictures of Māori life in New Zealand", whaikōrero, poi, haka and "love ditties" (Phillips 2014). The questions that these 19th and early 20th century examples of Māori performance raise around the control, distribution and exoticised consumption of Māori cultural content within a global entertainment sphere continue into the present.

In the contemporary theatre marketscape, Sharon Mazer (2013: 118) contends that, as with Haka, Māori theatre appears to dominate the "international imagination about New Zealand's national identity", although she adds the cynical qualifier that this is "perhaps less about empowerment than about branding". As Chapter 7 will detail, presenting Māori and Pasifika cultural products at Creative New Zealand's NZ at Edinburgh season at the 2014 Edinburgh Festival Fringe was part of a project to brand Aotearoa New Zealand with an inclusive multicultural image. The regionalist drive to establish Aotearoa New Zealand's unique national identity allies with and co-opts Māori cultural images in order to establish the nation's distinctiveness and global relevance. Even more so than plays from a Pākehā perspective, Māori theatre potentially offers consumable exotic cultural difference that can be sold and branded to overseas audiences. Playwright Hone Kouka (Ngāti Porou,

Ngāti Raukawa, Ngāti Kahungunu), whose plays have travelled to multiple countries, strongly criticises the treatment of Māori theatre as commodities within the global marketplace, likening it to the "land grab in New Zealand in the late nineteenth century or the self styled protectionism of anthropologists taking Māori taonga [prized treasure] for our own good" (2007: 238).

Ensuring that the global distribution of Māori theatre remains a mana-enhancing activity is a crucial concern. Māori theatre can also offer markers of identification and connection with other international Indigenous/ First Nations communities, a value that Tānemahuta Gray (Ngāi Tahu; Te Rūnanga o Koukourārata), Kahukura/chief executive of Taki Rua, identifies as a key value. Establishing networks of First Nations theatre practitioners and exchanging work and practice allows for the comparison of social and industry contexts: "how are we navigating it? How are you navigating it?" (Gray 2019). Gray (2019) advocates for reciprocity in any theatrical exchange between hosts and guests: it is not about buying product, but engaging with each other's worldviews, and "the potency of what an Indigenous viewpoint and Indigenous way of telling stories and sharing our perspectives can add to communities". This philosophy offers a path of resistance regarding the commodification of Māori theatre, emphasising instead the mutual learning and knowledge that can be gained when touring work globally to various communities.

Reflecting the challenge of ensuring that this reciprocal process, rather than market demand, is the primary motivation in the programming and production of Māori work in the global marketplace, there have been relatively few play texts toured overseas that present Te Ao Māori (the Māori worldview). In terms of other performance genres, dance has been represented on the world stage (contemporary Māori dance company Atamira has regularly toured overseas including USA and China, and Te Matatini's *Haka* was featured in the 2014 Edinburgh Festival Fringe), and there is an extensive history of Māori showbands overseas (a legacy continued by the Modern Māori Quartet, discussed in Chapter 7). Māori theatre, meanwhile, has been preoccupied with establishing visibility and recognition for its own place within Aotearoa New Zealand. While Māori culture will often be centrally presented on the global stage to project a desired image of a culturally enlightened nation for the world imagination, internally, Māori theatre has not had the support and prominence that is due in the spirit of Te Tiriti O Waitangi relationship. In the instances when Māori work has travelled, the response has provided inspiration and strength for the practitioners, providing contrasts between local and international receptions. Beginning with John Broughton's *Michael James Manaia* (1991), this chapter examines work by Māori playwrights toured beyond Aotearoa. *Toroihi rāua ko Kāhira* is then used as a major case study examining the meanings and receptions of Māori theatre in the global world, navigating issues of branding, audience gaze and agency in relation to concepts of universalism, exoticism and colonialism.

Māori playwriting abroad

Having found international success with a localised version of the canonical European play *Hedda Gabler*, Downstage's artistic director Colin McColl believed that the Wellington company needed to follow this by touring a New Zealand play internationally that was unknown to European audiences (McColl 1991). McColl selected *Michael James Manaia* (1991) by John Broughton (Ngai Tahu; Ngāti Kahungunu), a solo work performed by Jim Moriarty (Ngāti Toa, Ngāti Koata and Ngāti Kahungunu), who had played Lovborg in *Hedda Gabler*. Like McColl's version of *Hedda Gabler*, *Michael James Manaia* is set in New Zealand's past, in this instance the 1950s–1970s, and highly critical of the prevailing social pressures and their effect on the title character: the tensions in Michael James Manaia's dual Māori/Pākehā identity, the ongoing consequences of colonialism and Manaia's experiences as a soldier in the Vietnam War. While *Hedda Gabler*'s image was of a stifling 1950s New Zealand society, the classic status of Ibsen's text created distance from the societal representation. *Manaia*, though dealing primarily with the Vietnam era, was played with a force of cultural immediacy (and debuted concurrently with New Zealand's involvement in the first Gulf War). Downstage's *Michael James Manaia* played at the Traverse Theatre at the Edinburgh Festival Fringe in 1991 (one of the Festival's major venues). A two-week season at London's Covent Garden Festival following the Fringe had also been announced, but due to "prior commitments" this did not eventuate and no further international seasons of the Downstage production resulted (Calder 1991). Downstage's interpretation of an established Ibsen text had greater mobility in the Festival market than a new New Zealand play from a Māori playwright. Nevertheless, *Michael James Manaia* was a trailblazing production for Māori theatre overseas. Mei-Lin Te-Puea Hansen (2007: 963) credits Broughton's play for raising "the profile of Māori theatre". For Hansen, "the burgeoning of Māori drama is one of the most conspicuous and important developments in New Zealand theatre since 1990" (963), and Broughton would be followed by playwrights such as Briar Grace-Smith and Hone Kouka, whose work would also gain overseas performance.

Broughton – a dentist, member of the New Zealand Army Territorial Force and a professor at the University of Otago – had taken a playwriting course in 1988 led by Roger Hall, New Zealand's preeminent writer of Pākehā social comedy. It was during that programme that Broughton developed his first plays *Te Hara* and *Te Hokinga Mai* (the latter also containing a Vietnam theme). Broughton's playwriting was motivated by a goal to "to improve the health – in the widest sense – of Māori people" (Hotere 1995). He consciously synthesised Māori concepts in his dramaturgy. For *Michael James Manaia*, Broughton was influenced by whaikōrero (traditional oratory), and "tapu cleansing mechanisms" were "built into the script" to safeguard the spiritual health of audiences in the symbolic encounter with Hine Nui Te Po, the Goddess of Death (Hotere). Tapu is what is sacred and prohibited – it is offensive to violate tapu. The elements of tikanga Māori (system of values and practices) in the production were mediated by Pākehā director Colin McColl, particularly his interpretative decision to stage the play as if Manaia was participating in institutionalised group therapy.

The creative tension between the dramaturgy, direction and performance in *Michael James Manaia*'s debut at Downstage in February 1991 – a Pākehā-controlled venue – mirrored the title character's own identity conflict due to his dual Māori/Pākehā heritage. While Downstage's programming of Broughton's signalled an institutional engagement supporting the development and maturation of Māori theatre, the audience occupancy over the 20-show season was a disappointing 37.7%, suggesting a disconnect with attracting the Pākehā majority audiences who frequented Downstage (Smythe 2004: 323). Nevertheless, the play was influential in Jim Moriarty's development of his conception of Marae Theatre, where the theatre space is treated as a marae, into which the audiences are invited. Moriarty hoped Marae Theatre would "unite Pākehā unfamiliar with Māori protocol and Māori alienated by European theatrical traditions into a new audience for the performing arts" (Calder 1991). Through performing *Michael James Manaia*, the Edinburgh tour was an opportunity for Jim Moriarty to test how this could work in an international context. Elements of tikanga were employed to frame the performance, with a karanga (ceremonial call of welcome) as the audience arrived, and an invitation "to have a korero" (conversation) following the performance (Archie 1991).

In the play John Broughton presents a New Zealand–Māori identity in which violence through the consequences of war is in conflict with positive cultural values of tikanga (custom), whanaungatanga (family relationships), manaakitanga (care) and aroha (love and compassion). Broughton's play explores cyclical violence caused by war and colonial legacy, and how the sublimated trauma of both can be channelled into family violence. When Manaia returns from Vietnam, he realises the link between his father's violence and experiences in WWII: "No wonder you used to beat us with the horsewhip, through those whiskey mad rages of yours. You lost your mates too and you could never talk about it" (86). One of the most powerful scenes of the play is when Manaia, serving in Vietnam, enacts a mute Ka Mate haka as an act of defiance, the silence signalling his strength and mana against the imperialist forces of war. Nevertheless, he is traumatised by his experience in Vietnam. Christina Stachurski (1999: 125) notes that Manaia's "public expression of the pain and suffering engendered by myths of masculinity goes against New Zealand men's traditional emotional and vocal repression", which shocked "audiences into questioning a society which produces such individual violence and misery". After the war, Lizzie, Manaia's wife, has four miscarriages until eventually a son is born, who is described as having with the son is described as having a hole for a nose, a gaping mouth and tiny hands. Manaia uses whaikōrero (the height of oratory, which often employs metaphors) to liken the infant to a gingerbread man, but, like his father, threatens violence: "An' do you know what I do to gingerbread men? I take their fucking little heads off" (Broughton 1994: 101). Stachurski (1999: 131) observes that the miscarriages and the son's birth defects fundamentally challenged Manaia's identity and masculinity as he had "no means to continue history and value-systems into the future", whakapapa (ancestral lines) being a core aspect of Te Ao Māori.

The play's ending can leave an audience reeling. While Broughton's stage directions do not indicate how Manaia takes his son's life, in the original Downstage production the actor delicately cut the infant's throat and in the Taki Rua revival the actor squeezed the infant's throat. While the audience may have various reactions to the ethics of infanticide, Broughton sees this as Manaia's ultimate expression of love as the child had no hope of surviving (personal email March 1, 2019). The audience are able to understand Manaia's victimisation and alienation, and Manaia's act of sharing his story marks "an acceptance of some personal responsibility for his actions and attitude" (Stachurski 1999: 132). The audience can also see Manaia as a creation of New Zealand's colonial legacy, estranged from the dominant culture and a victim of generational violence at the hands of his father, and New Zealand's involvement in international wars.

When reading *Michael James Manaia* for markers of New Zealandness and the potential resonances of the play for local audiences within the feedback loop, it is clear that the play, as George Parker (2008: 115) states, "is not just another story about a Vietnam Veteran". *Manaia* brings the bicultural tensions of New Zealand Aotearoa's identity formation to the forefront of its drama, with Manaia unable to synthesise dual Māori and Pākehā identities. Stachurski (1999: 125) argues that Manaia's "personal story became political on another level when [...] performances at the 1991 Edinburgh Festival confronted British audiences with the consequences of imperialism". However, in Edinburgh, the New Zealand-specific meanings of the play became broadened in order to further accommodate the overseas audience. The poster for the Traverse Theatre season at Edinburgh overrides the play's local specificity with the statement that "he is all our fathers, uncles, brothers and cousins who've taken part in a war in a foreign land and come home battle-scarred and haunted by demons". This marketing also shifted the framing of the play from Vietnam-specific to all wars fought by New Zealand and British allies throughout the 20th century. It invited audience members into a cosmopolitan encounter through which they could make the play relevant to their own history, context and personal family history within the common space. *The Scotsman* critic recognised that "there must be almost as many stories of displaced trauma as there are surviving combatants" (Donald 1991). In invoking the principle of equivalence, overseas performance had the potential to destabilise the specific Aotearoa New Zealand regionalist elements of the play's identity.

The Vietnam genre was "all the rage" in the 1990s (Parker 2008: 147), but the New Zealand–Māori identity offered a distinct point of difference compared with other international plays and media that used the Vietnam War as their subject. Joyce McMillan (1991) acknowledged that Broughton and Moriarty's Māori and European ancestry "brings whole new worlds of imagery and body language to bear on the story of men brutalised by war, and drawn to war because they are brutalised", but, ultimately found that the play "simply retraces ground already well covered in great post-Vietnam plays like Emily Mann's *Still Life*, one of the festival hits of 1984". *Michael James Manaia* covers far greater ground than just Vietnam; however, McMillan's review exemplified how, overseas, it could be subsumed into a narrower subject, received primarily as Vietnam War story. As a play, *Michael James Manaia* makes a powerful statement about New Zealand's unique national identity having been influenced by still unresolved colonial trauma, but ironically, in showcasing the play internationally, this force was lessened with the meanings able to be redefined by the audience in Edinburgh.

Michael James Manaia was followed overseas by another play originating from Downstage, *Waiora Te Ū Kai Pō – The Homeland* by Hone Kouka which debuted as part of the New Zealand International Festival in 1996. With a touring entourage of 18, Kouka had not considered *Waiora* to be financially viable to travel, until he received an invitation to tour to the 1997 Brighton Festival in England (Rae 1997). *Waiora* was a resonant choice of play for an international tour to Britain. Like *Manaia,* it was set in New Zealand's past (in this case, the 1960s) and presented a troubling image of the ongoing fractures of colonisation on the Māori population. Kouka described the play's story as being about "those who leave their home" and "not just a Māori story, but an immigrant's story [...], something that so many New Zealanders might be able to relate to [...], all of us who have travelled from somewhere else" (Crooks 2006: 121). However, the migrants in *Waiora*'s context are internal migrants: a Māori whanau who have moved from their rural tribal home to an urban area and experience cultural estrangement as they attempt to conform to the Pākehā world.[2] The social commentary that Māori were being treated like immigrants in their own country offended some audiences during the play's 1996 Wellington debut; actor Nancy Brunning recalls the play "brought many Māori together and it angered many Pākehā who were turned off by the portrayal of Pākehā/Māori relationships" (Sears 2016).

The directors of the 1997 Brighton Festival had seen *Waiora* while scouting in Wellington. They told Kouka that "the play had opened their eyes to the effect of English colonialism on the land and the local people" (Rae 1997). Established in 1967, the Brighton Festival is one of the leading European Arts Festivals and has gained a reputation for experimentation ("About Brighton Festival" 2020). *Waiora* was one of the four plays programmed at the Brighton Festival that year, alongside two English works and a play from Israel which also dealt with the theme of displacement (Rae 1997). The season sold out prior to opening, demonstrating the interest by Brighton audiences towards engaging with an Indigenous play from Aotearoa New Zealand. Brighton critic Roger Love (1997) recorded a "prolonged ovation, much of it standing", after *Waiora*'s first performance in Brighton, and his own profound experience of chills "over the whole of my back, across my neck, and spreading to my sides". He attributed this reaction to "the blistering power of this play's climax, which combines intense human and spiritual emotions with Māori song and ceremony". A second account recorded that the "evocative Māori waiata/haka [...] stunned capacity festival audiences" (Whitehead 1997). The Brighton audience's encounter with unfamiliar elements of waiata and custom contributed to their elevated response to the play. According to Kouka, the Brighton audience responded to the play's "uniqueness" (Huria 1997: 6). Kouka commented that Māori theatre had "been in the shadows of New Zealand theatre", but "from a world viewpoint it's the other way around", and that the reception in Brighton made him "realise that we still haven't been completely accepted by New Zealanders", the divided responses towards the Wellington production absent in Brighton (6). Actor Rawiri Paratene says he will never forget the response from a Jewish boy who saw the production, who shared that the Māori family in *Waiora* reminded him of his own family, an example of strong identification with the play (Sears 2016: 6). *Waiora* was offered a European tour following Brighton, but this was turned down in favour of a New Zealand regional tour, as continuing to perform for home audiences was perceived as the most important goal for the production (Sherriff 1998).

The production did venture overseas one further time, on a Hawaiian Islands tour in 1999. Whereas the Brighton tour was described by Kouka as revealing the "results of colonisation to the colonisers", the Hawaiian tour was an opportunity to make connections with their "cousins": "like us, the Hawaiian people were colonised and the effects have been similar" (Oi 1999). *Waiora* in Hawai'i appealed to a perceived Indigenous experience-in-common; as stated by a representative of the Ilio'ulaokalani Foundation, which had sponsored the tour, the situations in *Waiora* had "a commonality with the history of Hawaiians [...], we share the same social problems in adapting to a Western culture" (Oi 1999). Kouka returned to Hawai'i in 2006 with *The Prophet* (2002), the third play in the *Waiora* trilogy; Kouka (2007: 244) found the response to be "overwhelming", confirming "the need for Māori to drive and create Māori work".[3]

Following Broughton and Kouka, Briar Grace-Smith (Ngāpuhi) has had productions of her plays *Nga Pou Wahine* (1995) toured in Sydney and Ireland in 1997 and *Purapurawhetū* (1997) at the International Women's Conference in Athens in 2000. Grace-Smith's main memory of the latter performance was of a Greek taxi driver who came to the performance and wept, despite not understanding English (O'Donnell 2007: 279). Witi Ihimaera's *Woman Far Walking* (2000) toured to Hawai'i in 2001 and Manchester and Wales in 2002. Tawata Productions toured *and what remains* (2005) by Mīria George (Te Arawa; Ngāti Awa; Rarotonga & Atiu, Cook Islands) and directed by Hone Kouka to the Pasifika Styles Festival in Cambridge, England, in 2007. Depicting a narrative in which the last Māori person left in New Zealand is preparing to fly out of a hostile country, George's provocative representation of an Aotearoa absent of Māori was intensively divisive in its Wellington debut at BATS theatre, but the play was expressly sought by the Festival curators in order to present British audiences with contemporary, politically charged Polynesian work, disrupting expected perceptions of what Māori theatre might be. For George, the reception to the Cambridge production reminded her of why the show was important, "that this kōrero was vital and should be told", and Hone Kouka recalled audience reactions from two young Irish women and a Turkish man that expressed cultural identification with the premise of the play (Goodall 2016).

Taki Rua (and later Cuba Creative) has toured *Strange Resting Places* (2007) to Australia, American Sāmoa, Singapore, London and Edinburgh. Written by Rob Mokaraka (Ngāpuhi; Tuhoe) and Italian-born New Zealander Paolo Rotondo, the play was inspired by the Māori Battalion's experience in Italy during WWII; like *Michael James Manaia*, the play provided a unique "Māori lens on [..] a world event" (Gray 2019). The play mixes Italian commedia dell'arte routines with whaikōrero and waiata to create a "Maui-esque mischief comedy" (Mokaraka and Rotondo 2012: 106). The Māori soldiers perceive cultural equivalence between an Italian monastery and their wharenui (communal house, the focal building on a marae), as both spaces record their respective culture's whakapapa. This becomes a source of conflict when the New Zealand soldiers are ordered to bomb the monastery. In the play's conclusion, the Māori soldier Anaru is accidentally shot and his body remains in Italy, registering the global resonances of Māori stories.

Coming full circle, Taki Rua also revived *Michael James Manaia* and toured to the Melbourne Festival, Australia, in 2012, where it was received with the status of a national classic: "a key text in New Zealand theatre" (Harkins-Cross 2012) and "part of a wave of important Māori plays redefining New Zealand's theatre" (Fuhrmann 2012). Notably, it was not the Vietnam context that dominated responses, as had been the case in the 1991 Edinburgh Fringe tour, but issues of masculinity, reflecting a contemporary focus on gender politics. As one reviewer stated, "Broughton is less concerned with the colonial encounter than with masculine inheritance and the fallout that follows men's silence across generations" (Harkins-Cross 2012). As evidenced with this latter comment, there again appeared to be a lack of recognition of how the contextual legacy of colonialism impacted the central character. The shifting responses to the play signal the fluidity of the common space created between audience and performers in which aspects of the play and story are registered and made visible. While the Māori context might be an appealing market proposition in allowing cosmopolitan audiences to engage with cultural difference, the specific context is broadened by audiences to find their own experience-in-common within the play. Nevertheless, these tours of Māori playwriting abroad have been mana-enhancing activities. Kouka's comments reveal a perception that overseas audiences valued the productions more highly than local audiences. While there is a demand for Māori theatre in the global marketplace, these touring experiences also motivated the artists to continue to develop Māori tinorangatiranga (agency and self-determination) in theatre back home.

Case study: *Toroihi rāua ko Kāhira*

Ngākau Toa's *Toroihi rāua ko Kāhira,* an adaptation into Te Reo of Shakespeare's *Troilus and Cressida* set in precolonial Aotearoa, is the highest profile Māori theatre production to date. It is exceptional in relation to the other works discussed in this chapter as it was created for the Globe to Globe Festival in London, rather than being produced for the domestic New Zealand market and then subsequently toured. It exists to satisfy a specific social and historical moment: the Globe to Globe Festival coincided with London hosting the 2012 Olympic Games and was part of the World Shakespeare Festival, organised for the UK's Cultural Olympiad programme of cultural events. The Globe to Globe Festival was intended to celebrate Shakespeare as a global treasure, with productions of all 37 of Shakespeare's plays in 37 different languages, performed at the Globe by companies from around the world. Over six weeks 100,000 audience members attended Shakespeare's Globe, 80% of whom had not previously attended the venue (Patterson 2012). The Festival promoted values of global togetherness through the arts, but did so by using the text of Shakespeare in translation, rather than inviting the representative companies to offer a work or "national playwright" from their own homelands to be performed on the Globe stage. Unlike the Downstage productions of *Michael James Manaia* and *Waiora*, Ngākau Toa was a Māori company, led by director Rachel House and producer and actor Rawiri Paratene (both of whom performed in the original *Waiora* touring production), able to pursue its own artistic tinorangatiranga. The performance of the work entirely in Te Reo was also exceptional for Māori theatre abroad, the linguistic difference complicating the process of identification for non-Reo speakers.

There has been a long history of non-English adaptations of Shakespeare, and "among the many postcolonial reworkings of canonical texts, Shakespeare's plays figure prominently as targets of counter-discourse" (Gilbert and Thompkins 1996: 19). In Aotearoa, Shakespeare's *Merchant of Venice* had previously been adapted as a text by Pei te Hurinui Jones in 1945, later used for Don Selwyn's 2002 film *The Māori Merchant of Venice*. In approaching the adaptation of *Troilus and Cressida* (written circa 1602) the creatives travelled into their own past, relocating Shakespeare's version of the Fall of Troy to a precolonial Māori setting, establishing a strong counter-discourse. Two iwi (tribes), Kariki (the Greeks) and Toroi (the Trojans) are in conflict. Nicola Hyland and Rob Conkie (2017: 158) note that rather than adapting Indigenous histories and performance praxes into Shakespeare's narratives, relocating Shakespeare to an Aotearoa context is a process "of making Shakespeare fit within Te Ao Māori". Te Haumihiata Mason translated the work first into modern English, then Te Reo Māori and finally into Kupu Tawhito, a formal poetic and precolonial form of Māori (158). The production was highly physicalised, with kapa haka and Mau Rakau (Māori martial arts) integrated throughout the stage action by co-director James Webster, and at times used in place of Shakespeare's text.

The Globe's promotional description emphasised that the production would "incorporate many aspects of Māori culture", featuring the "best Māori actors" and the "best composers and choreographers of Aotearoa" ("Troilus and Cressida" 2012). New Zealand Funding bodies supported the company in the context of the regeneration of Māori language and culture, with financial support from Te Puni Kokiri (the Ministry of Māori development) and Te Waka Toi (the Māori arts board of Creative New Zealand). Chris Finlayson, fittingly both New Zealand's minister of arts, culture and heritage and minister for Treaty of Waitangi Negotiations, stated that the production was "a great opportunity to demonstrate the strength of Māori theatre performance and to showcase Te Reo Māori" (Silverstone 2013: 36). The project was promoted institutionally as a national cultural export to a premiere arts venue, where overseas performance would grant cultural legitimacy. This could be viewed positively as a win for both nationalism and globalisation.

Despite this positive public relations spin, the company still faced a significant financial burden in order to perform at the festival, as the funding from these institutions was not enough to cover all production costs. The payment of wages was delayed during rehearsals, and it was announced late in the rehearsal process that Rachel House would have to remain in New Zealand as the company did not have the budget to also cover her travel and accommodation (Monsoon Pictures International 2013). Rawiri Paratene fronted an online crowdfunding campaign asking for individual donations to support the tour to London (fundraising performances were held at Te Papa in Wellington and the Auckland Town Hall), before leaving for London. Paratene acknowledged that although there were "whanau out there with real needs", he asked proud New Zealanders to donate as they would "fly our flag strongly" and would "represent New Zealand" (TangataWhenuaDotCom 2012). While acknowledging the hardship faced by many Māori communities with "real needs", Paratene's nationalistic appeal constructed the production as a representative of a united, bicultural country.

In practice, however, the politics of the representation within the work and the processes of reception when the production played overseas complicate this national inclusivity. At the conclusion of Christopher B. Balme's (1999: 275) study of syncretic theatre (which includes discussion of Māori theatre), Balme considers the difficulties facing a production when performed outside of its original performative context, "determined largely by receptive codes [which] determine how syncretized cultural texts are understood". Whilst *Toroihi rāua ko Kāhira* was created for Shakespeare's Globe in London, the production's reception in that context would still be determined in part by "the complex of cultural prejudices and categories of alterity that govern the reception of theatre in any cross-cultural situation" (275). As I will discuss in the following sections, the Globe performances of *Toroihi rāua ko Kāhira* negotiated complex issues of universalism, exoticism and colonialism, within a larger frame of globalisation.

Universalism

The Globe to Globe Festival platformed Shakespeare as a universal-humanist figure, in that the words and themes of his plays could be translated into any language and remain relevant, and in turn, remain accessible for diverse London audiences viewing, and hearing, these translations. Ngākau Toa's marketing described Shakespeare's plays as if they had been written in a transcendent proto-language: "Shakespeare is the language which brings us together better than any other, and which reminds us of our almost infinite difference, and of our strange and humbling commonality" (Ngākau Toa 2012). There is paradox here: infinite difference reveals commonality. This concept was reflected in reviews that located universal elements in a production that transcended cultural difference. Auckland reviewer Paul Simei-Barton (2012) claimed the production was a "remarkable testimony to the transcendent quality of Shakespeare's writing that is somehow able to speak across time and culture" and London's Dominic Cavendish (2012) wrote that "across the language barrier came hurtling, with ease, the universal aspects of the story and its tragicomic richness". House also identified universal aspects: "there are tones and expressions and emotions that are easily identifiable because they are so universal" (Masters 2012).

What the identification of universalism does not fully take into account is the translation process whereby an Elizabethan dramatisation of an ancient Greek myth is absorbed and reconstructed in Te Ao Māori context. Te Haumihiata Mason had already cut and reduced the text during its translation, which, together with the rehearsal process, emphasised what was culturally similar (or to put it another way, what was held in common between the text and the company) and discarded differences. The language of Shakespeare's poetry and classical Māori were equated through their mixture of high speech and bawdy; as Paratene stated, "it's got all the different forms of language that Shakespeare uses" (AFP 2012). The Trojan story was interpreted through the cultural lens of utu (retribution and reciprocity); actor Waihoroi Shortland said: "they [the Greeks] weren't there to claim land, but to take revenge", so it was "easy to give the story a Māori landscape" (Māori Television 2012). House believed the story fitted "with Māori culture like a glove", and went so far as to say, "it basically feels like one of our own stories, having explored the themes and given it our own interpretation"; this confluence was such that Shortland expressed, "we'd often forget this was a story from another country. It was embraced and treated entirely as Māori taonga" (Māori Television). Hyland and Conkie (2017: 159) identify the narrative of *Troilus and Cressida* as "paradigmatic" in a Māori context, connecting with key narrative themes of Paki Waitara (creation stories): whenua (land), wahine (women) and utu. This is expressed in the whakataukī (proverb) "He wāhine, he whenua, ka ngaro te tangata" (For a woman and land, men perish) – a statement that might summarise the message of Shakespeare's play. The apparent transcendent universalism that both the company and commentators discovered was an act of cultural translation that revealed the common space: what the company thought their culture shared with Shakespeare's text, and what the commentators and audiences perceived that they shared in common with the company's text and performance.

Exoticism

A universalised conception of the production was a prominent discourse surrounding the Globe presentation of the work, but, paradoxically, the production was also framed in a discourse of knowing exoticism. House expressed the desire to "show the sexiness of our culture" and suspected that "people will freak out about the tattooed bums" (Delilkan 2012). Her prediction proved correct, as the cast's stylised costumes and the men's semi-exposed buttocks became the object of an anthropological gaze by London reviewers: blogger David Nice (2012) described warriors performing with "incredible vigour, all feathers, bare chests and tattooed buttocks and thighs"; *The Guardian*'s Andrew Dickson (2012) wrote the performers prowled "across the stage like prize-fighting cocks, clad in loincloths, feathers, tattoos and precious little else"; *The Daily Telegraph*'s Dominic Cavendish (2012) mentioned the "panoply of barely clothed men, their thighs tattooed" had "some of the finest tattooed buttocks on the planet".

Balme (1999: 5) highlights the danger of exoticism in performance: when cultural texts are used for their surface appeal with no regard for the original cultural semantics, such texts can "mean little else than their alterity; they are no longer texts in the semiotic sense, but merely signs, floating signifiers of otherness". In the case of Ngākau Toa's *Toroihi rāua ko Kāhira,* an exoticising gaze was anticipated, and the production self-consciously signified its cultural difference on the London stage. While the production may have been received by some in the audience as a spectacle of cultural otherness, the production's aesthetics were working at a much deeper level, with the costuming supporting the characterisations of Shakespeare's text. The play's European origins were acknowledged in the costuming of the female characters, with "bodices and full satin skirts worn by some of the women" (Silverstone 2013: 36), which signified the way that the women were in bondage to the men, objects to be fought for and won, with Hērena (Helen) the ultimate prize. The men in this production were on full peacocking display, highlighting an important gender distinction in Shakespeare's text: war and battle were the ways men proved their sexual primacy. Hyland and Conkie (2017: 160) argue that the conscious and ostentatious parade of male bodies draws attention to the "continuing global

Image 3.1 Ngākau Toa Theatre Company performs *Toroihi rāua ko Kāhira* (*The Māori Troilus and Cressida*) at Shakespeare's Globe, London, UK, 2012. Credit: Tony Nandi/Lnp/Shutterstock

inability to praise performances by Māori men beyond their muscularity, or aesthetic masculinity" and deconstructed and subverted tropes of "stereotypical violent savages" and haka as metonymic of Māori performance. The company's visual spectacle was also used by the festival to promote itself in the media, and Catherine Silverstone (2013: 40) notes that double page spreads published by British media "offered spectacular images of cultural otherness on the Globe's stage", which contrasted with the globe's conventional publicity images of "white actors in period costumes". It is notable that while the production's costuming was highly stylised, and there was no concerted attempt at historical accuracy in the production's image of precolonial Māori society, the design was largely received by audience commentators as culturally authentic. This is due not to the clothes themselves, but the performers wearing them, who were subject to an othering gaze which constructed their Indigenous bodies as authentically real and different (see Image 3.1).

While reviewers were captured by the visual alterity, what was most significant about *Toroihi rāua ko Kāhira* was the way the production othered the drama of Shakespeare's play. Conventional scholarship categorises *Troilus and Cressida* as a problem play. It is believed to have not been performed in Shakespeare's lifetime and is one of his least performed today. For Hyland and Conkie (2017: 159) the problematic reputation of the Shakespeare's play made it an "ideal text to reclaim within a pre-colonial Māori setting and to relocate in the very heart of Empire". They argue that the narrative of *Troilus and Cressida* "actually makes more sense in Te Ao Māori", where the actions of the characters can be understood in the context of "critical beliefs and values from Māori culture" (159). This is a productive reading of the play that is accessible to audiences with knowledge of Te Ao Māori, but the critical response from the British press also overwhelmingly expressed the notion that the company's production transcended the flaws of Shakespeare's problematic play. Two separate critics agreed that this was the best version of *Troilus* since a Royal Shakespeare Company production 25 years before that had set the play during the Crimean War (Nice 2012; Wolf 2012). The fight scenes were identified as a particular strength, "usually the point at which even the best of British productions buckle a bit" (Nice 2012). The recontextualised Māori culture offered a new lens to view the gender politics in the play's drama:

> here it's not only Troilus and Cressida who find it impossible to admit their true feelings for each other; all the men on stage seem doomed to act out honour codes that leave little room for anything other than sound and fury.
>
> (Dickson 2012)

Cavendish's (2012) analysis is useful: "the production provides a way into a world removed from our own, which by its strangeness serves to comment on our own". By othering the play with Māori cultural signs, non-Māori audiences are enabled to reconceptualise their notions of the merits of Shakespeare's play. Ngākau Toa liberated the text from the confines of its language and British cultural context, allowing Globe audiences to rediscover the drama and revitalise both the Greek and Elizabethan contexts through the knowingly exotic Māori context.

House was also driven by a desire to make the work accessible to non-Reo speakers. Part of this strategy was an emphasis on the inherent sexual elements of the play. In a scene featured in *The Road to the Globe* documentary (Monsoon Pictures International 2013), the Globe audience are shown responding enthusiastically to the innuendo of Paratene's camp Pandarus, as he rhythmically bangs two pieces of bone together and makes noises of sexual pleasure during an interaction between Toroihi (Troilus) and Kahira (Cressida). Stereotypes of modern gayness are used to characterise Aikiri (Achilles) and Patokihi (Patroclus), depictions that Silverstone (2013: 41) criticises as "reductive representations". She argues the performances could have drawn "attention to the cultural specificity of takatāpui", an Indigenous concept of queerness. This was unlikely to have translated for audiences unfamiliar with takatāpui, and the production made the best choice for its audience. Though the company may have appeared to some in the Globe audience as a culturally authentic other, the production was also enacting modern and recognisable social roles in order to connect with the audience. House's direction was a canny modern reading of the text, emphasising that it is sexual desire that drives the action of the play, best exemplified by Pandarus's line in the original text, "hot blood, hot thoughts, and hot deeds" (Shakespeare 1602: 3.1, 128–129). By emphasising the innuendo in the text, non-Reo speakers were enabled to feel like they were in on the joke.

The need to both honour Māori culture and Te Reo, whilst providing an accessible performance for an international Globe audience in London, remained a tension in the company's work. While the Globe performance can be deemed to have successfully balanced these needs for the majority of their audience, especially those critics that identified transcendent universalism, there are some important counter-narratives from the London season where audiences were "doomed to spend large portions of this voyage around global Shakespeare somewhat at sea" (Dickson 2012). For Cavendish (2012), there were elements that "need little in the way of translation", but "others are far tougher to unpick". The use of surtitles in the Globe production was criticised for not providing any of Shakespeare's original lines and the "baldest of scene-summaries" (Nice 2012). Nice (2012) was bothered by his inability to follow key speeches and argued that Shakespeare's language was the "biggest casualty", except for Reo speakers, who "understood the impressive Māori translation". It is important to note that general audiences of Shakespeare in English may often find themselves "somewhat at sea" in attempting to follow the archaic language, with many English-language productions just as incomprehensible at times. When I saw the fundraiser production in Auckland, which provided no surtitles at all, as a non-Reo speaker I was able to discern enough of the action, and my own efforts of interpretation kept me doubly engaged. The decision not to include line-by-line translations was the correct one, as it would have drawn focus away from the action on stage. While the London reviews aesthetically analysed the cultural experience, none of them attempts to describe the quality of Te Reo itself. It is a curious absence that suggests an anxiety of comprehension, with an emphasis on both exotic and assessable visual cues, neglecting the performer's oratory and vocalised emotion.

Countering colonialism: mana enacted

The most significant outcome of the production was the way Ngākau Toa used the Globe performance as a site to assert their mana by championing tikanga Māori and Te Reo. In order to present their cultural testimony on the global stage, Ngākau Toa did so via a translation of another culture's story, just as Downstage had done with *Hedda Gabler*. The parameters of the Globe to Globe Festival positioned London as a global cultural centre, and the company worked within the institutional framework of a dominant former coloniser. This had been a willing collaboration, driven by Rawiri Paratene, who had previously performed at the Globe and whose dream as leader of the project was to "walk onto that stage with a bunch of Māori" (Monsoon Pictures International 2013). He compared the theatre and its relationship between players and audience to the marae: "it's intimate and huge all at once and the minute you start talking above the people, your argument is lost" (Smithies 2013). While Ngākau Toa was resident, the Globe was occupied as a meeting place between peoples where Māori voices could be heard and acknowledged. As Silverstone (2013: 43) argued, the production "privileges and affirms Shakespeare and the Globe [...] but also deploys these institutions and attendant cultural capital for its own ends of cultural and linguistic regeneration, so as to create and affirm networks and generate feelings of pride". While operating within a colonial paradigm, the work itself offered a site of resistance and opportunity to talk back to the former coloniser.

Setting *Toroihi rāua ko Kāhira* prior to European contact in New Zealand draws attention to the ongoing colonial legacy of New Zealand's settlement, depicting an unrecoverable precolonial and pre-globalisation Māori society, complicating the appeal to a united New Zealand nationalism in Paratene's crowfunding campaign. Ngākau Toa's image of precontact Aotearoa was not of some prelapsarian paradise, but a highly complex society of competing iwi, on par with the ancient Greeks and Trojans. As Hyland and Conkie write (2017: 159), the politics of war are deferred from the usual interpretation of conflict between Pākehā and Māori, concentrating "instead on ways that obligation to whanau (family) and responsibilities to iwi (tribe) are complicated by human desires". The imaginative decolonisation extends to the choice to present classical Kupu Tawhito Māori language rather than contemporary Reo. Gilbert and Tompkins (1996: 171) argue that "since even many Māori do not speak the language very well", the use of Te Reo in theatre signifies "only 'history' to some audiences, and a superseded past at that". While *Toroihi rāua ko Kāhira*'s classical Reo underlined the unrecoverable past, it simultaneously represented the future of a revitalised language.

Language regeneration was cited as a symbolic outcome of the performance. The majority of Ngākau Toa's performers were not fluent speakers of Te Reo. Shortland and Tweedie Waititi acted as mentors for the cast, improving their understanding and pronunciation of Te Reo (Māori Television 2012). For non-speakers, the production could provide an incitement for education. Rawiri Paratene reflected that Te Reo's health remains in trouble and felt it was their "duty to keep it alive" (Monsoon Pictures International 2013). Unlike other languages in the Festival which are in everyday use in their countries, for example, productions in Japanese and Russian, Te Reo is a threatened language that was being spoken by actors not necessarily fluent in the language. Through *Toroihi rāua ko Kāhira*, Ngākau Toa used the story and institutions of the colonising culture to regenerate their own connection to their language through the performance.

When the Globe to Globe Festival faced criticism for its programming decision to invite a company from Israel, the Festival argued that it was to be a "celebration of languages" rather than a "celebration of nations or states"; as *The Economist* correctly pointed out, this was a disingenuous statement as "a festival of this stature is a stamp of approval for what a culture is projecting about itself" (J.C. 2012). How language is used and expressed is an important aspect of constructing a cultural identity. Within New Zealand the company was celebrated as representing the nation's Indigenous (minority) culture. When placed on the Globe stage, kaupapa Māori represented the Aotearoa New Zealand nation, and the Indigenous culture was the culture of importance. Silverstone (2013: 43) warned that Ngākau Toa's showcase of culture risked "being consumed as exotic, universal or an object of cultural tourism [...], capable, variously, of both marginalising and homogenising difference". There were connections made with universal transcendence in the performance's reception, but the confident assertion of Māori culture within the production prevented the potential marginalisation of difference. The exotic gaze was a factor in the reception of the London season, evidenced through the focus on the theatricalised Māori costuming and othered body, although this was anticipated by the company and the performance self-consciously played with representations of exoticness. More significant was the cultural othering of the play itself. *Troilus and Cressida* is a bitter and ironic play that is underappreciated and rarely performed. Ngākau Toa was deemed to have surmounted the problems with Shakespeare's text and rejuvenated the play. The boldness of Rachel House's artistic vision made the production more than a vehicle for cultural tourism: it was an opportunity to see the performance as a definitive version of the play.

Silverstone (2013: 41) argues that "displaced 'local' audiences are also capable of expanding the range of meanings that a geographically dislocated production might generate in international festival contexts". This was evidenced in reactions to the curtain call, where the Māori in the audience responded to their performers with their own mihi and haka, confirming the prestige of the occasion and mana of the performers. London blogger David Nice (2012) recorded:

> There was an impromptu response at the end, too, as our neighbour-groundlings responded with their own earth-shaking tribute. At last we understood just how many audience members had been getting the verbal as well as the physical jokes; the Māori community in London must have joined the actors' devoted fans from New Zealand.

Māori and non-Māori audiences were involved in an example of performed mana and tikanga in practice, engaging with a living culture, on-stage and off. The company's imaginative relocation of *Troilus and Cressida* acknowledged Shakespeare's global primacy while equally offering Māori culture and Te Reo as *global* taonga.

Notes

1   Where possible I have provided in parentheses the iwi (tribal groups) that the Māori practitioners whakapapa to (affiliate with).

2 Māori urban migration represented a huge social shift within New Zealand – the Māori population switched from 83% rural to 83% urban between 1936 and 1986. See Derby, Mark. 2011. "Māori–Pākehā Relations – Māori Urban Migration". *Te Ara.* Last modified May 5, 2011. www.TeAra.govt.nz/en/maori-pakeha-relations/page-5

3 In addition to England and Hawai'i, Kouka's work has circulated to a number of markets: it has been produced by companies in Canada (*Waiora*, 1996), South Africa (*Homefires*, 1999), Illinois, USA (*Waiora*, 2016) and translated into French, Japanese and Russian. (Information provided by Playmarket director Murray Lynch on behalf of Hone Kouka, personal emails, November 27 and 28, 2019.)

References

Note: "CF:JB" or "CF:HK" indicates the source was accessed through Client File: John Broughton or Client File: Hone Kouka, Playmarket, Wellington.

"About Brighton Festival". 2020. *Brighton Festival.* Last modified January 7, 2020. https://brightonfestival.org/about/about_brighton_festival/

AFP. 2012. "Māori Troupe Kicks off Shakespeare Fest". *NZ Herald.* April 24.

Archie, Carol. 1991. "Every Marae Is a Theatre". *NZ Listener.* August 26. (CF:JB)

Balme, Christopher B. 1999. *Decolonizing the Stage: Theatrical Syncretism and Post-Colonial Drama.* Oxford: Oxford University Press.

Broughton, John. 1994. *Michael James Manaia.* Dunedin: University of Otago.

Calder, Peter. 1991. "Tree Blossoms in the Sacred Grove". *NZ Herald.* November 22. (CF:JB)

Cavendish, Dominic. 2012. "Māori Troilus and Cressida, Shakespeare's Globe, Review". *The Telegraph.* Last modified April 24, 2012. www.telegraph.co.uk/culture/theatre/theatre-reviews/9224440/Māori-Troilus-and-Cressida-Shakespeares-Globe-review.html

Crooks, Bridget. 2006. "Study Resource" in *The Prophet* by Hone Kouka. Wellington: Huia: 107–142.

Delilkan, Sharu. 2012. "Preview: Troilus and Cressida". *Theatre Scenes.* Last modified April 6, 2012. www.theatrescenes.co.nz/preview-troilus-and-cressida-auckland-town-hall-to-the-globe-theatre/

Dickson, Andrew. 2012. "Troilus and Cressida – Review". *The Guardian.* Last modified April 24, 2012. www.theguardian.com/stage/2012/apr/24/troilus-cressida-review

Donald, Colin. 1991. "Vietnam in Powerful Perspective". *The Scotsman.* August 15. (CF:JB)

Dromgoole, Dominic. 2013. "Foreword" in *Shakespeare beyond English: A Global Experiment*, edited by Susan Bennett and Christie Carson. Cambridge: University Press: xxiii–xxiv.

Fuhrmann, Andrew. 2012. "Michael James Manaia". *Time Out Melbourne.* October 29. (CF:JB)

Gilbert, Helen and Joanne Thompkins. 1996. *Post-Colonial Drama: Theory, Practice, Politics.* London; New York: Routledge.

Goodall, Adam. 2016. "A Woman, Leaving: An Oral History of 'and what remains'". *The Pantograph Punch.* Last modified July 18, 2016. www.pantograph-punch.com/post/a-woman-leaving-an-oral-history-and-what-remains

Gray, Tānemahuta. 2019. Interviewed by James Wenley. Wellington. October 30.

Hansen, Mei-Lin Te-Puea. 2007. "Maori Drama" in *The Columbia Encyclopedia of Modern Drama* (Vol. 2), edited by G.H. Cody and E. Sprinchorn. New York: Columbia University Press: 963.

Harkins-Cross, Rebecca. 2012. "Michael James Manaia". *The Age*. October 15. (CF:JB)

Hotere, Andrea. 1995. "John Broughton: Drama's Gentle Dentist". *North & South*, December (CF:JB)

Huria, John. 1997. "Mā Te Rēhia e Kawē". *Playmarket News*, 16, Spring: 2–7.

Hyland, Nicola. 2015. "Beyoncé's Response (eh?) Feeling the Ihi of Spontaneous Haka Performance in Aotearoa/New Zealand". *TDR: The Drama Review*, 59 (1): 67–82.

Hyland, Nicola and Rob Conkie. 2017. "Kissing and Drowning the Book Shakespearean Theatre in the Antipodes". *The Shakespearean World*, edited by Jill L. Levenson and Robert Ormsby. London: Routledge: 154–170.

J.C. 2012. "The Globe to Globe Festival: Tangling Tongues". *The Economist*. Last modified April 24, 2012. www.economist.com/prospero/2012/04/24/tangling-tongues

Kouka, Hone. 2007. "Re-Colonising the Natives: The State of Contemporary Maori Theatre" in *Performing Aotearoa: New Zealand Theatre and Drama in an Age of Transition*, edited by Marc Maufort and David O'Donnell. Germany: PIE Peter Lang: 237–245.

Love, Roger. 1997. "Chilling Climax Makes It Memorable". *West Sussex Gaze*. May 29. (CF:HK)

Māori Television. 2012. *Te Tēpu*. Broadcast on Māori Television. December 5.

Masters, Tim. 2012 "Globe to Globe: Māori Troilus and Cressida Puts Haka into Shakespeare". *BBC*. Last modified April 22, 2012. www.bbc.com/news/entertainment-arts-17769799

Mazer, Sharon. 2013. "A National Theatre in New Zealand? Why/Not?" in *Theatre and Performance in Small Nations*, edited by Steve Blandford. Bristol; Chicago: Intellect: 106–121.

McColl, Colin. 1991. Report prepared for Downstage Theatre Company. MS-Papers-8874-09:12. Downstage Theatre Company (Wellington): Records. Alexander Turnbull Library, Wellington.

McMillan, Joyce. 1991. "What's Wrong with Men?". *The Guardian*. August 16. (CF:JB)

Mokaraka, Rob and Paola Rotondo. 2012. "Introduction [to Strange Resting Places]". *Haruru Mai*. Wellington: Playmarket: 105–107.

Monsoon Pictures International. 2013. *The Road to the Globe: The Māori Troilus and Cressida*. Broadcast on Māori Television. April 21.

Ngākau Toa. 2012. "Globe to Globe". *The Māori Troilus and Cressida*. Last modified January 7, 2020. http://web.archive.org/web/20120510195520/http://themaoritroilusandcressida.com/

Nice, David. 2012. "Shakespeare's Māori Warriors". *I'll Think of Something Later*. Last modified April 26, 2012. http://davidnice.blogspot.com/2012/04/shakespeares-maori-warriors.html

O'Donnell, David. 2007. " 'Calming the Oceans': David O'Donnell Interviews Briar Grace-Smith" in *Performing Aotearoa: New Zealand Theatre and Drama in an Age of Transition*, edited by Marc Maufort and David O'Donnell. Germany: PIE Peter Lang: 269–282.

Oi, Cynthia. 1999. "Maori Theater Explores Social Injustice in 'Waiora'". *Star Bulletin*, September 16. (CF:HK)

Parker, George. 2008. "Actor Alone: Solo Performance in New Zealand". PhD Thesis, University of Canterbury, Christchurch.

Patterson, Christina. 2012. "Lost in Translation: The Globe's Shakespeare Season Offers a Surprising Insight into Different Cultures". *Independent*. Last modified June 7, 2012. https://www.independent.co.uk/arts-entertainment/theatre-dance/features/lost-in-translation-the-globes-shakespeare-season-offers-a-surprising-insight-into-different-7821169.html

Phillips, Jock. 2014. "Exhibitions and World's Fairs – International Exhibitions, 1900 to 1950". *Te Ara*. Last modified October 22, 2014. http://teara.govt.nz/en/zoomify/45436/advertisement-for-maggie-papakura-the-arawa-warriors-and-maori-maidens

Rae, Bernadette. 1997. "Rocking Brighton". *NZ Herald*. May, 8. (CF:HK)

Royal, Te Ahukaramū Charles. 2007. "Te Ao Mārama – The Natural world – Mana, Tapu and Mauri". *Te Ara*. Last modified September 24, 2007. www.TeAra.govt.nz/en/te-ao-marama-the-natural-world/page-5

Schultz, Marianne. 2016. *Performing Indigenous Culture on Stage and Screen: A Harmony of Frenzy*. Hampshire: Palgrave Macmillan.

Sears, Rachel. 2016. "Waiora Te Ū Kai Pō – The Homeland Education Pack". *The Court Theatre*. Last modified January 7, 2020. http://courteducation.org.nz/assets/Education-Packs/Waiora-Education-Resource-web.pdf

Shakespeare, William. 1602. "Troilus and Cressida" in *The Complete Works* (Second Edition), edited by Stanley Wells and Gary Taylor. Oxford: Clarendon Press. 2005: 744–776.

Sherriff, Val. 1998. "European Tour Turned Down in Favour of NZ". *Bay of Plenty Times*. July 9. (CF:HK)

Silverstone, Catherine. 2013. "Festival Showcasing and Cultural Regeneration" in *Shakespeare beyond English*, edited by Susan Bennett and Christie Carson. Cambridge: Cambridge University Press: 35–47.

Simei-Barton, Paul. 2012. "Theatre Review: The Māori Troilus & Cressida, Town Hall". *NZ Herald*. Last modified March 23, 2012. www.nzherald.co.nz/entertainment/news/article.cfm?c_id=1501119&objectid=10794079

Smithies, Grant. 2013. "All the World's a Stage for Rawiri". *Sunday Star Times*. Last modified April 21, 2013. www.stuff.co.nz/entertainment/8561153/All-the-worlds-a-stage-for-Rawiri

Smythe, John. 2004. *Downstage Upfront*. Wellington: Victoria University Press.

Stachurski, Christina. 1999. "Michael James Manaia: The Personal Is Political". *Journal of New Zealand Literature*, 17: 125–138.

TangataWhenuaDotCom. 2012. "The Māori Troilus and Cressida Fundraiser Appeal". *Youtube*. Last modified March 20, 2012. www.youtube.com/watch?v=N3YsJLWZYPI

"Troilus and Cressida". 2012. *Globe to Globe*. Last modified January 7, 2020. http://globetoglobe.shakespearesglobe.com/archive/2012/plays/troilus-and-cressida/english-19

Whitehead, Jan. 1997. "Waiora". *The Stage*. June 12. (CF:HK)

Wolf, Matt. 2012. "Globe to Globe: Troilus & Cressida, Shakespeare's Globe". *The Arts Desk*. Last modified April 24, 2012. www.theartsdesk.com/theatre/globe-globe-troilus-cressida-shakespeares-globe

4 *Skin Tight*'s world flight

The production of New Zealand plays by international companies

Which New Zealand play has been most regularly programmed by international theatre companies? Mark Amery (2013: 101) identifies *Skin Tight* (1994) by Gary Henderson as the most produced New Zealand play internationally. In *Skin Tight*, rural farmers Tom and Elizabeth negotiate differing perspectives around their marriage and lives spent together against a backdrop of the South Canterbury plains. Gary Henderson is represented by New Zealand's Playmarket agency, who issued 33 separate licenses to international companies to stage productions of *Skin Tight* between 1997 and 2018.[1] Among these, 13 were produced by companies in the UK, 12 in the USA, 5 in Australia and 1 each in South Africa, Germany and Belgium. In addition, a French translation of the play was produced in Montreal, Canada, in 2016, and *Skin Tight* made its Republic of Ireland debut in Dublin in 2019.[2] There is, however, another work that – on face value – also has a claim of being the most produced New Zealand play internationally: *Ladies Night* (1987) by Stephen Sinclair and Anthony McCarten. Commercially popular in New Zealand and overseas, four working class Kiwi blokes become male stripper act the Raging Rhinos. Unlike "pumped up foreigners with their silicon inflated biceps", the Rhinos give their punters "the real thing [...], genuine prime Kiwi beefcake" (Sinclair and McCarten 2003: 50). During the same 1997–2018 period, Playmarket licensed nine productions of *Ladies Night* in Australia, but Sinclair and McCarten used a separate agent for licensing productions in the Northern Hemisphere. Co-writer Sinclair estimates at least 28 further productions in countries including England, Italy, Russia, Greece, Scandinavia, Iceland, Poland, Ukraine, Belarus, Spain, Brazil, Argentina, Canada (performed in both French and English) and an illegal unlicensed production in Costa Rica (personal email December 9, 2014). In France, *Ladies Night* won the Molière Award for best stage comedy of 2001, and it "had an on-going life in Germany for almost 20 years" (Sinclair, personal email). Having been translated into 12 languages, *Ladies Night* is the most widely travelled play from New Zealand (Circa Theatre 2016).[3]

Low-brow and populist, *Ladies Night* represents a different type of theatre to the poeticism of *Skin Tight*. *Ladies Night*'s categorisation as a New Zealand play, however, is problematised by its history of overseas productions. McCarten states that he and Sinclair are "very flexible in terms of allowing the play to be adapted to local conditions" (McCarten and Balme 2017: 40). The text is transposed and translated for each local cultural context where it is produced; therefore, Kiwi beefcake becomes Deutschland Muskelprotze and so on in an endless line-up of country-specific strippers. In the Manchester version of the sequel, *Ladies Night 2: Raging On* (1993), one character, performing a drag routine, says he can "speak 20 languages and can't say no in any of them" (Sinclair and McCarten n.d.: 2). *Ladies Night* and its less regularly produced sequel wear cultural drag so convincingly that international audiences would not realise that these plays were originally created in Aotearoa New Zealand. *Skin Tight*'s South Canterbury location, in contrast, travels with the play in productions across Australia, the UK and USA. The sense of place is crucial in the play, and Amery argues that *Skin Tight* as a New Zealand play has "one of the strongest evocations of Pākehā grounding in the land" (Amery 2013: 101).[4] *Skin Tight* provides a case where plays with a strong New Zealand identity can appeal to theatre companies in other parts of the world. *Ladies Night* makes a counterclaim: in order to achieve commercial success, it is desirable for companies to have the option to replace a New Zealand context with their own. As a populist comedy *Ladies Night* is less bound to place, and by exchanging cultural references, the male strippers become generalised archetypes of masculinity, a national "imitation without an origin" (Butler 1999: 175). As a serious work about the couple's relationship, *Skin Tight*'s Tom and Elizabeth are harder to uproot from a New Zealand cultural and historical context without major rewrites. In *Skin Tight*, markers of New Zealand identity have been retained in performances by overseas companies. In *Ladies Night*, New Zealand identity is stripped away and replaced with another.

New Zealand plays performed by international companies have often been adapted ala *Ladies Night* under this commercial pressure in the belief that localising the script will make it more relevant to audiences and, therefore, be more successful at the box office. As detailed in Chapter 1, in the 1979 West End production of *Middle Age Spread* (1977), Roger Hall exchanged the original play's Wellington setting for Thatcherite England. The prestige of performance at London's West End was privileged over retaining the representation of New Zealand society. Bruce Mason provided a contrasting example, insisting that any international productions of his work were presented true to label, that is, retaining their original representation of New Zealand society. These two poles of permissive adaptation (*Middle Age Spread*, *Ladies Night*) versus true to label representation (plays by Bruce Mason, *Skin Tight*) are a further manifestation of New Zealand's anxious and insecure national identity, presenting an existential tension between desiring international production, visibility and validation, which is undermined by a potential market-driven demand to transpose cultural contexts and make New Zealand representation invisible. Playwright Stuart Hoar (2012: 26) reflects on this tension in an article in the 2012 *Playmarket Annual*, noting that the cultural privileging of overseas markets remains an influential factor in the international experience of contemporary New Zealand playwriting: "[W]hile in New Zealand we happily accept plays set elsewhere, I think it's equally true that the rest of the world doesn't have that same comfortable feeling with NZ plays". Hoar asks his peers, "if the price to pay for getting a London production was to change the setting from Ekatahuna to Luton would you do it?" and answers for himself in the affirmative (26).

For a playwright hopeful for production by international companies, the use of an agent to distribute scripts to companies on their behalf is a typical tactic. Playmarket actively distributes client plays to international companies. Playmarket issued 382 separate licenses for performances of New Zealand work overseas between 1997 and 2018. A minority (57) represented licenses issued to New Zealand companies touring to overseas destinations, but the majority was for amateur and professional overseas companies or schools performing a New Zealand work. Agents lobby producers and companies with their clients' scripts, take a commission on the playwright's royalties and can advocate for the playwright's financial and legal interests. Australia is the main overseas market that Playmarket licenses to, followed by the UK and USA. As Figure 4.1 indicates, Playmarket has rarely licensed client plays beyond the Anglo-world. James Belich (2009: 49) describes the Anglo-world as a "transcontinental, transnational entity" in which "transfers of things, thoughts, and people" – and in this case, theatre – "lubricated by shared language and culture" flowed more easily from countries within the Anglo-world than from without. It is not surprising that Playmarket's data demonstrates a very Western, and colonial, route for the New Zealand play to travel.

Playmarket's international licensing data provides an impression of what kinds of New Zealand play have been programmed by international

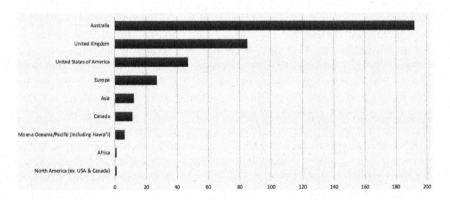

Figure 4.1 Playmarket international licenses issued by region (1997–2018)
Source: Playmarket

companies and the tensions around retaining a true to label national representation. Ranked at the top of Playmarket's list of most internationally licensed scripts, Gary Henderson's *Skin Tight*, a play with highly visible markers of New Zealand identity, does not undergo textual changes when performed by international companies. *Ophelia Thinks Harder* (1993) by Jean Betts, a feminist reimagining of Shakespeare's *Hamlet,* follows at 19 productions, with 13 in Australia, 4 in the USA and 2 in Singapore. With 18 international productions (mostly across Australia), the third is *Chook Chook* (1994) by Fiona Farrell, featuring four chickens who dream of escaping their cages. The play's young adult female cast and minimalist staging are likely reasons for the play's appeal, as well as the play's non-specific setting. It has proved popular in high schools, where the play is also commonly performed in New Zealand. Duncan Sarkies's *Lovepuke* (1993) ranks fourth at ten productions, seven of which have been in Australia. *Lovepuke* is promoted as a play that "taps directly into the relationship concerns of contemporary young adults everywhere" (Playmarket n.d.). While New Zealand cultural references in *Ladies Night* are exchanged in order to work for the overseas companies' home contexts, *Chook Chook*, *Ophelia* and *Lovepuke* fill theatrical niches and are not firmly identified with Aoteaoroa New Zealand. These factors increase their potential appeal to overseas production and aid easy assimilation into alternative cultural contexts. At nine performances, *Daughters of Heaven* (1991) by Michelanne Forster, about the Christchurch Parker/Hulme murder case that was also the basis for Peter Jackson's 1994 film *Heavenly Creatures,* completes the top five (equalled with nine Australian licenses for both *Ladies Night*'s and Roger Hall's *Footrot Flats: The Musical*, set on a New Zealand farm). Henderson's, Hall's and Forster's plays are the minority of these most licensed works, retaining a specific New Zealand setting when performed by overseas companies.

In all cases, international companies choose to emphasise aspects of the play they perceive will resonate with their own audience of "model spectators", and this adaptation is completed when the performed text meets the real audience. Certain meanings and identity markers are received and understood within the feedback loop generated between the performance and audience. Some markers may match the play's original context, but when placed in front of an audience outside of New Zealand, the possibility for different meanings and points of identification occurs, based on the perception of what is held in common. The commercial, cultural and social factors that go into deciding which play to programme and produce are numerous and resist simplification, but the cultural, artistic and economic assumptions that prompt a New Zealand company to programme a local New Zealand work, or even tour a work overseas, will differ from an overseas company programming the same work, who desire work that will appeal to their immediate social, cultural and market context. This chapter uses two plays written by Gary Henderson as contrasting case studies to explore the production of Aotearoa New Zealand plays by international companies and the meanings that are produced for and by their local audiences. The first is the aforementioned *Skin Tight*, which has been performed true to label by companies across multiple locations. The second, *Mo & Jess Kill Susie* (1996), was transposed to a Canadian context when it was produced by companies in Edmonton and Toronto.

Skin Tight as true to label?

As the most licensed New Zealand play to international companies *in which the originating New Zealand cultural context is retained*, *Skin Tight* has demonstrated itself to be extremely portable across various geographic locations (see Map 4.1). The play's two-actor format (with a third actor who appears at the conclusion of the play), and the suggested staging of "a number of gym mats", lends itself to flexibility and adaptability (Henderson 2007: 15). What is not immediately clear is how the play's strong evocation of a Pākehā/Anglo-New Zealand sensibility could extend to the same thematic flexibility in overseas staging. Gary Henderson built *Skin Tight* with a number of cues and clues that a knowing New Zealand audience can identify, and identify with, stimulating the potential New Zealand audience's sense of national identity through the feedback loop.

The first clue is the names of central characters Tom and Elizabeth, borrowed from Denis Glover's 1939 poem "The Magpies". Glover stages a narrative of settlement as ever-present magpies, who chant "Quardle oodle ardle wardle doodle", witness Tom and Elizabeth working their farm, "while the pines grew overhead". Despite their toil, the farm is seized by the bank, Elizabeth dies and Tom goes "light in the head", the couple's New Zealand dream unfulfilled (Glover 1939: Poem 30). In *Skin Tight*, Tom and Elizabeth similarly lose the farm and Elizabeth approaches death, but while the poem views their stories from the detached vantage point of the magpies, Henderson positions the drama with the immediacy of Tom and Elizabeth's own experience. In doing so, Henderson experiments with the temporality of the drama. The bodies of the characters are in their "prime" (Henderson 2007: 14), and Henderson has the couple engage in "brutal" fights where they "punch, kick, slap each other" (15) as a heightened expression of their complex relationship. But their minds and memories are of their older selves, allowing the characters a longer view of their histories as they negotiate an agreed narrative of what their marriage has meant to each other and attempt to delay the inevitability of Elizabeth's death. Towards the end of the play, Tom and Elizabeth make light of their situation:

ELIZABETH: Not me. My body. I'll be gone. Flying away with the magpies. Once around the farm for a last look, then away.
TOM: Where to?
ELIZABETH: Somewhere only magpies know about.
TOM: Oh! Oamaru! (39)

Map 4.1 Productions of Gary Henderson's *Skin Tight* by international companies (1999–2019)

Invoking Glover, this is a self-referential joke, about the perceived obscurity of Oamaru, that undercuts the pathos and that the local audience in the know can appreciate.

Tom and Elizabeth symbolise the New Zealand experience-in-common, their "1940s or 1950s" dress style reminiscent of a nostalgic New Zealand yesteryear, changing the WWI context of Glover's poem to WWII. Elizabeth describes reuniting with Tom when he returned from war: "I ran to you, and it was the first time that I'd seen you cry. And I, deceived again, thought the horror was over" (26). The war's trauma leaves a psychic scar on the characters, and by extension, the nation. It was also during Tom's absence that Elizabeth had an affair with another man, which Elizabeth finally confesses to in the course of the play's action. When Tom asks what kind of man he was, in a further specific feedback loop cue, Elizabeth replies, "a sheep shearer" (32). This challenges the comforting myth of the New Zealand rural paradise, which is challenged again when we learn Tom and Elizabeth's daughter is living in self-imposed exile in metropolitan London. Tom and Elizabeth represent a corroded New Zealand, whose reality does not match the myth of the country as an egalitarian paradise that New Zealanders tell about themselves.

The way Tom and Elizabeth feel and relate to the land is a marker that potentially offers the strongest identification for the local audience. Lisa Warrington (2009: 77) observes that "the Pākehā protagonists are both figuratively and literally locked into the landscape which they love and belong to with a fierce and emotional passion". Henderson develops this sense of the Pākehā's "grounding" in the land (as Amery put it) when Elizabeth imagines her aged body taking on the characteristics of the New Zealand landscape:

> Sooner or later your life becomes parched. Its rivers run thin. Its mountains have melted into the distance as blue and cool as memories. It gathers its cracked old skin and peers thirstily at the wall of black thunderheads coming from the south.
>
> (Henderson 2007: 44)

Elizabeth evokes a view of her mortality, but by linking herself to the landscape, her body can live on. The characters of *Skin Tight* are bound with the land they come from, a statement of Pākehā's insistence of belonging.

Mark Amery (2013: 101) claims that "producers elsewhere in the world equally sympathised with [the play's] connection to the land". It is feasible that Tom and Elizabeth's connection with place could be understood in terms of audiences' and producers' feelings towards specific relationships with place and landscapes of significance in their parts of the world. Johnny Oleksinski (2012), a critic in Chicago, imaginatively substituted Canterbury for "farmland reminiscent of Eugene O'Neill's rocky settings". When the Shaky Isles Theatre Company (formed in 2006 by New Zealand expats living in London) produced *Skin Tight* in London in 2009, an actor from Newcastle played Tom with a Geordie accent. Director Stella Duffy (2015) found this worked "perfectly" for London audiences as there existed a stereotypical perception that people from Newcastle "know about the land". Duffy (2015) informed me this choice did not work for some audience members from New Zealand, for whom the dissonance proved too distracting, although many immigrants living in New Zealand have British accents.

Lyn Gardner (2013), in her review of a 2013 London production, is one of the few critics to mention how the play constructed "a loamy sense of place – New Zealand's Canterbury plains and surrounding mountains". More often, the land becomes generic "rural farmland" (Pender 2010). In the 2000 Sydney production, a reviewer commented that the references to the land produced a distancing effect, "raves about the land and the sound of magpies squawking really gives no palpable sense of time, place and history" ("Dance of Love and Hate" 2000), ironic since these magpies would have been introduced from Australia. *Skin Tight*'s use of Glover's "Magpies" fits into Lorenzo Veracini's (2010) description of the typical "settler narrative of adaptation, struggles against a harsh environment, economic development and integration of migrants". When produced internationally, Tom and Elizabeth can become displaced from the land, the South Canterbury landscape standing in for settled land across the Anglo-world.

The sense that *Skin Tight* operates beyond both national and temporal borders is a common response. The New Zealand context is entirely absent from some overseas reviews. Two British reviews of the same 2013 London production did not find the New Zealand setting or origins of the work an important enough aspect to even briefly mention or discuss (Brown 2013; Bayes 2013). *Skin Tight* is effectively absorbed into the British culture. Two Perth reviewers failed to mention New Zealand (Turner 2003; McNeill 2003), with one (McNeill) situating the show as "a love story outside conventional time frames". A Cincinnati reviewer mentioned the "rural New Zealand" setting, but emphasised that "*Skin Tight* really happens in a place of no time – or, rather, a timeless place", which the minimalist set reinforces (Pender 2010). This was a sentiment shared by Síofra Ní Shluaghadháin (2019), who in reviewing the Dublin premiere, contended that "apart from occasionally mentioning names from their native land, Tom and Elizabeth give us little cause to believe that this play is not simply set anywhere, at any time", overlooking the specific historical context of WWII and how that impacted Tom and Elizabeth's relationship. Shluaghadháin expressed that the play had "a universality". Tom and Elizabeth are often situated as universal figures in reviews, "two ordinary people [...] with just enough detail left out to be any one of us" (Kessler 2010), with the audience able to "understand their universal commonalities" (Oleksinski 2012) (Image 4.1).

The cumulative impression from the critical archive of the play's international production is the potential for an intense audience identification with these "universal" characters. There are reports of *Skin Tight* provoking a profound emotional impact in various audiences: the "raw, emotional portrayal of a very real, intimate relationship [...] reduced many in the audience

Image 4.1 59E59 Theaters' production of *Skin Tight* by Gary Henderson, NYC, USA, 2012. Credit: Carol Rosegg

to tears by the end of the show" (Kessler 2010); a "genuinely moving work about the course of love over a lifetime […]. I found a little trace of something in my throat" (Razer 2011); and even this experience in the Sydney production in 2000:

> One audience member who perhaps had his own war scars tried to leave during a particularly emotive scene and passed out on his way, stalling the performance for a few minutes. The friend I was with, shed tears of joy and sadness for the show's finale.
>
> (Merrill 2000)

What these descriptions of audience responses reveal is not universality, but the operation of the common, the markers of identity which the audiences perceive that they share with the characters, thereby supporting the work's international portability. For a local, knowing audience, the New Zealand regional specific cues stimulate recognition through the feedback loop, providing a context for understanding these characters – the parallel story of the Glover poem of Pākehā settlement – in addition to the potential catharsis the raw and sensual love story allows. Overseas, the New Zealand context (if it is even deemed important in the response) is a context only for these two characters to exist; as a Chicago reviewer expressed, "understanding the actual story becomes secondary to just being immersed in this tumultuous eroticism" (Walsh 2012).

Veracini (2010: 187) argues that "in the consolidating settler 'Angloworld' [...] the ultimate results of settler colonialism were thought to be inherently comparable, a matter of local variation on a common theme". When produced outside of Aotearoa, *Skin Tight* is accepted within a similar frame where local or regional divergence and specific difference is limited. The critical archive reveals a perception that the story could take place anywhere and is relevant everywhere, even though the text could not literally be re-set without substantial textual adaptation. The consistent licencing of *Skin Tight* by Playmarket to international companies is based on the play's artistic merit, the simplicity of its staging and its potential to produce a strong cathartic effect in audiences. *Skin Tight* does not change, but its audiences do, identifying with some of the possible readings, but not recognising others. In other words, the label may stay the same, but overseas audiences do not necessarily read the label the same way.

Margin to Margin: *Mo & Jess Kill Susie*

The Canadian experience of another of Gary Henderson's works, *Mo & Jess Kill Susie* (1996), provides a vastly different example of international production. Northern Light Theatre, who presented the play in Edmonton in 2008, and Harley Dog Productions, who presented it in Toronto in 2013, adapted the script into their own cultural context. Reflecting postcolonial concerns whereby theatre that originates from one ex-British colony is translated by another ex-colony, Māori characters Mo and Jess became Indigenous Canadians in these productions. Henderson approved the adaptation but was uninvolved in the changes.

In its Aotearoa New Zealand context, *Mo & Jess Kill Susie* examines tensions within the myth of bicultural harmony between Māori and Pākehā. Set four years in the future from when it was originally written in 1996, Mo and Jess are two Māori activists, part of an unidentified protest movement resisting government land seizures. They have abducted and taken Susie, a Pākehā police officer, as a hostage, a trump card in their protest group's showdown with police. Mo and Jess await a phone call which may order them to release, or kill, their hostage. Set in a claustrophobic room in an empty building, as the play unfolds we learn about the characters' backgrounds and motivations for their action. There are a number of New Zealand specific references, including the 1995 Moutoa Gardens protest, a 79-day occupation in Whanganui, which the characters cite as an impetus for more radical protests: "Moutoa changed things" (Henderson 2007: 69).

When the Northern Light Company (2018) produced *Mo & Jess Kill Susie* in Edmonton, the stated goal, as explained on the company's website, was to "introduce a play that is unheard of in our region, and to show the similarities in culture".[5] The choice to present a transposed version of the play arguably undermines this intention. Performing the original version of the script might have allowed the cultural specificity of the New Zealand context to work as a distancing effect, which may have provoked recognition of a Canadian cultural history through audience comparison.[6] Instead, any similarities are simultaneously upheld and removed when cultural specificity of one kind is replaced by another. Northern Light Theatre, in the words of a Canadian reviewer, "effectively altered" the play "to make it sound and feel more Albertan" (Maclean 2008). The company emphasised the experience-in-common between Canada and New Zealand on their website: "the situations of the Māori and Aboriginal peoples are amazingly comparable, and, while the play could just as easily be performed by three Caucasian actresses, the racial aspect brings a specificity that makes another, larger statement" (Northern Light Theatre 2008). The adaptation attempted to universalise the similarities of the political experience of First Nation peoples by translating the New Zealand context into the Canadian context. However, the Canadian audience was presented with only a specific Canadian experience that overwrote the New Zealand point of view. This process reduced Henderson's commentary on specific New Zealand issues: the history of Māori land rights and protest, and the expression of a Pākehā fear that these factors could lead to a potential violent response. The suggestion that the play could "just as easily" be performed by Caucasian characters further challenged the play's New Zealand specificity, and would substantially change the subtext of the play and undermine its politics.

The second Canadian production, presented at the Toronto Fringe 2013 by Harley Dog Productions – an independent theatre company in Toronto – did not mention the play's New Zealand origin in its marketing. Instead, it was promoted as culturally specific and relevant to the Canadian context: "Set in present day Ontario, *Mo & Jess Kill Susie* is more relevant than ever" (BWW Newsdesk 2013). With this frame, one review described the play as "a story of two First Nations women and their bound, gagged white hostage" that addressed "the difficult topic of Canada's treatment of our Native citizens, and asks if it is possible to break the cycles of violence we find ourselves part of unwittingly" (Shaw 2013). The claim of "our Native citizens" expressed the extent to which the recontextualised play was perceived to represent and reflect a Canadian consciousness.

Marc Maufort (2003: 18) finds similarities in Australian, Canadian and New Zealand drama because the nations represent "prominent instances of settler-invader colonies of the former British empire which share a number of historical, political, cultural and even literary characteristics". This partly explains the ease with which the political situation in *Mo & Jess* can be transported to the Canadian setting; the general positions of the two nations as settler-invader colonies, both sharing an "acute sense of social and intellectual inferiority towards the centre of the Empire", open general commonalities of experience (19). Of relevance to this discussion is the approach taken by playwright Albert Belz (Ngati Porou, Nga Puhi, Ngati Pokai) in preparing both a New Zealand and Australian version of his play *Astroman*, which debuted concurrently in productions by Melbourne Theatre Company and Christchurch's Court Theatre in 2018. The Christchurch production told the story of Jimmy, a young Māori boy finding his place in Whakatāne during the 1980s; in Melbourne, it was Jiembra, a young Australian aboriginal boy finding his place in Geelong. A Melbourne reviewer expressed that there was "something disconcerting about that, as if specific Indigenous experience was ultimately a narrative plaything that could be transferred, comfortably interchangeable" (Byrne 2018).

An issue shared by Belz's *Astroman* and the Canadian *Mo & Jess Kill Susie* adaptations is that they remove the possibility of the audience's own cosmopolitan agency to question the extent of the interchangeability or otherwise between cultural contexts, that is, if the Māori/Pākehā relationship represented in *Mo & Jess Kill Susie* is analogous to the Indigenous Canadian/European Canadian relationship, or if there are differences in each country. Instead, it was the Canadian producers that had decided that the cultural contexts were equivalent. The Canadian adjustments of *Mo & Jess Kill Susie* both generalised and specified, narrowing possible meanings.

Locating New Zealand

The production of New Zealand plays by international company largely minimises the cosmopolitan encounter. Whereas touring productions signal they are not of this place, and thereby promote "a conscious attempt to be familiar with people, objects and places that sit outside one's local or national settings" (Kendall, Woodward and Skrbiš 2009": 113), non-New Zealand companies consciously programme and place the work in a context that they believe will be accepted by their own local audiences. The Canadian productions of *Mo & Jess Kill Susie* had the potential to open a cosmopolitan zone, allowing audiences to draw connections and distinctions between Canada and New Zealand's colonial histories within the common, but instead transplanted the action of the play to their own local context, foreclosing this possibility. Explicit adaptation by the Canadian companies in *Mo & Jess* or the numerous international productions of *Ladies Night* more overtly guide, and limit, the way their audiences see the plays. It suggests an anxiety from the producing companies that a cosmopolitan transfer, in which their audiences are invited to interpret the cultural images of others, cannot occur without their help. The circulation of *Skin Tight* in the Anglo-world, with international companies performing their own representations of New Zealand, is exceptional. The cultural origins of other plays regularly licensed internationally by Playmarket – *Ophelia Thinks Harder*, *Chook Chook* and *Lovepuke* – are largely irrelevant. These plays already have a Westernised non-specific cultural context, or a known Shakespearean setting, which allow them to be staged from country to country.

Even when plays like *Skin Tight* are presented true to label, an implicit process of adaptation takes place. Overseas companies and audiences empha- sise certain aspects of the play over others in order to meet their own criteria for identification. In *Skin Tight*, Tom and Elizabeth's relationship dominates overseas responses, and subtextual markers of New Zealand identity – such as a Pākehā conception of place – are not read by audiences overseas in the same way they potentially can be by a home audience. However, there is potential for a wider range of meanings, or different meanings, to become available for overseas audiences. In cases of both explicit and implicit adaptation, it is not the New Zealand context itself that is the primary appeal for the inter- national companies, but what the plays can say about their own contexts. The spectrum of possible meanings both expands and contracts, limiting or even absenting entirely the New Zealand context, but simultaneously allowing for other interpretations, meanings and cultural identifications. This process is aided, however, by the cultural similarities or the perception of a local vari- ation on a common theme between the Anglo–New Zealand mainstream and the cultures where the plays have been produced overseas, particularly in Britain, Australia and North America. In general, cultural equivalence is emphasised over local and special regionalist difference.

Notes

1 Licensing data provided by Playmarket. By comparison, there were 18 local licences of *Skin Tight* issued to New Zealand companies over the same period to 2015.
2 The original New Zealand production of *Skin Tight* was also toured internationally to the Traverse Theatre at the Edinburgh Festival Fringe in 1998.
3 McCarten and Sinclair settled privately with the producers of the 1997 British film *The Fully Monty*, subsequently adapted as a stage show, following a law suit alleging the male stripper plot and themes of the film had been taken from *Ladies Night*.
4 This reflects Michael King's (2004: 239) conception of Pākehā as someone "who identifies as intimately with this land, as intensively and as strongly, as anybody Māori".
5 Northern Light Theatre programmed *Mo & Jess Kill Susie* after the com- pany produced *Cherish* (2003) by Ken Duncum the previous year and requested Playmarket to send them further New Zealand scripts to consider.
6 Although doing so could potentially present a challenge around how to cast the play culturally appropriately.

References

Note: "CF:GH" indicates the source was accessed through Client File: Gary Henderson, Playmarket, Wellington.

Amery, Mark. 2013. "Pākehā and Palagi: New Zealand European Playwriting 1998– 2012" in *Playmarket 40*, edited by Laurie Atkinson. Wellington: Playmarket: 99–103.
Bayes, Honour. 2013. "*Skin Tight*". *The Stage*. July 19. (Proquest Database)

Belich, James. 2009. *Replenishing the Earth: The Settler Revolution and the Rise of the Anglo-World, 1783–1939*. Oxford: Oxford University Press.

Brown, Peter. 2013. "*Skin Tight* – Review". *London Theatre*. Last modified July 18, 2013. www.londontheatre.co.uk/reviews/skin-tight

Butler, Judith. 1999. *Gender Trouble: Feminism and the Subversion of Identity*. New York: Routledge.

BWW Newsdesk. 2013. "Harley Dog Productions to Present *Mo & Jess Kill Susie* at Toronto International Fringe Fest, 7/3–13". *Broadway World Toronto*. Last modified June 14, 2013. www.broadwayworld.com/toronto/article/Harley-Dog-Productions-to-Present-MO-AND-JESS-KILL-SUSIE-at-Toronto-International-Fringe-Fest-73-13-20130614#.U6I17PmSxg0

Byrne, Tim. 2018. "*Astroman* Review". *Time Out*. Last modified November 5, 2018. https://www.timeout.com/melbourne/theatre/astroman-review

Circa Theatre. 2016. "Spotlight On ... Anthony McCarten". *Circa Theatre*. Last modified March 9, 2016. www.circa.co.nz/spotlight-on-anthony-mccarten/

"Dance of Love and Hate". 2000. *Sydney Star Observer*. December. (CF:GH)

Duffy, Stella. 2015. Interviewed by James Wenley. London. July 7.

Gardner, Lyn. 2013. "*Skin Tight* – Review". *The Guardian*. Last modified July 22, 2013. www.theguardian.com/stage/2013/jul/22/skintight-theatre-review

Glover, Dennis. 1939. "The Magpies" in *100 New Zealand Poems*, edited by Bill Manhire. Auckland: Godwit. 1993: Poem 30.

Henderson, Gary. 2007. *Three Plays: Skin Tight; Mo & Jess Kill Susie; An Unseasonable Fall of Snow*. Wellington: Playmarket.

Hoar, Stuart. 2012. "Substitute Luton for Eketahuna". *Playmarket Annual*. Wellington: Playmarket: 26.

Kendall, Gavin, Ian Woodward and Zlatko Skrbiš. 2009. *The Sociology of Cosmopolitanism: Globalization, Identity, Culture and Government*. Hampshire: Palgrave Macmillan.

Kessler, Jenny. 2010. "Know Theatre's *Skin Tight* Offers Passionate Look at Love". *UrbanCincy*. October 14. (CF:GH)

King, Michael. 2004. *Being Pākehā Now: Reflections and Recollections of a White Native*. Auckland: Penguin.

Maclean, Colin. 2008. "On the Edge of Killing". *Edmonton Sun*. September 16. (CF:GH)

Maufort, Marc. 2003. *Transgressive Itineraries: Postcolonial Hybridizations of Dramatic Realism*. Bruxelles; New York: PIE Peter Lang.

McCarten, Anthony and Christopher B. Balme. 2017. "Whanganui to Wiesbaden". *Playmarket Annual*. Wellington: Playmarket: 40–42.

McNeill, Sarah. 2003. "Love Story Has Compelling Depth". *Subiaco Post*. March 29. (CF:GH)

Merrill, Miles. 2000. "Real Lives Given Beauty". *The Hub*. December 7. (CF:GH)

Northern Light Theatre. 2008. "Mo & Jess Kill Susie". Last modified January 10, 2020. http://web.archive.org/web/20081225190914/http://www.northernlighttheatre.com/season/play1.htm

Oleksinski, Johnny. 2012. "Review: *Skin Tight*/Cor Theatre". *New City Stage*. September 3. (CF:GH)

Pender, Rick. 2010. "Onstage: *Skin Tight* at Know Theatre". *City Beat*. October 5. (CF:GH)

Playmarket. N.d. "Lovepuke". *Playmarket*. Last modified January 10, 2020. www.playmarket.org.nz/bookshop/playmarket-manuscripts/lovepuke

Razer, Helen. 2011. "Erotic Play Hits the Spot". *The Age*. February 7. (CF:GH)

Shaw, Colette. 2013. "The Hostage". *The Charlebois Post*. July 4. (CF:GH)

Shluaghadháin, Síofra Ní. 2019. "*Skin Tight* Stays Tense". *The Theatre Times*. Last modified August 15, 2019. http://thetheatretimes.com/skin-tight-stays-tense/

Sinclair, Stephen and Anthony McCarten. 2003. *Ladies Night* (July 2003 rewrite). Wellington: Playmarket.

———— *Ladies Night 2: Raging On* (Manchester Version). 2007. 2007-250-221. Playmarket: Records. Alexander Turnbull. Wellington.

Turner, Martin. 2003. "Passion Play". *Western Suburbs Weekly*. March 25. (CF:GH)

Veracini, Lorenzo. 2010. "The Imagined Geographies of Settler Colonialism" in *Making Settler Colonial Space: Perspectives on Race, Place and Identity*, edited by Tracey Banivanua Mar and Penelope Edmonds. New York: Palgrave Macmillan.

Walsh, Katy. 2012. "Review: *Skin Tight* (Cor Theatre)". *Chicago Theater Beat*. Last modified August 31, 2012. http://chicagotheaterbeat.com/2012/08/31/review-skin-tight-cor-theatre/#review

Warrington, Lisa. 2009. "Landscape, Body, Memory and Belonging in the Plays of Gary Henderson". *Australasian Drama Studies*, 55: 75–87.

Wright, Steve. 2005. "Review – *Skin Tight*". *Venue Magazine*. May 6–15. (CF:GH)

5 Beyond biculturalism

Touring Pasifika and transnational theatre

In Red Leap Theatre's inventively physical and visual debut work *The Arrival* (2009), created by Julie Nolan and Kate Parker, the protagonist traveller departs from his homeland, oppressed by black tentacles that circle above his home, and arrives in a new world looking for work in order to support his wife and daughter back home. The traveller learns the strange customs of the new world, and his integration is complete when his family joins him to live in the new world. Amanda Rogers (2015: 97) writes that the concept of "transnationalism, with its evocation of cross-border movement away from a location of origin", is often viewed as containing a "tension between displacement and emplacement [...], particularly through the notion of belonging to a home or homeland". The displacement/emplacement tension is also performed in the devised adaptation process of *The Arrival* in which the 2006 graphic novel by Australian artist Shaun Tan is displaced and emplaced by New Zealand's Red Leap Theatre, in a theatrical medium. The displacement/ emplacement binary is complicated further through the international performance of the work across multiple cultural contexts in the Asia-Pacific region (New Zealand, Australia, Singapore, South Korea, Hong Kong and Taiwan). As Fiona Wilkie (2015: 2) suggests, mobility, as "the act of moving between locations", inherently "involves a displacement".

The intensification of neoliberal globalisation has resulted in an increased interaction between cultures, ideas and products that extend beyond the boundaries of nation states: "transnationalism describes this act of border-crossing [...], allowing us to apprehend how the relationship between culture, people and place is reconfigured as national territories no longer automatically provide the main locus of identification and belonging" (Rogers 2015: 7). The traveller in *The Arrival* exists as a border figure, exiled from the old world, displaced in the new world and belonging to neither. As a theatrical fable in which the setting is fantastic rather than specific, he is also a border figure in that he can represent multiple cultures and points of departure depending on the contexts of those receiving the narrative. Though Nolan and Parker were largely faithful in using Tan's graphic novel as a story board for their theatrical images and physical storytelling, alternative meanings are constructed through the displacement of the text in performance. As a transcultural adaptation, the work is not made to align with Aotearoa New Zealand identity specifically, but the programme notes parallel the show with an image of Aotearoa New Zealand as a nation of travellers, both coming to and departing from the nation (Red Leap Theatre 2012). My own review of the 2012 Auckland production concurred: "*The Arrival*'s story of a traveller (Jarod Rawiri) seeking out a new land, speaks to something of our collective New Zealand experience" (Wenley 2012). This rhetoric of Aotearoa as a land of immigrants is used to support acceptance of multiculturalism, but can also be employed to limit notions of national citizenship; what constitutes a New Zealander, and when does a migrant become a New Zealander? This was a question Frank Sargeson asked in his 1940 short story "The Making of a New Zealander", in which the narrator meets a Dalmatian migrant who confides that he "was a New Zealander, but he knew he wasn't a New Zealander. And he knew he wasn't a Dalmatian anymore. He knew he wasn't anything anymore" (104). Though transnationalism is associated with contemporary globalisation, Sargeson's earlier text eloquently speaks to transnational confusion around the migrant's locus of national identification and belonging.

New Zealand adopted biculturalism as a government policy in the 1980s, embedding the principles of Te Tiriti o Waitangi in legislation and emphasising the partnership between Māori and the Crown. The reality is complicated: while New Zealand remains formally tied to Britain with the British monarch as the head of state, as Sharon Mazer (2013: 110) puts it, New Zealand is "not so much a bicultural country as a hybrid nation, as such no longer colonial, really, and yet not quite postcolonial, officially bicultural but both less and more than that in practice". The quasi-bicultural arrangement generates particular tension between cultural and national identities for those "living outside the English/Māori (i.e., coloniser/colonised) binary" (110). Frameworks of biculturalism and postcolonialism are limited in their applicability to a multicultural population and power relationships beyond the historical colonial network of relations between Māori and settler-descended Pākehā. In an Aotearoa New Zealand theatre context, Marc Maufort (2012: 257) observes that the "vast array of multicultural voices on the New Zealand stage" reflects the "increasingly pluri-ethnic set-up of a traditionally bicultural, Pākehā and Māori culture", which forces a redefinition of "the very concept of a monolithic national literature".

This chapter utilises transnationalism to analyse theatrical works that redefine the national and move beyond a bicultural binary. The transnational is associated with "migrant, diasporic and refugee communities not directly emerging from the colonial experience" (Ashcroft, Griffiths and Tiffin 2007: ix) – although this should be modified to recognise that such communities may also have been affected in complex ways by colonial histories in their place of departure. The danger with transnationalism is when it is used to hail the "racial other" by another name, that is, reductively associating transnational theatre with ethnic minorities. Conversely, where it can be introduced to disrupt ideas of the monolithic nation, and investigate hybridity and concepts around the politics of interweaving cultures, it is a valuable tool. As Homi Bhabha (1994: 38) advocates, scholarship needs to pay attention to the *inter* of international culture, "based not on the exoticism of multiculturalism or the diversity of cultures, but on the inscription and articulation of culture's hybridity"; for Bhabha, it is the "inter" as an in-between space "that carries the burden of the meaning of culture".

Transnational narratives offer the possibilities of hybrid in-between identities, synthesising old and new homelands. Gilbert and Lo (2007: 167) argue that "diasporic cultures that are ambivalently positioned between cultural homelands and current hostland [...] tend to produce and enact signs of cultural hybridity", and theatrical performance can "index the tensions (and pleasures) of diasporic belonging". These signs of cultural hybridity can challenge hegemonic notions of national identity. Gilbert and Lo emphasise that hybridity reveals identity formation to be "a fluid and provisional process and offers an alternative organising category for a new politics of representation that is informed by an awareness of diaspora and its contradictory, ambivalent and generative potential" (170). As this chapter will demonstrate, transnational migrant narratives have been particularly prominent in the work toured from Aotearoa New Zealand in the global world, highlighting the processes of emplacement and displacement as an active site of contestation for identity formation. As Sargeson's story asked, at what point does your point of arrival, rather than your point of departure, constitute your identity?

Globalisation, changing migration and demographic patterns, and a promotion of multiculturalism have influenced the construction of broader identities represented in Aotearoa New Zealand theatre over the past 30 years, with a wave of playwrights since the 1990s that brought "more global perspectives" (O'Donnell 2011: 334). These playwrights are often more willing to acknowledge transnationalism and intersections between cultures in their plays, compared with the Pākehā impulse to construct a naturalised and stable identity of belonging. Marc Maufort (2007: 13) identifies that the New Zealand identity is in transition as it increasingly "evades the rigid imperialistic, exclusively Pākehā discourses of the past to extend into a fruitful hybridisation of different races, classes and genders". Lisa Warrington and David O'Donnell (2017: 210) argue that Pasifika theatre (created by artists of Pacific Island-descent working in Aotearoa) has been the site of particular energy and social agitation, illustrating "all the complexities of the fluid sense of cultural identity in migrant societies, and provides a dynamic exemplar or how migrant theatre movements can contribute to arts and culture on both local and international levels". While it is true that New Zealand theatre over the past three decades reflects a greater diversity, Maufort's "fruitful hybridisation" threatens to reinforce a European fantasia of multiculturalism which overlooks ongoing power imbalances.

This chapter investigates the shift towards transnationalism in the global world as Aotearoa New Zealand continues to negotiate its bicultural colonial legacy alongside a multicultural identity, while globalising forces further complicate national concepts. Recognising the significance of the development of Pasifika theatre in Aotearoa, the first section, "Navigating Moana Oceania", follows the circulation of this work across Moana Oceania (the Pacific) and beyond. The second section, "Narratives of migration", offers a comparative analysis of a range of toured transnational texts that represent migrant experiences. The third section, "Touring the transnational", explores the meanings that are emplaced and displaced when such transnational dramas travel to overseas destinations, and the chapter closes with a case study of the international journey of *The Factory* (2011) by Vela Manusaute to Australia and Scotland, analysing the shifting responses that can be generated as transnational theatre reflects and confounds cultural expectations when viewed within different geographic markets.

Navigating Moana Oceania

Beginning in the early 1990s, a significant movement in Aotearoa drama has been what Diana Looser (2014: 59) describes as "a flourishing of work by a wide variety of Pasifika artists [...], some of which has toured back to the artists' respective home islands and further afield". These home islands include Sāmoa, Tonga, Fiji, Niue and Kūki 'Āirani (Cook Islands), originally populated by the Indigenous peoples of Moana through feats of navigation. Pacific Underground, formed in Christchurch in 1992 by a collective of artists (Simon Small, Oscar Kightley, Erolia Ifopo, Mishelle Muagututi'a, Tanya Muagututi'a and Michael Hodgson), toured their debut play *Fresh Off the Boat* (1993) by Oscar Kightley and Simon Small to Apia, Sāmoa, in 1994. Lisa Warrington and David O'Donnell, authors of *Floating Islanders: Pasifika Theatre in Aotearoa* (2017), which records the dynamic variety of Pasifika theatre, describe the Sāmoa tour as a "significant step" for Pacific Underground which "engendered a different perspective on the play" (87). Pacific Underground discovered that placing *Fresh Off the Boat* in Āpia substantially shifted the resonance of the work, observing a difference between the characters audiences in Christchurch and Āpia broadly identified with. Audiences in Āpia responded to the character of Charles, portrayed by David Fane, who arrives from Sāmoa (hence, "fresh off the boat") to live with his Kiwi-Sāmoan relatives, while the audience laughed at the New Zealand-born Sāmoans, as "they were the foreigners this time" (Kightley and Small 2005: viii). In New Zealand, these general audience affinities had been reversed, and it was Charles who was received as a comic figure. Fane discussed the performance with his uncle, who saw the play as a tragedy about failure, telling Fane that, in Charles, Sāmoa had sent "a perfectly good product over to you [in New Zealand], and they came back as broken, we don't understand it" (quoted in Warrington and O'Donnell 2017: 87). The differing geographic and cultural vantagepoints shifted the potential meanings audiences could generate from the performance. After taking *Fresh Off the Boat* to Sāmoa, Pacific Underground performed the play in Brisbane in 1995 where they met Australian company Zeal; the two companies subsequently created *Tatau: Rites of Passage* (1996), "the first Pacific theatre international performance collaboration" (Warrington and O'Donnell 2017: 91). The play was produced in both Auckland and Sydney, connecting the Pacific diaspora. Christopher B. Balme (2007: 192) highlights how the play's live application of the traditional practice of tautau (tattooing) on the body of an actor acts as a means of transcending cultural dislocation "and repairing the ruptures caused by it".

Another milestone in Pasifika theatre in Aotearoa and abroad was *Frangipani Perfume* by Makerita Urale, who grew up in Sāvai'i, Sāmoa, before moving to Aotearoa. The "first Pacific play to be written by a woman writer for an all-female cast", *Frangipani Perfume* debuted at BATS theatre in 1997 (O'Donnell 2004: i). Under the direction of Rachel House, in 2006 *Frangipani Perfume* was toured to the Dreaming Festival in Queensland, Australia, and the Native Earth Festival in Toronto (plus four other venues in Canada), and in 2007 was programmed (with Mīria George's *and what remains...*) in the Pasifika Styles Arts Festival in Cambridge, UK.[1] Dianna Fuemana, an original cast member of *Frangipani Perfume*, has been another influential Pasifika practitioner, born in Auckland to an American Sāmoan mother and Niuean father, who was driven to take her work overseas because she perceived that the "pool is bigger and ideas around 'what theatre is' are more vast than small-town Auckland with all its 'white' British – and American-produced plays" (Fuemana 2008: 13). A playwright and performer, Fuemana has toured and starred in her solos *Mapaki* (1999), which went to America and Greece, and *Falemalama* (which paid tribute to her mother's migration story), commissioned by Pangea World Theatre artistic director Dipankhar Mukerherjee and premiered at Pangea World Theatre in Minneapolis in 2006 as part of their tenth Indigenous Voices series. Fuemana's *The Packer* (2003), starring Jay Ryan, has toured Australia and to the Edinburgh Festival Fringe, and *Birds* debuted at the Niue Culture & Arts Festival 2011 and played the eleventh Festival of Pacific Arts in the Solomon Islands in 2012. Scripts by Pasifika playwrights have also been produced within Hawai'i, such as Kumu Kahua Theatre productions of Albert Wendt's *The Songmaker's Chair* (2003) in 2006 and Victor Rodger's *My Name Is Gary Cooper* (2007) in 2015 and *Puzzy* (2016) (in collaboration with Hawai'i-based playwright Kiki).

The Conch, founded by Nina Nawalowalo and Tom McCrory in 2002, has consistently pursued connections across Moana Oceania. For Warrington and O'Donnell (2017: 141), it represents "a distinctive aesthetic that is the result of a unique intercultural vision", fusing "Pacific cultural forms with physical theatre, mime, illusion, dance, music and lighting, informed by Nawalowalo's Fijian cultural heritage and the performance skills both partners gained in Europe and Aotearoa". The Conch's first production, *Vula* (2002), debuted at BATS and was subsequently toured to multiple locations including the Festival of Pacific Arts in Palau (2004); the Charter Day Festival Guam (2005); Vaka Vuku Conference, Suva, Fiji (2006); the Sydney Opera House (2006), a tour of Holland (2008); and the Barbican Centre in London (2008). A predominant movement and image-based work originally performed solely in Gagana Sāmoa (Samoan language), *Vula* explores Pacific women's relationship with moana (the ocean), incorporating intercultural stories from Fiji, Aotearoa, Sāmoa and Tonga (Warrington and O'Donnell 2017: 144).[2] In touring the work, producer/operator Salesi Le'ota found that people interpreted *Vula* in many different ways, but "Pacific Islanders will always find more behind it" (146). When the Conch performed in the Netherlands, a large audience of Pacific people living in Europe came to see the work; Le'ota recalls that "they sang along, it was like a rock show, and at the same time it was deeply spiritual and humbling for us as performers" (146–147). The Conch sold out their ten-show season at London's Barbican Centre, symbolising for McCrory how far the company had travelled since their BATS debut; McCrory described the Barbican season as a "a huge moment of arrival – we all shed tears because the women were so moved to be the first of their people to bring their stories to such an internationally acclaimed centre" (147).[3] The Conch's one of the most significant projects is *Stages of Change* (2013), in which the company partnered with the Solomon Islands Planned Parenthood Association and the British Council to offer workshops in the Solomon Islands. Using theatre as a social tool to reduce violence against women, the Conch collaborated with survivors of domestic violence to create *Stages of Change*, which was performed from 2013 to 2014 in the Solomon Islands, Papua New Guinea, Sāmoa and the European parliament in Brussels (the European Union partly funded the work) (150).

It is appropriate at this point to recognise Salā Lemi Ponifasio's MAU company, which makes avant-garde work using Pasifika practices for the high-end International Festival touring circuit. *I AM* (2014) was a centrepiece of the NZ at Edinburgh season at the 2014 Edinburgh International Festival, and MAU was performed at the "most prestigious opera houses and arts festivals in the world", including the Théâtre de la Ville in Paris, Festival d'Avignon, Prague Quadrennial, Venice Biennale, Holland Festival, Adelaide Festival, Lincoln Centre in New York and the Santiago a Mil International Festival in Chile (Warrington and O'Donnell 2017: 137). MAU feature a "unique pan-Pacific performance style from diverse influences, including Sāmoan dance, tikanga Māori and Japanese butoh" that is "inherently connected to Pacific spirituality and communities" (136). MAU's hybrid performances challenge reductive application of formal categories of theatre or dance, and are worth acknowledging as a product of the global Festival system. Although drawing from the culture of Aotearoa and Moana Oceania, MAU is often produced in the European-America axis, one of the most regularly Festival-programmed international performance exports connected with Aotearoa.

The circulation routes of many of these Pasifika works to European markets demonstrate how Pacific exoticism has cultural currency in the global theatre marketplace, where works "of cultural difference circulate as valuable commodities" (Gilbert and Lo 2007: 9). But arguably the circulation of the works across Moana Oceania has been of far greater significance, (re) establishing transnational and Indigenous connections. The latter emphasis towards Moana Oceania decentres the colonially premised prestige associated with the Northern Hemisphere market, flipping the axis the other way up and centring what Epeli Hau'ofa (1999: 28) describes as "our sea of islands". An important destination for performance from Aotearoa New Zealand has been the four-yearly Festival of Pacific Arts. With no ticket fees charged, it stands in opposition to highly commercial marketplaces such as Edinburgh. In recent festivals New Zealand has been represented by theatrical work that includes Briar Grace-Smith's *Ngā Pou Wahine* (1995) in Noumea in 2000; Ihimaera's *Woman Far Walking* (2000) and the Conch's *Vula* in Palau 2004; and Dianna Fuemana's *Falemalama* and Taki Rua's *Strange Resting Places* (2007) in American Sāmoa in 2008.

Indigenous Māori and Pasifika work have travelled side by side representing Aotearoa New Zealand, the Festival registering the complex relationship between Pasifika migrants in New Zealand and Māori; Pasifika people are "technically tauiwi (visitors), but many Māori consider themselves to have a closer kinship with Pasifika people than Pākehā" (Warrington and O'Donnell 2017: 17). Within the wider Festival, Ian Gaskell (2009: 132) identifies a tension between representations of "pre-contact" cultural traditions and Westernised forms. Warrington and O'Donnell (2017: 208) argue that "contemporary Pasifika theatre has used the tensions Gaskell mentions to create innovative artistic practice and to foster debate about the role of performance in society". For the 2016 New Zealand delegation to Guam, Creative New Zealand supported a development season of Nathaniel Lee's *Fale Sa*, which deals with the creation legend of the Pacific and the coming of Christianity, Māori urban comedy *Party with the Aunties* (2011) directed by Erina Daniels, alongside "clay artistry, waka navigation, tā moko, weaving, kapa haka, carving and traditional music" (Chung 2015). Ian Gaskell (2009: 132) argues that the festival's intention is to protect Indigenous culture against the perceived threat of globalisation. New Zealand's involvement in the festival has been a postcolonial attempt to move beyond the Anglo-world towards the Polynesian world, where Māori and Pasifika can find common interest through a pan-Pacific/Moana identity. In December 2019 Creative New Zealand announced the new Moana Nui a Kiva fund as part of CNZ's Pacific Arts Strategy in partnership with the Ministry of Foreign Affairs and Trade (MFAT). Enabling Pasifika artists based in Aotearoa to collaborate with communities in Moana Oceania, it is a significant new policy direction for the funding body that will enable more projects like The Conch's *Stages of Change*, prioritising projects that "address issues confronting the Pacific region such as climate change, heritage, language and culture, identity, environmental sustainability, LGBTQI, women, youth and the empowerment of indigenous peoples" (Lisi 2019). The activity focused towards Moana Oceania by New Zealand-based Pasifika groups re-orientates the conventional perception of Britain and America as theatrical centres by instead positioning

Aotearoa New Zealand, as Christopher B. Balme (2007: 191) has argued, as a theatrical centre of the Pacific.

Narratives of migration

A striking development in Aotearoa New Zealand drama toured to the global world in the past three decades has been the number of plays that deal with transnational migration narratives. Diana Looser (2014: 59) notes that Sāmoan theatre in Aotearoa has been particularly focussed on the "immediate experience of migration", although this has shifted over time. In *Fresh Off the Boat*, Charles felt that coming to New Zealand from the islands was like "getting out of prison after twenty years" (Kightley and Small 2005: 62), but his new-found freedom leads to displacement and self-destructive choices. In Makerita Urale's *Frangipani Perfume*, three sisters hold low-paying jobs as cleaners and, "like many other Pacific Island plays, the immigration process is characterised by alienation and dysfunction, mourning the loss of tradition and finding dramatic conflict in the struggle to adjust to Palagi [the Sāmoan term for white New Zealander] society" (O'Donnell 2004: iii). Kila Kokonut Krew's musical *The Factory* by Vela Manusaute is set in 1974 during a period of hostility to Pacific migration within New Zealand and anxiety about "over-stayers", and depicts the struggle against assimilation demanded by the factory's Palagi boss.[4] Other transnational stories of immigration and arrival, such as Toa Fraser's *No. 2* (1999), Jacob Rajan's *Krishnan's Dairy* (1997) and Red Leap's *The Arrival*, have toured extensively. All of these dramas, used as comparative case studies in this section, raise questions about belonging and identification with the New Zealand nation, and the position of being a New Zealander, but not being a New Zealander.

Diana Looser (2014: 59) states that the Sāmoan corpus reflects concerns common to other immigrant theatre and lists these as "the challenges of adjusting to an alien, often unsympathetic host culture; racism and stereotypes; various relationships with the homeland; conflicts between first-generation and later-generation migrants; and personal and communal identity". This is a useful list, as these concerns emerge in varying combinations, and in contextually and culturally specific ways, throughout the transnational narratives of migration toured from Aotearoa New Zealand. For example, the traveller's experience in *The Arrival* offers possibilities for identification, as the production enacts a series of common signifiers of the immigrant experience, including the search for work and the formation of new social bonds. Red Leap Theatre's image-based method, which uses movement and design (including puppetry) to tell the story, lends itself to the disorientation of encountering and decoding a new culture: at any moment the landscape may change or objects will respond in an unexpected manner.[5] A jazz soundtrack plays as border controls do invasive checks: migration officials cover the traveller's eyes when he needs to see and cover his ears when he needs to hear. *The Arrival*'s new world is a generic global world, and for the most part is given positive values, in contrast to the highly negative old world which is represented as a mono-chromatic, bleak, industrial city. With the arrival of the traveller's family at the end of the play, his belonging in his new home is narratively complete, and his connection with the old homeland is severed. In the journey away from home towards not-home, there is a state of limbo, but not-home eventually becomes home, displacement leading to an eventual emplacement. The transnational becomes the national and the old world is left behind.

Krishnan's Dairy by Jacob Rajan (see Image 5.1) offers a nuanced representation of adjusting to a new homeland, the ongoing relationship with the old homeland and the tensions between these two positions. Rajan was born in Malaysia of Indian heritage and migrated to New Zealand with his parents when he was four. *Krishnan's Dairy* was influenced by Rajan's cultural displacement, as "a boy raised in the west trying to understand his parents' relationship" (Warrington 2007: 384). Rajan's play, which he began to develop while training as an actor at Toi Whakaari New Zealand Drama School and which debuted at BATS in 1997, centres on husband and wife Gobi and Zina, who have migrated to New Zealand and established a dairy (a New Zealand colloquialism for corner shop or convenience store). Gobi advocates conformity with the new society while Zina insists on returning to India – "I'll never like it here", she declares (Rajan 2005: 35). Zina tells their baby Apu the story of

Image 5.1 Red Leap Theatre's *The Arrival*, Brisbane, Australia, 2018. Credit: Darren Thomas

Shah Jahan and Mumtaz Mahal, who married for love, whereas Gobi and Zina's marriage was an arranged one, and they have had to learn to love each other, highlighting not only religious but also class issues. *Krishnan's Dairy's* opening song acknowledges that Gobi and Zina come from a different cultural framework than the Anglo–New Zealand mainstream: "They met on their wedding day – please suspend your judgment" (29). There is an assumption of difference built into the text between the implied model spectators and the characters and their cultural practices. At the end of the play Gobi is killed during a robbery, which resonates with a history of violent crime in New Zealand perpetuated against dairy owners. Shah Jahan constructs the Taj Mahal as a tomb to his deceased wife, whereas Zina continues to run the dairy as a living monument to her husband's memory and his wish for them to make a new life in New Zealand. Rajan summarises the play as "telling the immigrant's dream and nightmare" and "starting a new life, with a new opportunity, while longing for home" (Forster and Plumb, 2013: 24). Not-home also eventually becomes home, but *Krishnan's Dairy* dramatically shows that this transfer is accompanied by loss. The death of her husband forces Zina to embrace New Zealand as home.

Kila Kokonut Krew's *The Factory*, described by the creators as the world's first Pasifika musical, depicts the challenges of integration with a host culture, particularly in relation to stereotyping and racism. The musical, which debuted at Māngere Arts Centre in 2011 and was substantially rewritten for a 2013 Auckland Arts Festival production, was inspired by the story of playwright Vela Manusaute's father, who arrived in New Zealand from Niue in the 1970s and worked at a bed factory (Manusaute 2015). The catalyst for Kavana and his daughter Losa's migration is a cyclone that devastates their village in Sāmoa and kills Kavana's wife. The pair moves to New Zealand to work in a factory in order to send money home to their remaining family. Losa deals with the loss of two mothers, "the memory of her mother" and "Sāmoa her mothertongue", but begins to find "a new home in unfamiliar territory" (Manusaute 2014: 39). Richard Wilkinson, the factory owner, asserts an ideology of capitalist assimilation, promoting the values of "English and Money" (15–16), anglicises the names of his Pacific workers, and forbids them from speaking their Indigenous languages. "What Do We Have" is the show's *West Side Story* (1957) "America" moment, as the ensemble attempts to reconcile the disconnect between their "milk and honey" dream and their reality: "We got a house but it's got no wall / We got no phone so how do we call?" (43). Inviting reflection about ongoing inequalities for Pacific peoples in Aotearoa New Zealand, *The Factory* articulates the challenges of making a new home as a minority in a new culture; as in *Krishnan's Dairy*, Niu Sila is the dream and the nightmare.

A recurring anxiety around identity in these migrant dramas involves generational displacement: concerns about the children of migrants losing connection with their heritage. Tien, the narrator of Dianna Fuemana's semi-biographical *Falemalama*, was not allowed to learn Sāmoan or Niuean as a child, and the act of sharing her mother's story allows her to reconnect with her heritage. In *Fresh Off the Boat*, the teenage characters "don't know anything about our culture" (Kightley and Small 2005: 50). The character Samoa, named for his homeland, is obsessed with radical American figures like Malcom X, but when asked if he knows about Tamasese and the Mau, referencing the Sāmoan independence movement, he replies "I've heard of them – they were boxers in the sixties weren't they?" (55). In *Frangipani Perfume*, Pomu's ignorance about her heritage is highlighted through her mistaken notion of how Frangipani perfume is prepared. Pomu feels alienated from her Sāmoan heritage, and it is only when the "hidden mystery" of the traditional process for the creation of the perfume is revealed that she can feel complete (Fuemana 2008: 35), making it clear that for Pomu and her sisters, "memories of Sāmoa and connections with their mother and female ancestors will sustain these women through the challenges of their lives in Aotearoa" (Warrington and O'Donnell 2017: 112). In contrast, in Toa Fraser's play *No. 2*, a solo in which actor Madeleine Sami portrays multiple members of a Fijian-Indian family living in Mt Roskill, Auckland, the second generation are absent, as is the anxiety about losing touch with culture. Instead, we see the third generation, the grandchildren of Nanna Maria, who came from Fiji to settle in New Zealand. Her grandchildren feel largely at ease in their hybrid Pacific–New Zealand identities.

Fraser was born in London to a Fijian father and English mother, raised in Hampshire and moved to New Zealand when he was 14. In *No. 2*, which debuted at Auckland's Silo Theatre (now the Basement Theatre) in 1999, Fraser recognises cultural identity to be fluid and subject to global cultural influences.[6] Soul, who at the end of the play is named by his grandmother Nanna Maria as her successor, claims to be "teaching realness" (Fraser 2007: 72). The play, however, questions what is culturally real and authentic. Nanna Maria wants singing, dancing and a big feast to mark her choice of successor to head the family and continue its traditions before she passes on, but when Father Francis asks Soul if naming a successor is a "Fijian tradition", Soul replies, "I don't know, it's just a Nanna thing, I think … she's trying to make it a real European thing" (75). Similar to the way Rajan switched between different characters' masks in *Dairy*, actor Madeleine Sami adopted multiple personas to play the entire *No. 2* family, destabilising fixed senses of identity and emphasising how we perform our identities: you create your own "realness".

Gilbert and Lo's (2007: 168) point that hybridity can hold "a stabilising function and works to settle cultural differences" is borne out in these texts; though they critique the position and treatment of migrants in society, they are ultimately narratives of successful migration, with the conclusions settling cultural differences. In *The Arrival*, the traveller's homeland was one of oppression and hardship, the new world is of safety and prosperity. In *The Factory*, the outdated racist attitudes die with the death of the factory owner from a faulty electrical wire, due to his own negligence of health and safety.

It is up to the new generation to make a change, and the owner's son Edward, in partnership with Losa, vows to rebuild the values of the factory, a typically celebratory musical theatre ending presenting an ideal vision of a relationship of equality between Pasifika and Pākehā cultures. Maria's death at the end of *No. 2* represents a further displacement from the homeland left behind, but marks a revitalised sense of belonging for her grandchildren for whom New Zealand is home. In the epilogue of *Krishnan's Dairy*, Zina's dairy has thrived, and we see teenaged Apu, played by Rajan sans mask with a Kiwi accent, pointing towards Aotearoa New Zealand's multicultural future. The period of displaced limbo has dramatic potential, but the narratives demonstrate the pressure placed on conceptions of identity, and the conclusions to the plays insist on resolving this conflict. Longing for a lost homeland is replaced by belonging in the new homeland. But they also challenge fixed notions of national identity by promoting the value that anyone from any culture has the right to belong in New Zealand, and in their own terms.

Touring the transnational

Emma Cox (2014: 27) observes that theatre that engages with migrant stories is implicated and troubled by "power relationships within the broader society". As a microcosm of societal power dynamics, the demographics of a theatre audience attending such work will sit on a spectrum between "people for whom the representation of migration is a story of others or otherness", and people "who perceive the work as about their own community" (27). This binary can become especially pronounced when transnational work is toured. Rogers (2015: 10) argues that performances "acquire multiple meanings as they move between localities, operating as forms of travelling culture that reflect and disrupt cultural expectations". As works of cultural displacement, further questions of emplacement and displacement arise when these transnational works are toured outside of a New Zealand context. These stories can resonate in other locations in the global marketplace, through the perceived experience in common. As I have previously emphasised, this is not the same as universalism, though instances where universality is claimed by productions and audiences reveals the perception of these connection points.

Red Leap Theatre (2012) promoted *The Arrival* on the basis of what they called its universal narrative:

> Set in a fantastical time and place but is a universal story. Whether you are a refugee, migrant or have simply been on an OE you will appreciate what it like to be a fish out of water, to decipher strange languages, to navigate unfamiliar streets, to grapple with foreign customs.

Invocations of universality were a noticeable trend when *The Arrival* played at the Sydney Festival in 2010. Jack Tiewes (2010) said it was "one of the best examples of truly *universal* theatre that I've seen in recent memory" (his emphasis) and Emma Bell (2010) claimed that "actual words aren't needed because the message is a universal one". As a fantastic allegory of global migration, rather than the depiction of a specific locality, *The Arrival* invites such response, although these claims of universality are reductive. The production's abstracted style opens itself to fluid readings and discoveries of cultural equivalence within the common space, that which the subject perceives they share with the other.

While the graphic novel tells its story without words, Red Leap's inclusion of language in the touring production became problematic. For the production, Red Leap Theatre created a language for the people in the new world to speak. As Tiewes (2010) wrote, "everyone in the audience is put in the same position as the protagonist, able only to infer intent and context without any understanding of the actual words". Responding to audience feedback from the premiere season of *The Arrival* for the Auckland Arts Festival in 2009 that some had found the production difficult to follow, the company added brief English phrases for the traveller to speak ("I am here safe, I have a new friend, I miss you..."). This aligns the traveller in New Zealand and Australia with the mainstream Anglo-culture and language, reinforcing societal power relationships. For Tiewes (2010), the use of English "universalises the experience of being a foreigner in a new land so that anyone can understand what it would feel like to be lost amidst a foreign language and culture", but for Gord Sellar, an audience member who saw the production in Seoul during Red Leap's season at the LG Arts Centre in May 2012, the English language broke identification. Sellar (2012) felt that the inclusion of English "shook me out of the performance", though he did acknowledge the "interesting reversal of it being an English-speaker who is a refugee and immigrant in a strange land where he must struggle to learn the language". Sellar's frustration attested to the potential disruption that the use of language had to the abstracted setting and the audiences' ability to project their own meanings and resonances within this.

The space for audiences to draw equivalence in common with Gobi and Zina in *Krishnan's Dairy* is one reason that play has been so portable and popular with overseas audiences for two decades, and is New Zealand's longest touring theatrical export. A review from the 1999 Edinburgh Festival Fringe season claimed that Gobi's life "might belong to Wishaw or Watford as much as to Wellington" (Lockerbie 1999). In a review for a season at Tasmania's inaugural Ten Days on the Island Festival in 2001, another critic found local and global relevance in *Krishnan's Dairy*'s story:

In New Zealand, a corner store often is owned by an Indian family. But their culture is as invisible to the general Kiwi population as the Hmong's is to most Tasmanians. Rajan wanted to make their culture visible, while lifting the veil on the difficulties all migrants face in adjusting to being outsiders.

(Poos 2001)

Krishnan's Dairy had invited cosmopolitan engagement, which, by presenting the specific experiences of Indian immigrants in New Zealand, could draw attention to the local echoes in the play's touring locations.

The critical response to *No. 2*'s season at the 2000 Edinburgh Festival Fringe meanwhile emphasised the Fijian aspect of the play over its wider transnational context. Max Szalwinksa (2000) called the play "a slice of Fijian life with a lot of spice". Susannah Clapp (2000) exoticised the play as a "gentle Fiji romance" and "South Seas bubble" that "wires you directly into another culture's psyche". Actor Madeleine Sami spent two years after Edinburgh touring *No. 2* to overseas destinations, negotiated by producer Fenn Gordon. The *Evening Post* reported: "from Jamaica to Israel, from Wellington to Edinburgh, audiences are queuing up and raving. Even the Aussies understand and love it" (Bisley 2001). "What better way to brand New Zealand around the world as a leader in cost-effective creativity, ingenuity and innovation?" asked New Zealand critic John Smythe (2001). A two-show performance for the Festival Internacional Cervantino in Guanajuato, Mexico, in October 2001 had major sponsorship and support from New Zealand's MFAT and the New Zealand Dairy Board, utilising the play as cultural diplomacy to increase political and business ties between the countries. A Mexican reviewer stated that the production provided a contrast with "the magnitude of the Cervantino" and its "super-productions", reminding the writer that "theatre is purely and simply an audience, an actor and a story" (Meza 2001). Neither of the two reviews of this season focussed on the particularism of *No. 2*'s story or setting, noticeably lacking the exoticism of the British response. When *No. 2* toured to London in 2003, reviewers identified particularism while also extending the family as universal figures: "Fraser has drawn a family who are at once uniquely Fijian-New Zealanders, and very much the average clan" (North 2003). Another reviewer claimed that the play's "nature resonates in all family situations of this type. Each character reminds you of someone you know" (Shenton 2003). As a solo play *No. 2* could be highly mobile and portable, enabling a wide range of overseas audiences to identify equivalences within the common, albeit complicated by an exotic gaze.

Reworking *The Factory* for the marketplace

In promoting the 2014 Edinburgh season of *The Factory*, producer Stacey Leilua said,

> the migrant experience, coming to a new country in search of a better life is one that people all over the world can relate to [...]. I think European audiences will love it – at the end of the day themes like family, love, and justice are universal.
>
> (Heerde 2014)

This is arguable, as cultural perspectives on these concepts may differ. *The Factory* tells a very specific story in a very specific time and place (Auckland,

1974), but uses a conventional musical theatre formula with the intention of appealing to a global audience. Rogers (2015: 9) warns that "local specificity can [...] become lost as performances become global in reach". The development and production history of *The Factory* played out a tension between representing local specificity and emphasising "universal" elements in the hopes of appealing to a global market.

The first season of *The Factory* in 2011, directed by Vela Manusaute and Anapela Polata'ivao and performed at the Māngere Arts Centre, was set in the present day, with the workers opposed by a Polynesian boss and his daughter. There was a romantic subplot involving Losa, and a fellow factory worker, but it was the community of workers as an ensemble that drove the narrative. The themes here were of internal oppression, a culture exploiting their own migrant workers. Dramaturge Jonathan Alver encouraged radical changes for the 2013 Auckland Arts Festival season. The setting was changed to 1974, a period when demand declined for Pacific Island workers who had filled labour shortages since the end of WWII, and "tolerance towards migrant workers on temporary permits from Western Sāmoa, Tonga and Fiji came to an end" (Beaglehole 2015). By making the boss, Mr Wilkinson, a Palagi, a different racial and cultural tension was added. The boss's daughter was now a son, Edward, and the new *Romeo and Juliet* romantic plot between Edward and Losa was at the centre of the drama. Five new songs with a period disco vibe were added by *The Factory*'s composer Poulima Salima. Critics compared the play to well-known musical theatre works from the Western canon, for example, the "Pacific Les Mis", due to its depiction of inequalities between social classes (McAllister 2013). My own review of that season described the musical as "*West Side Story* meets *Saturday Night Fever* with a Pasifika flavour" (Wenley 2013). It was a Moana-Aotearoa story, but told within a familiar Western musical theatre form and genre.

The producers of *The Factory* targeted Australia for the show's international debut. Within the Asia-Pacific region, entry into the Australian market for touring work remains less accessible than the geographical and cultural closeness of the countries might promise. In recent years CNZ has supported New Zealand delegates to the APAM, which promotes theatrical work to Australian venues and presenters. *The Factory* team benefitted from that strategy, securing a tour of five Australian venues in June/July 2014 after pitching their work at APAM. The production premiered in Australia at the Adelaide Cabaret Festival, followed by seasons at the Riverside Theatres in Paramatta, Canberra Theatre Centre, Merrigong Theatre in Wollongong and the Gold Coast Arts Centre.

On its Australian tour *The Factory* was celebrated for its Pacific content and innovation as New Zealand's first-ever Pasifika musical. Stevie Zipper (2014) deemed it "worthy of tours internationally" and believed the "deeply soulful" Pacific heritage would "spark deep interest in audiences who enjoy musicals that portray uniqueness and promote cultural diversity and history". Deborah Hawke (2014) concluded her review with the statement that because "audiences in the region are so used to seeing American and European productions" it was "hard to believe that any musical produced from this neck of the woods could ever have popular appeal – I'm glad to be proved so wrong, and that the Pacific has found its voice". *The Factory* was both new and familiar, and the critics were energised by the display of Pasifika song and dance. The production attracted strong interest from Pacific communities within Australia. Kila Kokonut Krew (2014) shared heartfelt feedback from an audience member in Canberra:

> We are the only fobs in our small country town, it was great connecting with our culture [...]. Just like most islanders it was a true life story. My dad passed away in his factory job in Sydney when I was 18. He was always working for his 10 kids and I couldn't stop crying on my drive home [...,] thinking of the sacrifices he made to provide for us in NZ.

The Factory's story found connection with a diasporic audience, eager to see equivalent histories represented back to them. The story of Sāmoans coming to New Zealand was enlarged to cover family histories of Pacific peoples working in New Zealand and Australia. The Australia tour was a success, facilitating an outpouring of pride and diasporic ownership.

While articulation of a Pasifika perspective was celebrated in Australia and New Zealand, in Edinburgh at the 2014 Fringe, playing at Assembly Festival's Main Hall as part of a CNZ-supported NZ at Edinburgh showcase, the show was only of passing exotic curiosity to most critics. David Pollock (2014) found interest in *The Factory*'s "packaging of a slice of New Zealand's social history, which is doubtless largely unknown outside of the country itself". Fiona Orr (2014) separated issues surrounding migration from the "more 'human' issues of relationships and status", as if migration is only an ethnic issue. Michael Coveney (2014) gave *The Factory* a one-star review for *What's On Stage*. He invoked stereotyping in his description of the "bushy-haired menfolk" with the "threatening physical presence of the Samoan rugby team", and cultural ignorance in calling the fa'afafine character a "domestic servant in drag – a tranny nanny".[7] Coveney predicted that the "Sāmoan samba and the Polynesian polyphonies will not be gate-crashing the West End any time soon". *The Factory* may have presented "a time, a place and a people we're unused to seeing on a British stage", as Pollock (2014) put it, but Coveney too easily dismissed a culture he did not understand, perpetuating the racial stereotyping that *The Factory* critiqued. *The Factory* did not find a home in Scotland. Critics did not make a cosmopolitan connection with Scotland's own history of oppression by the English.

The critics were largely aligned in their reaction that, rather than offering a unique cultural perspective, *The Factory* was too familiar, offering a tired example of formulaic musical theatre. Pollock (2014) labelled it "popcorn theatre", and said the "song and dance sequences never quite hit a height of invention so as to be extremely memorable after the fact". For Lyn Gardner (2014), her musical theatre comparison of choice was not *Les Misérables* or

West Side Story, but "*High School Musical* with added 70s and Polynesian vibes" (a maligned and shallow musical compared to the canonical greats) and she concluded her two-star review, "[*The Factory*] is innocuous to the point of blandness". These critics identified legitimate weaknesses in the show that New Zealand and Australian critics were prepared to overlook because of the cultural significance of the production for the region; however, the response by the Edinburgh critics was also framed by Eurocentrism. *The Factory* offered an alternative Pacific perspective, but because the form was so familiar and, therefore, not perceived to be culturally authentic, the critics dismissed it as a show they had seen before, exposing an expectation of exotic difference that was unfulfilled.

Finding a home

The Factory and the other transnational texts discussed in this chapter display local and contextually specific permutations of a global migrant experience. They reveal the tensions generated by the movement between nations and cultures and the attempt to establish a new home – tensions which are further highlighted when the productions themselves move between locations and attempt to find their own home in other geographic marketplaces. These transnational dramas are ultimately hopeful narratives, which, perhaps based to an extent more in idealism than reality, offer a final vision of a tolerant and accepting Aotearoa New Zealand homeland to overseas audiences. As observed with the overseas tours of *No. 2*, *Krishnan's Dairy* and *The Arrival*, they have often been understood through the experience in common, wherein the specificity of the texts is enlarged by the audience framing their interpretation of the texts via the relevance to their own localities and experiences. *The Factory*'s Edinburgh tour was an example of when the cosmopolitan encounter broke down: audiences and critics expected to encounter significant cultural difference and they would have hoped to find within the difference some points of commonality. However, *The Factory*'s particularism was negated by the clichéd and highly recognisable musical theatre form and story, which, exacerbated by a Eurocentric gaze, precluded the impact of the cultural differences of the content and the potential cosmopolitan transfer.

The plays featured in this chapter have embraced transnationalism over nationalism, rejecting monolithic identity and recognising the potential fluidity and hybridity of identity in relationship to national belonging. These dramas offer a powerful resistance to the globalising pressures of homogeneity from a pluralist range of perspectives. By signalling that culture is constantly undergoing a process of hybridisation, they challenge attempts to create a coherent national identity, exposing it for the fantasy that it is.

Notes

1 *Frangipani Perfume* has also travelled to Sāmoa (2013) and Hawai'i (2015).

2 Remounts of *Vula* also included Fijian language in the production.
3 In addition to *Vula*, The Conch toured internationally with *Masi* (2012), which played at the Oceania Centre ITC Theatre in Suva, Fiji (2012) and the Seymour Centre as part of the Sydney Festival (2013).
4 This was characterised by the government's disruptive dawn raids on households suspected to contain over-stayers.
5 My description of *The Arrival* is based on the recording of a performance at the Wellington Opera House in March 2010, provided by Red Leap Theatre.
6 Fraser subsequently adapted *No. 2* into a film, released in 2006.
7 An important Sāmoan cultural practice, fa'afafine is a biologically male sex person who takes on feminine-gendered roles and ways (sometimes categorised as a third gender or non-binary person).

References

Note: "CF:TF" indicates the source was accessed through Client File: Toa Fraser, Playmarket, Wellington.

Ashcroft, Bill, Gareth Griffiths and Helen Tiffin. 2007. *Post-Colonial Studies: The Key Concepts* (Second Edition). London; New York: Routledge.
Balme, Christopher B. 2007. *Pacific Performances: Theatricality and Cross-Cultural Encounter in the South Seas*. Hampshire: Palgrave Macmillan.
Beaglehole, Ann. 2015. "Immigration Regulation – Controlling Pacific Island Immigration". *Te Ara*. Last modified August 18, 2015. www.TeAra.govt.nz/en/immigration-regulation/page-6
Bell, Emma. 2010. "The Arrival by Shaun Tan". *Stage Whispers*. Last modified January 9, 2020. www.stagewhispers.com.au/reviews/arrival-shaun-tan
Bhabha, Homi K. 1994. *The Location of Culture*. London: Routledge.
Bisley, Alexander. 2001. "Toa! Toa! Toa!". *The Evening Post*. February 6. (CF:TF)
Chung, Jasmyne. 2015. "Creative New Zealand Announces Delegation to Festival of Pacific Arts 2016 (Guam)". *Creative New Zealand*. Last modified September 15, 2015. www.creativenz.govt.nz/news/creative-new-zealand-announces-delegation-to-festival-of-pacific-arts-2016-guam
Clapp, Susannah. 2000. "Come Up and See". *The Observer*. August 20. (CF:TF)
Coveney, Michael. 2014. "The Factory (Edinburgh Fringe)". *What's on Stage*. Last modified August 15, 2014. www.whatsonstage.com/edinburgh-theatre/reviews/the-factory-nz-at-edinburgh_35406.html
Cox, Emma. 2014. *Theatre & Immigration*. Hampshire: Palgrave Macmillan.
Forster, Michaelanne and Vivienne Plumb. 2013. *Twenty New Zealand Playwrights*. Wellington: Playmarket.
Fraser, Toa. 2007. *Two Plays [Bare; No. 2]*. Wellington: Playmarket.
Fuemana, Dianna. 2008. *Two Plays [Falemalama; The Packer]*. Wellington: Playmarket.
Gardner, Lyn. 2014. "The Factory – High School Musical with Polynesian Vibes". *The Guardian*. Last modified August 20, 2014. www.theguardian.com/stage/2014/aug/20/the-factory-review-assembly-hall-edinburgh-fringe
Gaskell, Ian. 2009. "Truth, Identity and a Sense of 'Pacificness'". *Australasian Drama Studies*, 55: 132–149.

Gilbert, Helen and Jacqueline Lo. 2007. *Performance and Cosmopolitics: Cross-Cultural Transactions in Australasia*. Hampshire: Palgrave Macmillan.

Hau'ofa, Epili. 1999. "Our Sea of Islands" in *Inside Out: Literature, Cultural Politics, and Identity in the New Pacific*, edited by Vilsoni Hereniko and Rob Wilson. Lanham/Oxford: Rowman and Littlefield: 27–38.

Hawke, Deborah. 2014. "The Factory". *The Barefoot Review*. Last modified June 24, 2014. www.thebarefootreview.com.au/menu/theatre/120-2014-canberra-reviews/978-the-factory.html

Heerde, Rosie van. 2014. "The Factory: Magnificent Voices Soar in Musical Journey". *The Clothesline*. Last modified June 3, 2014. http://theclothesline.com.au/factory-magnificent-voices-soar-musical-journey/

Kightley, Oscar and Simon Small. 2005. *Fresh Off the Boat*. Wellington: Play Press.

Kila Kokonut Krew. 2014. Facebook update. June 27, 2014. www.facebook.com/92837192322/photos/a.10150095273117323.303062.92837192322/10152601783387323/?type=3&theater

Lewis, Justin. N.d. "Justin's Notes". *Indian Ink*. Last modified January 9, 2020. http://indianink.co.nz/production/krishnans-dairy/

Lisi, Paul. 2019. "Moana Nui a Kiva Fund a New Opportunity for Collaborative Arts Projects between Aotearoa and Oceania". *Creative New Zealand*. Last modified December 16, 2019. www.creativenz.govt.nz/news/moana-nui-a-kiva-fund-a-new-opportunity-for-collaborative-arts-projects-between-aotearoa-and-oceania

Lockerbie, Catherine. 1999. "The Little Shop of Wonderment". *The Scotsman*. August 14. (CF:TF)

Looser, Diana. 2014. *Remaking Pacific Pasts: History, Memory, and Identity in Contemporary Theater from Oceania*. Honolulu: University of Hawai'i Press.

Manusaute, Vela. 2014. "The Factory". MS provided by Manusaute.

———— 2015. Interviewed by James Wenley. Auckland. September 12.

Maufort, Marc. 2007. "Performing Aotearoa in an Age of Transition" in *Performing Aotearoa: New Zealand Theatre and Drama in an Age of Transition*, edited by Maufort and David O'Donnell. Bruxelles; New York: PIE Peter Lang: 13–16.

———— 2012. "Positioning Alterity: Multi-Ethnic Identities in Contemporary New Zealand Drama". *Cross/Cultures*, (149): 257–277.

Mazer, Sharon. 2013. "A National Theatre in New Zealand? Why/Not?" in *Theatre and Performance in Small Nations*, edited by Steve Blandford. Bristol; Chicago: Intellect: 106–121.

McAllister, Janet. 2013. "Review: The Factory". *NZ Herald*. March 7. (CF:TF)

Meza, Luis. 2001. "She Talks a Bit about Everything". English translation of unidentified Mexican review. (CF:TF)

North, Madeleine. 2003. "No. 2". *Time Out London*. February 12. (CF:TF)

O'Donnell, David. 2004. "Introduction" in *Frangipani Perfume/Mapaki*. Wellington: Play Press: i–x.

———— 2011. "Beyond Post-Colonialism? Transactions of Power and Marginalisation in Contemporary Australasian Drama" in *Old Margins and New Centers: The European Literary Heritage in an Age of Globalization*, edited by Marc Maufort and Caroline De Wagter. Bruxelles, BEL: Peter Lang AG: 325–341.

Orr, Fiona. 2014. "The Factory – Edinburgh Festival Fringe". *Musical Theatre Review*. Last modified August 5, 2014. http://musicaltheatrereview.com/factory-edinburgh-festival-fringe/

Pollock, David. 2014. "The Factory". *The List*. Last modified August 9, 2014. http://edinburghfestival.list.co.uk/article/63562-the-factory/

Poos, Margaretta. 2001. "Look Out from Our Islands". Unidentified Australian newspaper. (CF:TF)

Rajan, Jacob. 2005. "Krishnan's Dairy" in *Indian Ink: Krishnan's Dairy; The Candlestickmaker; The Pickle King*. Jacob Rajan and Justin Lewis. Wellington: Victoria University Press.

Red Leap Theatre. 2012. *The Arrival* Programme. Auckland Season.

Rogers, Amanda. 2015. *Performing Asian Transnationalisms: Theatre, Identity and the Geographies of Performance*. New York: Routledge.

Sargeson, Frank. 1940. "The Making of a New Zealander" in *The Stories of Frank Sargeson*. Auckland: Penguin Books, 1982: 99–105.

Sellar, Gord. 2012. "도착 (The Arrival) – The Red Leap Theatre Performance". *Gordsellar*. Last modified May 5, 2012. www.gordsellar.com/2012/05/05/%EB%8F%84%EC%B0%A9-the-arrival-the-red-leap-theater-performance-seoul-5-may-2012/

Shenton, Elizabeth. 2003. "No. 2". *Online Review London*. (CF:TF)

Smythe, John. 2001. "No. 2 Kicks off Welcome Binge of Homegrown Theatre". *National Business Review*. February 2. (CF:TF)

Szalwinka, Max. 2000. "Keep It in the Family". *The Scotsman*. August 8. (CF:TF)

Tan, Shaun. 2006. The Arrival. South Melbourne: Lothian Books.

Tiewes, Jack. 2010. "The Arrival". *Australian Stage*. Last modified January 12, 2010. www.australianstage.com.au/201001123106/reviews/sydney-festival/the-arrival-%7C-red-leap-theatre.html

Urale, Makerita. 2004. *Frangipani Perfume/Mapaki*. Wellington: Play Press.

Warrington, Lisa. 2007. " 'We Want to Create Work That Is Funny, Sad and True': Lisa Warrington Interviews Jacob Rajan" in *Performing Aotearoa: New Zealand Theatre and Drama in an Age of Transition*, edited by Marc Maufort and David O'Donnell. Germany: PIE Peter Lang: 383–390.

Warrington, Lisa and David O'Donnell. 2017. *Floating Islanders: Pasifika Theatre in Aotearoa*. Otago: Otago University Press.

Wenley, James. 2012. "Astounding Journey Continues". *Theatre Scenes*. Last modified July 17, 2012. www.theatrescenes.co.nz/review-the-arrival-red-leap-theatre/

———— 2013. "Pacific Side Story". *Theatre Scenes*. Last modified March 8, 2013. www.theatrescenes.co.nz/review-the-factory-auckland-arts-festival/

Wilkie, Fiona. 2015. *Performance, Transport and Mobility: Making Passage*. London: Palgrave Macmillan.

Zipper, Stevie. 2014. "The Factory". *Theatre Unzipped*. Last modified June 19, 2014. http://theatreunzipped.wordpress.com/2014/06/19/the-factory/

6 Exporting culture
Indian Ink Theatre Company

Formed by Jacob Rajan and Justin Lewis in 1997 as the "first theatre company speaking with an Indian New Zealand voice" (Rajan 2017: 12), Indian Ink Theatre Company is a prolific international touring company based in New Zealand, having visited Australia, Singapore, UK, Germany, USA mainland and Hawai'i, Canada, Fiji and India. Exporting Indian Ink's work to these overseas markets has been a crucial factor in allowing Rajan and Lewis to sustain their company and practice for the past two decades. Collaborators since *Krishnan's Dairy* (1997), Rajan and Lewis bonded over their shared interest in mask and their mutual training from Australasian director John Bolton, who was in turn trained by influential French mime and actor Jacques Lecoq. Rajan wrote *Krishnan's Dairy* and Lewis directed, with all subsequent Indian Ink plays co-written between the pair. Financially supported with recurrent funding from Creative New Zealand and private patronage, it takes on average two years to develop an Indian Ink show. Rajan and Lewis collaborate with Murray Edmond, a poet and playwright who worked with the Lecoq-influenced Theatre Action group in the 1970s, who has been the dramaturge for all of their shows. Their work blends Western and Eastern influences through the use of Italian commedia dell'arte mask traditions and later forms from Balinese theatre and mask-making traditions.

Stuart Young (2006: 495) credits Indian Ink's "playful hybridity combined with the novelty of their provenance" as providing "ready appeal in the global marketplace". In 2010 Indian Ink signed with an American agent, David Lieberman, which was the first time that a New Zealand company (as opposed to a playwright) had been signed to a major US agent (Cardy 2010). On Lieberman's website, Indian Ink has been profiled as a paradigm of global success:

> Indian Ink has become one of New Zealand's most successful touring theatre companies performing in every major New Zealand theatre and city since 1997; from intimate black boxes to 800+ Lyric theatres. Return seasons sell out before opening, and the company has broken box office records on the way to a total audience of more than 175,000 people.

Indian Ink has toured internationally to great success and has won two Fringe First Awards from its two trips to Edinburgh.

("Indian Ink Theatre Company" 2015)

In recognition of Indian Ink's exceptional track record as a New Zealand company in the global theatre marketplace, this chapter presents a case study of how Indian Ink exports its productions for mobility and portability in a range of markets. The following discussion appraises Indian Ink's evolution as an international touring company: from a change in market destinations for its work to how the identities expressed in the work have shifted from a transnational New Zealand–Indian focus towards a global orientation. Indian Ink's most recent international touring work, *Guru of Chai* (2010), *Kiss the Fish* (2013) and *Mrs Krishnan's Party* (2017), are analysed in relation to the receptions to these works that have been produced in various market contexts.

Entering the marketplace

Indian Ink's touring capacity was built on its success with *Krishnan's Dairy* (discussed in relation to transnationalism in Chapter 5) at the Edinburgh Festival Fringe in 1999. Justin Lewis informed me that the company had wanted to go to Edinburgh to:

> test our mettle in that big bear pit of a place. But we also had ambitions and dreams and aspirations of our work having a bigger, longer life. And of touring more internationally. We always saw Edinburgh as a market-place where we could make more things happen from.

(Lewis 2016)

The Indian Ink team had conversations about whether to change the name of the play to "Krishan's Corner Shop" and the currency from "dollars and cents to pounds and pence", but decided against making any changes because, as Rajan believed, "to muck around with [the cultural context of a show] destroys its soul" (Mead 2011). *Krishnan's Dairy* received a number of positive reviews, the influential Fringe First award from *The Scotsman* newspaper, and sold out its four-week season. The critical notices proved crucial for the future touring life of the show, as the company found that reviews from UK publications carried "far more weight than any of the New Zealand press or success" (Lewis 2016). Indian Ink returned to the Edinburgh Fringe with *The Pickle King* (2002), in 2003, and again won a Fringe First Award. The company had hoped to use this as a springboard to enter the British market, a "big ambitious goal of something commercial, of being on the West End" (Lewis 2016). Lewis (2016) recalled how Indian Ink had a West End venue booked, the money lined up, but they did not commit after concluding it was "too big a risk".[1] Indian Ink began touring to Singapore from 2004, which became an important international market. In 2007 *The Pickle King* played at Singapore's DBS Arts Centre, performing three shows daily over 18 days. Though initially attracted by the prestige of the London centre, Indian Ink in this period pivoted away to explore other markets, including Singapore, Australia and Germany's Festival Theaterformen with *The Candlestickmaker* (2000), in 2006.

A research trip to Bali in 2009 influenced a new phase in the life of the company and the development of Indian Ink's next two touring works, *Guru of Chai* (2010) and *Kiss the Fish* (2013). Lewis and Rajan spent two weeks in Bali where they trained in the art of Balinese-masked dance with practitioner Nyoman Sukerta, who would become one of the inspirations for Kutisar, the narrator of *Guru of Chai* (Edmond 2016: 6). For *Kiss the Fish*, Indian Ink used both stock-and-custom-commissioned Balinese Bonres style masks (traditionally used in comic masked dance), carved by Balinese mask-maker Wayan Tanguuh. Lewis (2016) describes Balinese mask as a "preserved-in-aspic, dead tradition"; as a New Zealander, he felt free to "mess with stuff and make it up" and reinvent the form for a contemporary Western audience

Image 6.1 Promotional image for Indian Ink Theatre Company's *Kiss the Fish*, 2013.
Credit: John McDermott

(see Image 6.14). Here, a New Zealand status is claimed as granting ethical immunity for appropriating other traditions, due to a perceived absence of theatrical tradition within New Zealand.

Lewis and Rajan began writing *Guru of Chai*, adapting the "Punchkin" story, about a fakir and seven princesses, from Joseph Jacob's *Indian Fairy Tales* (1912). As a financially driven response to a downturn in local theatre audiences following the 2008 Global Financial Crisis, *Guru of Chai* was first performed in private homes, community halls, drama classrooms and church auditoriums in 2010.[2] While Indian Ink remained committed to the domestic market, the team recognised that the company's ongoing "survival depended on extending our reach beyond these shores" (Rajan 2017: 13). *Guru of Chai* was subsequently presented in professional theatres in New Zealand, Australia and Singapore where it played to a collective audience of around 5,000 (Christian 2011). It would also become the first of Indian Ink's plays to tour in the North American market, after Indian Ink signed with David Lieberman following a presentation of *Guru of Chai* at the APAM, held in Adelaide in February 2010. Indian Ink's first USA tour of *Guru of Chai* went to Los Angeles in August, Virginia, in September, and St Louis in November 2011.

As Indian Ink had once set its sights on London's West End, the ultimate goal was now New York's Broadway. In 2012 Indian Ink began a crowdfunding campaign to raise money for a showing of *Guru of Chai* in the Barrow Group's off-Broadway theatre to coincide with the APAP arts market in January 2013. With a "top US agent" behind them, Indian Ink (2012) told would-be backers that "once the hotshot producers and presenters see *Guru of Chai* live, they'll love it and we'll be on the road with tours throughout USA and elsewhere". The company requested NZ$18,000 for airfares, venue hire and accommodation. To accompany the campaign, Indian Ink prepared an image of Times Square. Next to posters of Broadway blockbusters *Wicked*, *Jersey Boys* and *Shrek the Musical* were three photoshopped posters of Rajan as *Guru of Chai*'s Kutisar overlooking Times Square, grinning through his bad teeth. The outcomes from the New York showing did not match Indian Ink's hyperbole. Lieberman struggled to sell the show, and he and Indian Ink concluded that "two foreign words in one title was too much" (Lewis 2016). While *Krishnan's Dairy* remained *Krishnan's Dairy* overseas, the pragmatic decision was made to change *Guru of Chai*'s title to *The Elephant Wrestler* for subsequent North America tours. While potentially enticing (who is this wrestler and why would they battle elephants?), the replacement title is only tenuously connected with the actual content of the story (there is no person who literally wrestles elephants, although the Indian God Ganesh does appear briefly), but the commercial practicalities won out.

Indian Ink has continued to make repeated trips to America, with *Kiss the Fish* taken to Minnesota and Kansas in 2015 and multiple tours of *Mrs Krishnan's Party* to the USA and Canada between 2018 and 2020. Though the American tours are an impressive achievement for the company, the closest

Indian Ink has got to Broadway so far remains the photoshopped billboard. This expansion into the North American market has been lucrative for the company, but a symbolically meaningful new market has been entry into India, with Indian Ink touring *Guru of Chai* in 2014 and *Krishnan's Dairy* in 2016 (to be discussed in the following section). Meanwhile, *Guru of Chai* has been regularly toured to Australia (using the play's original title) including Sydney (2017), Adelaide (2018) and Darwin (2019) and was also supported by the New Zealand High Commission to give free performances at the University of the South Pacific, Laucala Campus, Suva, Fiji, in November 2019 (see Map 6.1).

Global identities

As Indian Ink's market focus was transforming at the beginning of the 2010s with the debut of *Guru of Chai*, so too was the work itself. Indian Ink's original trilogy had focussed on the transnational interplay of New Zealand and India, led by Rajan's fascination with his own Indian heritage. In *Krishnan's Dairy*, Gobi and Zina had left India to come to New Zealand. In *The Candlestickmaker*, a New Zealand Indian student visits India, and in *The Pickle King*, Wellington's Empire Hotel attracts immigrants and exiles from India. George Reaper, a character in *The Pickle King* who has been away from India for 21 years, says that "we are all more than just the product of our families, we also take on the flavour of those things around us. We are ingredients in a jar. Here I preserve the essence of the universal soul" (Rajan and Lewis 2005: 140). This quotation acknowledges identity as a confluence of past and present circumstances. It is a fitting metaphor for the early Indian Ink work, as the company mixed Indian and New Zealand identity markers, with the addition of Italian commedia dell'arte mask traditions. Indian Ink's hybridised work (in content and form) attempted to provide something of a transcendent universal human experience for its audiences, performing stories that are beautiful, funny, sad and true:

> We tell human stories. They are tales about love, happiness, facing your fears. It just so happens that the characters are mostly Indian and the situations and setting reflect that [...]. Our job as theatre makers is to tell the stories, to throw a light on the dark corners of humanity and to lead the audience into a new and exotic world, the world of the plays.
>
> (15)

Indian Ink's first three touring works all featured exoticised tales of India, but anchored with a New Zealand context, providing local audiences with a familiar gateway to enter the stories. For overseas audiences, these New Zealand markers would not have provided the same familiar resonance. Indian Ink did not include New Zealand markers in its next two international touring works *Guru of Chai* or *Kiss the Fish*.

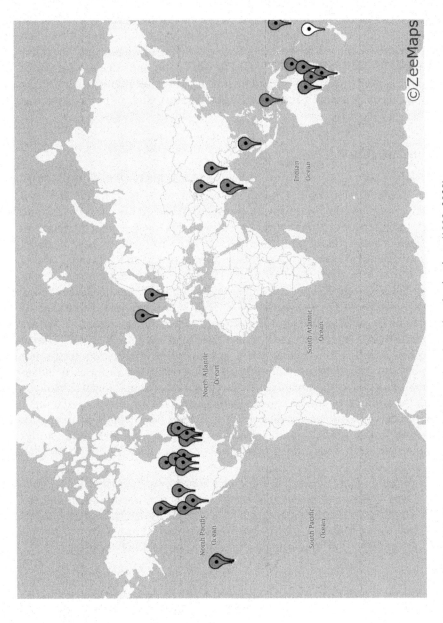

Map 6.1 Indian Ink Theatre Company's international touring destinations (1999–2020)

Guru of Chai consciously engages with its audiences in the "here and now" (Edmond 2016: 22). Kutisar, the chai seller and narrator, totters onto the stage, and through his prominent bad teeth (Indian Ink had reduced the principle of mask from the earlier plays to false teeth worn by Rajan) announces that the artistic director of their venue has advised him:

> Kutisar, my audiences are all unhappy. Their lives are meaningless. They work hard, they have stress at work, but their work is meaningless. They fill their empty lives with foolish distractions. They drink coffee because they are tired. They go to the gym because they are fat. They buy things that have no use. They drink too much. They chitty chatty about nothing. Their marriages are going down the toilet. Their children are all on drugs. Kutisar, my audience is full of fat, useless, drunks – help them!
>
> (Rajan and Lewis 2016: 23)

This opening recognises the specific location of the performance, but unlike the plays of the original trilogy, it does not assume that its prime audiences are New Zealanders. The audiences are characterised humorously in this address, but this generic description of malaise is designed to be porous enough that they can find some resonances with their own various dissatisfactions in their lives. Edmond (2016: 11) explains that "we, the audience, come to the Guru's presence as people come to a séance, in hope of hearing the truth". The relationship established between the narrator and the audience plays into stereotypes of Westerners who look to Eastern gurus for spiritual enlightenment. This is made explicit with the introduction of Dave, the musician, whom Kutisar met in India. Instead of finding enlightenment, Dave found "vomiting and diarrhoea"; Kutisar says that they are brothers and India is their common mother, though "Dave is adopted", he can never completely belong (Rajan and Lewis 2016: 24–25).

Having drawn attention to the audience's specific locality, *Guru of Chai* then invites the audience to imaginatively transport themselves to India. Kutisar describes the scene:

> Bangalore Railway Station, 6 am, 40 degrees. White gibas, brightly coloured saris, porters' blue uniforms, saffron robes – the holy man with the sandalwood paste. Early morning rush hour, trains: ka tak ka tak ka tak. Porters: "marra dee, marra".
>
> (26)

Rajan observed that:

> imaginatively, everyone has their own India [...]. It's so lovely when people come up to me after [seeing *Guru of Chai*] and say, "I know that railway

station, I've been to that railway station". Everyone has a different picture of all those people, the beggars, hawkers, priests.

(Hay 2011)

The sprinkling of Indian terms and the performance of songs in Malayalam throughout the play offers Western audiences a degree of exotic flavour. The Punchkin fairytale is transposed to a global contemporary India. Kutisar remarks how they have a "KFC in Bangalore" (Rajan and Lewis 2016: 39). Kutisar the chai seller is symbolic of local resistance to globalising homogenising forces. He affectionately criticises Dave as a symbol of the West: "Dave is the West. I am the East. I give Dave yoga, mental and physical wellbeing, I give Dave spirituality. Dave give me Starbuck. Stupid, Dave!" (49). The play draws attention to how people worldwide are linked by forces of globalisation and standardising "McDonaldisation".

In *Kiss the Fish*, the narrator, an unnamed Fisherman, explicitly characterises his audiences as tourists, welcoming them to Karukam Island: "You can switch off your mobile phone now, just relax, no more stress, stress. You come to see the monkey, ah? Yah, plenty here" (111). As Edmond (2016: 11) states, "the play is a guided tour in which The Fisherman takes us through the events that have led to the present state Karukam Island is in, with its abandoned resort and its small-scale eco-tourism". The island is "Indian-esque", but never firmly placed; the setting was inspired by an experience Lewis had in Malaysia when he saw an abandoned resort that was "entirely occupied by monkeys" (Calman 2014). In the play, developer Kingsley wants to make an "ecologically sustainable paradise" for "big travellers, large group bookings", but he needs control of the spring on rice farmer Bapa's land (Rajan and Lewis 2016: 116). Jasmine, ex-wife of Bapa's son Sidu, arrives on the island as a satire of the tourist's ethnographic gaze. She raves:

> Wow, such a sense of community [...]. I came here with all this anxiety and stress and it's gone, it's just, like, gone. Oh my gosh, I have no idea how long I've been here now [...]. This is paradise. I think I've been travelling my whole life to find this place. I point my camera anywhere and it's, like, *National Geographic*.

(150)

Jasmine is the anti-cosmopolitan traveller, but the audiences are invited by the Fisherman to become cosmopolitan citizens, consciously attempting to become familiar with a non-local culture. While Jasmine looks with a superficial gaze, the Fisherman offers us understanding and access as a cultural insider, albeit to a hybrid culture from Indian Ink's fictional imagination.

Guru of Chai and *Kiss the Fish* are designed in theory to allow audiences of any place insider access to the world of their stories. When *Guru of Chai* was invited to Virginia, the company was asked to give a "cultural presentation" to explain the cultural context of the show to "an audience possibly less knowledgeable about New Zealand or India than some others"; Indian Ink declined, and it was reported that "the audience loved what they saw without a prior explanation" (Christian 2012). This makes sense, as the local knowing audience for the work is assumed to be a generic Western one. When *Guru of Chai* toured to Vancouver in 2016 as *The Elephant Wrestler*, the marketing blurb promised a play in which "the contradictions of modern India, with its iPhones and ancient gods, come alive in this funny, heartbreaking, and beautiful romantic thriller" (The Cultch 2016). The critical response leaned on exoticised preconceptions of India: "Rajan brings a warm and sunny taste of southern India to dark, rain soaked Vancouver" (Ledingham 2016); "this show is like a dazzling, whirlwind ride on a magic carpet!" (Cairney 2016). One review seemed entirely unaware of the show's New Zealand connection, writing how the play showcases the "diversity of Hindu theatre" (Harbottle 2016). This is an instance where, despite its highly hybridised nature, the work (a New Zealand incubated, Bali-influenced, intercultural fairytale) had been packaged and made consumable for a Western audience, reflecting, rather than disrupting, cultural expectations and, therefore, critically received in Vancouver within a familiar and narrow band of "authentic" cultural stereo-types. That is not to say *Guru of Chai* is received thus everywhere: Vancouver's exoticism, for instance, was not a feature of reviews of the 2017 Belvoir season in Sydney. *Kiss the Fish,* meanwhile, has proven less portable. Lewis explained to me that in America the work, "with its questions about modernising and tourism", plays as a "cultural curiosity" rather than something that resonates in the American context. Lewis said that in the "vast land that looks inward, they don't tend to think about tropical islands" (Lewis 2016).

The limits of *Guru of Chai*'s portability were exposed when the play was toured to India.[3] Rajan had been making imaginative trips to India in his performances since *Krishnan's Dairy*, and his work can be read as diasporic longing for the homeland. Rajan gave the following account of the experience:

> In sweltering 32°C heat, in a 600-seat theatre in Thrissur, we performed *Guru of Chai* to an audience seeing – for the first time – a prodigal son telling them a story [...]. At the end they did something extraordinary. Our composer, David Ward, had written a song using an Indian raga. Suddenly the audience recognised the rhythm and started swaying in their seats and clapping along. They erupted at the curtain call. We were all draped with ceremonial shawls and blessed by a silver-haired, dignitary. It was strange but wonderful.
>
> (Asia New Zealand Foundation 2014)

Guru of Chai, which Lewis agreed was written for a non-Indian audience, "sat very differently in an Indian context" and despite the reception at the curtain call, "didn't resonate so well in some ways". Corruption is one of the issues that backgrounds the play, but Indian Ink found that because "corruption is a real issue over there in a way we don't understand it here, that it is endemic and it does affect people's lives in quite visceral ways", there was "longing amongst some people for that to be treated as a much more of a serious issue [...] rather than being a vehicle for a love story" (Lewis 2016). The Indian culture had been made digestible for a Western audience, but some audiences in India found that the corruption in Indian society had been dealt with too flippantly.

In 2016 Rajan returned to India with *Krishnan's Dairy*, supported by the New Zealand High Commission with an agenda of marketing New Zealand to India. A tight touring schedule and the distances between Calcutta, Bangalore and New Delhi meant that local carpenters in each location were contracted to construct identical versions of the play's set; this was more cost efficient than freighting the set from New Zealand (Rajan 2017). A preview of the play in the *New Indian Express* commented, "how often do you hear stories of Indian immigrant dairy owners in the West. Rarely, if ever" (Shantaveeresh 2016). A blogger who watched the performance identified the specificity of the ethnic group of Gobi and Zina as Malayali, lost on most Western audiences unfamiliar with Indian communities, and named it number one of the "9 Must-Watch plays of all time for theatre-lovers in India" (Rao 2016). Another viewer lavished praise on the play and reported that it "deeply satisfied those who watched the show at Ranga Shankara" (Mohan 2016). *Guru of Chai* reflected an immediate image of Indian society that did not match Indian audiences' lived reality, whereas *Krishnan's Dairy* played better in India because the distanced New Zealand setting allowed audiences to imaginatively place themselves in the characters' positions without experiencing the cultural dissonance of *Guru of Chai*.

Diversifying the output

Since 2016 Indian Ink has increased its production and touring output by pursuing a strategy of product diversification. The reliance on using Jacob Rajan as a performer had limited its opportunities for market expansion; therefore, new works *The Elephant Thief* (2016) and *Mrs Krishnan's Party* (2017), as well as a revival of *The Pickle King* for a New Zealand national tour celebrating Indian Ink's twentieth anniversary in 2017 were performed with new casts, allowing Rajan to tour *Krishnan's Dairy* and *Guru of Chai* overseas while the other productions toured New Zealand.[4] *Mrs Krishnan's Party*, a sequel to *Krishnan's Dairy*, represented the company's first new play to feature a New Zealand setting in 15 years, although this is complicated in its overseas presentation as the setting is transposed for each geographic location it plays in.

Mrs Krishnan's Party revisits the character of Zina Krishnan 20 years after the events of *Krishnan's Dairy*, as Zina (played by Kalyani Nagarajan) prepares to welcome her adult son Apu back home for the harvest festival of Onam. Indian Ink's major innovation for this production is the deployment of an immersive form, situating the audience within the store room of the dairy, thus flipping the imaginative offstage space of *Krishnan's Dairy* (in

Mrs Krishnan's Party the dairy front store where *Krishnan's Dairy* was set becomes the unseen backstage). The audience are characterised as guests of Zina's boarder James (Justin Rogers), a university student who has organised a surprise party for Mrs Krishnan for Onam. The play's dramaturgy is built around both the audience's diegetic role (events happen in real time and any dialogue must be believable to be uttered in front of us) and the time required for the preparation and cooking of daal during the play (offered to the audience at the end of the play). Thematically, Indian Ink returns to the tension introduced in *Krishnan's Dairy* between staying in the new homeland or going back to the old, with Zina uncertain about whether she should accept an offer to buy the dairy that would allow her to return to India. When Apu phones to explain that he will not be able to visit for Onam due to work, a heartbroken Zina exclaims, "what was the point of doing all this if he has to work just as hard uh?", although the subsequent revelation that Apu is actually at another party leads Zina to reevaluate her own steadfast dedication to the dairy.[5] As *Krishnan's Dairy* used the romance of Shah Jahan and Mumtaz Mahal as a parallel to Gobi and Zina's relationship, in *Mrs Krishnan's Party* the sacrifice of King Marveli to prevent Vishnu from destroying Marveli's kingdom is equated with Gobi's death, sacrificing himself for his family. Marveli's return from the underworld, the basis of Onam, expresses the importance of rebirth. This is manifested in the play as dark farce, with James mistaking the ashes of Gobi for pepper and adding this to the daal; while Zina's realisation that what has occurred is both excruciating and highly amusing, it functions as a signal to resist stasis and let go of the reverence to the dairy (and the earlier play); at the end of the production Zina announces that "you will have to buy your milk from somewhere else" and entertains the possibility of a new suitor, confirming her desire for rebirth.

Actor Justin Rogers reported that performances of *Mrs Krishnan's Party* in North America "felt different from the New Zealand shows because there were a few cultural differences" (Indian Ink Theatre Company 2019). While *Krishnan's Dairy* travelled with its representation of a transnational New Zealand context intact, the logic of the immersive form meant that when *Mrs Krishnan's Party* is performed overseas, it is transposed for each local context, an extension of *Guru of Chai*'s gesture of engaging with each theatre audience in the "here and now". Therefore, in *Mrs Krishnan's Party*'s January 2019 season at the Culture Lab at the Cultch, Mrs Krishnan's Dairy became a Vancouver convenience store, with Zina having migrated to Canada from Kerala. The character of James retains his New Zealand identity, and his "New Zealand accent is explained by his being a friend of a friend of a distant relative who lives in New Zealand who'd asked Mrs. K. to let her son James board with her while he goes to university" (Graves 2019). *Mrs Krishnan's Party* was made portable by offering audiences a local gateway (a hometown convenience store) that potentially allows access to both New Zealand and Kerala identity, a value proposition that a Vancouver reviewer expressed as "not only a show but a cultural experience, *Mrs. Krishnan's Party* will teach you the true meaning of Onam complete with music, dancing, and food" (Tisdale 2019).

The marketing for the production's 2019–2020 North America tour emphasised the unifying potential of theatrical encounter, with a production that "bridges cultures and expands boundaries", magically transforming "strangers into friends through laugher, tears, good music and great food" (Green Music Centre 2019). Himself dressed in a costume representing King Marveli, James enlists audience members to help hand out garlands, scarves and bindi, costuming the audience with markers of Indian culture, an inclusive gesture that overlooks the politics of cultural appropriation and the appropriateness of being so adorned by a non-Indian performer. James announces: "Tonight we are all one people. Christian. Hindi. Buddhist. Muslim. Atheist. Black. White. Young. Old. Successful. Yet to reach their full potential. All one tribe united in this time and space". This gesture towards transcendental universalism is complicated by the specificity engendered by engaging with the particular time and space constituted by each particular audience. James follows by asking who has been to Onam before (a tiny minority of four people put up their hand in the recording of a performance in Auckland that I viewed). When James later asks if anyone has been to Kerala, where he says he visited during a gap year, one audience member replied that they were from there, and James asks if they had checked on their family following recent floods. A Vancouver reviewer found that the spontaneity of the performances kept the audience "firmly rooted in the present moment", including an interaction between vegetarian Mrs Krishnan and a "chatty kid" who declared his favourite Indian dish was butter chicken (Thomas 2019). These interactive improvisatory elements recognise specificity and the multiplicity of the common space, calling attention to varied life experiences within each audience. Indian Ink's ethos of connecting through difference is exemplified by Zina's observation that "different races, strangers becoming friends, this is what Onam should be". Similarly, James speaks for Indian Ink's production aims when he states that "when you get the atmosphere right people connect. At the end of the day that's what everyone wants". These sentiments were reflected in reviews from the Vancouver and USA seasons, with a number of reviewers commenting on how the experience brought the audience together as family. One reviewer observed that "the feeling of common experience and casual friendliness was most evident after the show was over and most of the audience lingered to chat, eat daal, and bask in the welcoming atmosphere that was created in the space" (Perkins 2019).

Concurrent with the development of *Mrs Krishnan's Party*, Indian Ink's partnership with California's South Coast Repertory Theatre represented a new strategy for making work for the global market. Representing the Repertory's first international collaboration, the company commissioned a new play by Rajan and Lewis, *Welcome to the Murder House*. Indian Ink viewed this an opportunity to create a show set in the USA to specifically resonate with Americans, as well as work with higher production values and a larger sense of scale. Rajan and Lewis went to California to hold an initial workshop with the company, and Lewis reported that he and Rajan were "fascinated in terms of the cultural contexts and resonances that we don't understand" (Lewis 2016). Indian Ink ran a crowdfunding campaign for the *Murder House* project on *Boosted* and raised NZ$27,344 to fund workshop costs and collaborator fees. In a video on the page, Lewis said that South Coast were "one of the biggest producers of new writing in the United States", and Rajan mentioned how "a number of South Coast Rep's commissions have transferred to Broadway" (Indian Ink Theatre Company 2016). Indian Ink premiered *Welcome to the Murder House* in Wellington, New Zealand, in 2018 with Rajan making a return to the stage; however, South Coast Repertory is yet to programme its own production and Broadway remains a distant dream.

Indian Ink's work attempts to move beyond postcolonial anxieties, asserting a perceived ethical freedom and flexibility as New Zealanders, without being weighted by tradition, to appropriate and adapt stories and theatrical practices from across the world. Murray Edmond (2016: 18) notes that Indian Ink's mask theatre:

> draws from French and Italian and Kiwi and Balinese training. It draws from Indian stories that are part of widely disseminated tales. Bali itself is a unique creation of cultural syncretism, which in turn has had a significant influence on the world of modern global theatre cultures. Jacob and Justin's plays take their place in this world.

Through its plays Indian Ink's global influences from India, Europe and the Pacific are shown to be mixing, hybridising, mutating. Indian Ink's New Zealand context infuses the work, but in Indian Ink's transformation into a global touring company its work has generally been uninterested in interrogating New Zealand (trans)national identity, so even Zina Krishnan becomes a local migrant wherever *Mrs Krishnan's Party* is produced. Indian Ink's knowing and playful theatrical hybridity resists easy impositions of national or cultural categories. Indian Ink utilises a mutating hybridity as a foundation in both theatrical form and narrative content, further influenced by canny business strategy as to how they can sustain its practice within the limitations of New Zealand's theatrical infrastructure and sell its product across geographic markets.

Notes

1 *The Pickle King* was instead adapted into a tepid BBC radio drama using a British cast, which Lewis (2016) described as a "strange terrible thing".
2 Including the University of Auckland's Drama Studio, where I first encountered the play.
3 The tour of *Guru of Chai* to India was funded by Creative New Zealand, the Asia New Zealand Foundation and Indian group Theatre Connekt.

4 Highlighting that the "national" is never static, the 2017 version of *The Pickle King* was specifically reworked to reflect contemporary Aotearoa, changing the play's original heterosexual central love story to involve a same gender couple.
5 My account of *Mrs Krishnan's Party*, including quotes, has been sourced from a private recording of a 2018 Auckland Q Theatre performance provided by Indian Ink Theatre Company.

References

Asia New Zealand Foundation. 2014. "'Feeds Works to Come' Says Playwright". *AsiaNZ*. June. Last modified January 6, 2020. https://web.archive.org/web/20160211020543/http://www.asianz.org.nz/bulletin/indian-visit-feeds-works-come-says-playwright

Bennett, Susan. 2005. "Theatre/Tourism". *Theatre Journal,* 57 (3): 407–428.

Calman, Matt. 2014. "Malaysian and Indonesian Inspirations Infuse Indian Ink's Latest Play". *AsiaNZ*. Last modified January 6, 2020. https://web.archive.org/web/20160211020609/https://www.asianz.org.nz/bulletin/malaysian-and-indonesian-inspirations-infuse-indian-ink%E2%80%99s-latest-play

Cairney, Sharon. 2016. "The Elephant Wrestler". *Review Vancouver*. Last modified January 6, 2020. www.reviewvancouver.org/th_elephant_wrestler2016.htm

Cardy, Tom. 2010. "US Agent Signs Up Kiwi Act Indian Ink". *The Dominion Post*. Last modified September 8, 2010. www.stuff.co.nz/entertainment/arts/4105562/US-agent-signs-up-Kiwi-act-Indian-Ink

Christian, Dionne. 2011. "US Tour Means Indian Ink's Cup Runneth Over". *NZ Herald*. June 25.

———2012. "Theatre Success Playing Away from Home". *NZ Herald*. July 7.

The Cultch. 2016. "The Elephant Wrestler". *The Cultch*. Last modified January 6, 2020. https://thecultch.com/events/elephant-wrestler/

Edmond, Murray. 2016. "Introduction" in "The Balinese Trilogy". Unpublished manuscript provided by Murray Edmond: 6–18.

Graves, Lorraine. 2019. "Do Not Miss the Krishnan Party". *Richmond Sentinel*. Last modified January 23, 2019. www.richmondsentinel.ca/article-detail/391/do-not-miss-the-krishnan-party

Green Music Center. 2019. "Center Stage: Mrs. Krishnan's Party". *KSRO*. Last modified November 4, 2019. www.ksro.com/2019/11/04/center-stage-mrs-krishnans-party/?fbclid=IwAR3zDFPb2vDNLkwi7p9wA9gjcZxmC8aiJG93lyYsrSdOnsf4j8MsEI8zRRU

Harbottle, Sean. 2016. "The Elephant Wrestler Stands as Fine Addition to Vancouver's Diwali Fest and the Cultch's Creative Legacy". *The Ubyssey*. Last modified November 10, 2016. https://www.ubyssey.ca/culture/the-elephant-wrestler-review/

Hay, Natasha. 2011. "Indian Ink Interview". *NZ Listener*. June 17. Last modified January 6, 2020. www.noted.co.nz/archive/listener-nz-2011/indian-ink-interview/

Indian Ink Theatre Company. 2012. "Help Indian Ink's Dreams Come True in New York City". *PledgeMe*. Last modified November 19, 2012. www.pledgeme.co.nz/projects/641

——— 2015. *David Lieberman Artists Representative.* Last modified August 20, 2015. www.dlartists.com/2015/08/20/indian-ink-theater-company/

——— 2016. "Welcome to the Murder House". *Boosted.* Last modified January 6, 2020. https://web.archive.org/web/20180220123632/https://www.boosted.org.nz/projects/welcome-to-the-murder-house

———— 2019. "DJ Jimmy J and the Party in America". *Indian Ink*. Last modified January 6, 2020. https://indianink.co.nz/news/dj-jimmy-j-and-the-party-in-america/ ?fbclid=IwAR2vvbsUOCrbYvypVb8_JymEw-RG-xf5qFgfwcdlz8HoBNoc1fB_ Yc6J4AU

Ledingham, Jo. 2016. "The Elephant Wrestler". *Jo Ledingham Theatre Reviews*. Last modified November 3, 2016. http://joledingham.ca/the-elephant-wrestler/

Lewis, Justin. 2016. Interviewed by James Wenley. Auckland. November 16.

Mead, Kate. 2011. "Gurus of Centre Stage". *Sunday Star Times*. Last modified August 21, 2011. www.stuff.co.nz/sunday-star-times/features/5476176/Gurus-of-centre-stage

Mohan, Deepa. 2016. "Theatre Review: *Krishnan's Dairy*, by Indian Ink, Ranga Shankara". *Citizen Matters*. Last modified November 16, 2016. http:// blogs.citizenmatters.in/deepa-s-jottings/theatre-review-krishnan-s-dairy-by-indian-ink-ranga-shankara-16-nov-2016–8823

Perkins, Tessa. 2019. "Mrs. Krishnan Knows How to Throw a Damn Good Party". *Centre Stage*. Last modified January 6, 2020. www.tessaperkins.ca/index. php?option=com_content&view=article&id=393:mrs-krishnan-knows-how-to-throw-a-damn-good-party&catid=82&Itemid=473

Rajan, Jacob. 2017. "Still Pioneers" in *Playmarket Annual*. Wellington: Playmarket: 12–13.

Rajan, Jacob and Justin Lewis. 2005. *Indian Ink: Krishnan's Dairy; The Candlestickmaker; The Pickle King*. Wellington: Victoria University Press.

———— 2016. "The Balinese Trilogy: *Guru of Chai*; *Kiss the Fish*; *The Smalls*". Unpublished manuscript provided by editor Murray Edmond.

Rao, Phalguni Vittal. 2016. "MY VIEW: 9 Must-Watch Plays of All Time for Theatre-Lovers in India". *The Better India*. Last modified December 13, 2016. www. thebetterindia.com/77553/theatre-best-plays-must-watch/

Shantaveeresh, Pratima. 2016. "Love Tales from Taj Mahal, Immigrants in NZ". *New Indian Express*. Last modified November 16, 2016. www.newindianexpress. com/cities/bengaluru/2016/nov/15/love-tales-from-taj-mahal-immigrants-in-nz-1538963.htm

Thomas, Colin. 2019. "*Mrs. Krishan's Party*: Accept This Invitation". *Colin Thomas/ Substantive Editor*. Last modified January 18, 2019. https://colinthomas.ca/2019/ 01/18/mrs-krishnans-party-accept-this-invitation?fbclid=IwAR3mEeCvwXIwH4J ez6vnF1CorzMX5zcgxyz8qXlaTHeBXAkAyZthgfgOw

Tisdale, Ash. 2019. "My Two Cents". *Two Cents & Two Pence*. Last modified January 6, 2020. www.twocentstwopence.com/mrskrishnansparty

Warrington, Lisa. 2007. "'We Want to Create Work That Is Funny, Sad and True': Lisa Warrington Interviews Jacob Rajan" in *Performing Aotearoa: New Zealand Theatre and Drama in an Age of Transition*, edited by Marc Maufort and David O'Donnell. Germany: PIE Peter Lang: 383–390.

Young, Stuart. 2006. "Review of *The Pickle King, Krishnan's Dairy, The Candlestickmaker*". *Theatre Journal*, 58(3): 491–495.

7 Selling the nation at the Edinburgh Festival Fringe

For many New Zealand performers, the Edinburgh Festival Fringe is perceived as the gateway for entering the global theatre marketplace. Edinburgh's Fringe, the largest multi-performance event in the world, is a destination we have already visited multiple times over the preceding chapters. It was there, in 1963, that Bruce Mason sought international validation through his tour of *The End of the Golden Weather*, performing the first half of his show in a late night slot. It was there, in 1991, that Downstage toured *Michael James Manaia*, with a confronting representation of Māori identity ravaged by war and colonialism. It was there in 1999 that Indian Ink Theatre Company's *Krishnan's Dairy* was recognised with a prestigious Fringe First Award from *The Scotsman* newspaper and subsequently achieved extensive international touring. And it was there, in 2014, that Kila Kokonut Krew toured *The Factory* as part of Creative NZ's NZ at Edinburgh season and received a Eurocentric response from some critics. New Zealand theatre makers desiring international performance of their work inevitably arrive in Edinburgh. The mythos of the Edinburgh Festival Fringe dream is tantalising: against impossible odds your underdog show from a country at the bottom of the world receives rave five star reviews, sells out its season, and is picked up by a hotshot international producer who lines up years of future international tours – and maybe even a TV deal. For some, presentation in Edinburgh can indeed lead to further touring opportunities and local prestige for "making it" overseas. For others, Edinburgh's profoundly uneconomic market conditions results in the Fringe marking the end of the overseas journey.

Despite – or perhaps because of – the challenges of geographical proximity and financial solvency, the Edinburgh Fringe has become *the* rite of passage for New Zealand theatre makers to test their work abroad, and artists go to great lengths to get there. To take one example from 2018, *Valerie* (2016), an autobiographical work that explored hereditary mental health issues through a gig-theatre format created by Robin Kelly, Tom Broome and Cherie Moore, was programmed by Summerhall, a prominent Fringe venue associated with socially conscious and alternative performance work. While the producing company Last Tapes Theatre received funding from CNZ to support flights, Last Tapes identified that it needed to supplement the institutional funding with an additional NZ$40,000 beyond the projected box office return. Last Tapes held a crowdfunding campaign through New Zealand platform *Boosted*, produced an Auckland fundraising season of *Valerie*, and the father of one of the creators raised $8,000 by cycling the length of New Zealand in eight weeks. On its *Boosted* page, Last Tapes Theatre Company (2018) team outlined why it was targeting the Fringe:

> Taking our work to Edinburgh is a big deal. Not just because it's a work that deals with mental health issues (which are a big deal), but because Edinburgh Fringe is a BIG deal. It's the largest performing arts festival in the world. It has launched international careers (Tim Minchin, Rhys Darby, Flight of the Conchords), and provided a platform for countless artists to establish themselves internationally. We believe we're ready to be seen on the international stage.

At the 2018 Fringe *Valerie* was one of 20 shows awarded Fringe First Awards by *The Scotsman*, alongside another New Zealand work, *The Basement Tapes* (2017) by Stella Reid and Jane Yonge. Meanwhile, New Zealand comedian Rose Matafeo was awarded the Fringe's Best Comedy Award. The Fringe First awardees selected by *The Scotsman* represented 0.56% of the 3,548 total shows presenting at the Fringe that year. For Creative New Zealand, the two New Zealand award winners represented 25% of the eight theatre works the funding body had supported to tour to the 2018 Fringe. As a recognition of quality, these awards represent an outstanding achievement for the New Zealand artists and one indicator by which the value of touring to the Fringe can be measured. Another indicator could be whether the Fringe destination is connecting or terminating: *The Basement Tapes* secured a 2019 UK tour following the Fringe; however, *Valerie* is yet to book any further international seasons.

The arts purist within me recoils at applying such market-driven criteria to the values and outcomes of touring work to the Fringe: the ultimate worth of a production should be around the multivalent ways audiences experience a work, what a work can mean for audiences and what it means for the artist in sharing it. This kind of individual level engagement is devalued due to the difficulty of measuring such responses as they fall outside of economic paradigms and beyond the transaction of purchasing a ticket. An outcome-led assessment of the Edinburgh Fringe, however, is necessitated by the need to scrutinise the powerful factors motivating New Zealand's market emphasis on the Fringe in recent years. One influential factor is the colonial premise of Edinburgh presentation: access to the UK market is privileged over the cultivation of audiences closer to home within the Asia-Pacific region, including the Adelaide Fringe and Perth's Fringe World in Australia, currently the self-claimed second and third largest performance markets in the world next to Edinburgh (Wayne 2019). Retracing colonial routes, Edinburgh is the idealised sight where the New Zealand theatre maker seeks to prove their worth within a global context and acquire increased status once they return home having "made it" in Edinburgh.

From the late 1990s a wave of New Zealand plays gained high-profile seasons at the Fringe, consolidating the mythos of Fringe as a must visit destination for New Zealand theatre makers. Prolific UK producer Guy Masterson brought Tim Balme's *The Ballad of Jimmy Costello* (1997) to the Edinburgh market in 1997, and continued to showcase New Zealand work at subsequent Fringes: Gary Henderson's *Skin Tight* (1994) in 1998, Toa Fraser's *Bare* (1998) and Jacob Rajan's *Krishnan's Dairy* (1997) in 1999, followed by Fraser's *No. 2* (1999) in 2000 and Stephen Papps and Stephen Sinclair's *Blowing It* (1999) in 2003. Masterson's market knowledge was critical for driving audience to these shows via his established network and brand. Other New Zealand productions travelling to the Fringe during his period included: *Bleach*, a co-production between Trouble (NZ) and Boilerhouse (UK) companies in 1999, *The Naked Samoans* in 2002, Indian Ink's *The Pickle King* in 2003 and *Flight of the Conchords* (comedy duo Jermaine Clement and Brett McKenzie) from 2002 to 2004. Queer Māori cabaret artist Mika played multiple Fringes over this period (1997, 1998, 1999, 2003): his sold-out *Mika and the Uhuras* cabaret was the darling of the 1997 Fringe, mixing "faux foreignness – the grass skirts and painted faces, waiata and haka [...] with familiarity: sequins and fluffy hair, pop tunes and disco steps" (Mazer 2019: 134–135).[1] At the turn of the millennium, Edinburgh could experience a plurality of voices from Aotearoa (however, despite the greater range of cultural identities, a masculine hegemony remained). Many of the shows gained overseas attention and prestige at the Fringe (*Skin Tight, Krishnan's Dairy, No. 2* and *The Pickle King* were all recognised with Fringe First Awards from *The Scotsman*), which helped them book further tours in other markets, whilst Flight of the Conchords leveraged their Fringe break-out status to create a hit television sitcom for HBO (2007–2009).

Funding from Creative New Zealand has driven an accelerating wave of productions from New Zealand travelling to Edinburgh since 2013, the first year that CNZ invested in a cluster of five independent works to perform at the Fringe. Edinburgh has become a key market for achieving CNZ's strategic goal of New Zealand arts gaining international success with "distinctive, high-quality, internationally viable work [being] presented overseas" (Arts Council "Item 3.11..." 2013). In moving from one-off project funding towards substantially investing in presentation at the Edinburgh Fringe by annually supporting a suite of shows, this policy change has been a decisive factor in Edinburgh becoming the most common overseas market to view New Zealand theatre. The New Zealand government via Creative New Zealand has invested in branded NZ at Edinburgh seasons of work at the Fringe in 2014 and 2017 in an attempt to bring attention to New Zealand theatre and opportunities for the artists within the ultra-competitive market context of Fringe. In addition, CNZ has supported artists to attend professional development programme Momentum (instituted in 2013 and subsequently relaunched as

Edinburgh Intensive in 2018) held during the Fringe in order to upskill their touring capability and form international networks.

CNZ's funding assists with the viability of Fringe presentation for independent companies; however, as funding covers only a portion of costs and with no underwriting offered, it is the independent companies, not CNZ, that face the risk of considerable financial exposure. The complementary forces of colonial validation and institutional emphasis encourage theatre makers to travel to Edinburgh. This chapter, therefore, seeks to analyse the funding and market drivers of Edinburgh presentation, and the positions of the artists within these economic and institutional paradigms. I evaluate the experience and outcomes of the first NZ at Edinburgh season in 2014 and how Creative New Zealand's Edinburgh strategy has developed as a result. How has Aotearoa New Zealand theatre attempted to stand out, sell itself and get seen by audiences within the oversaturated Edinburgh marketplace? What are the risks for artists in doing so? And what does it mean for a national government funding agency to support a suite of the work to tour to the Fringe each year? As I argue in this chapter, touring to Edinburgh has become a complex and often fraught nationalistic enterprise, highlighting the challenges of marketing and performing a stable and coherent national identity to audiences within this market.

The Fringe as market

Edinburgh Fringe is the pinnacle representative of the global performance marketplace, bringing together "hundreds of different shows, people, cultures, and economies for a brief period of time in the compressed space of one city" (Harvie 2005: 75). The "promotional and codified status" of the Fringe today is at odds with its economic and political origins as an alternative counter to the high culture programme of the inaugural 1947 Edinburgh International Festival (Jamieson 2004: 66). The omission of any Scottish drama in the official Festival programme was answered in part by six Scottish groups, who together with two English groups "turned up 'uninvited and unheralded'" and organised their unauthorised performances, the companies' "rebellious and provocatively playful character" pitted against the "legitimate and civilizing International Festival" (67). This famous origin story of the Fringe established a democratising ethos as a key feature of the Festival, with an open access policy that welcomed any kind of work from anywhere to take part, contrasting with the International Festival's curated and sanctioned taste-making progamme.[2] This originating ideal, however, has been morphed by late-capitalist logic that prizes exponential growth over sustainable enterprise. The growth in the Fringe can be tracked over key stages of New Zealand's involvement. In 1963 Bruce Mason's *The End of the Golden Weather* was one of 52 shows at the Fringe. This seems a miniscule number today, but as an antagonist to the funded International Festival, Mason (1963) speculated that the "air of wild improvisation over overwhelming odds on the Fringe circuit" was perhaps "the secret of its appeal" – a comment which might still be applied to the contemporary Fringe. By 1979 when UK-based New Zealand company Heartache and Sorrow was awarded New Zealand's first Fringe First from *The Scotsman*, Heartache and Sorrow's season of works represented 5 out of 700 Fringe events. Twenty years later, the number of Fringe events had more than doubled: in 2000 actor Ian Hughes wrote that "*Bare* is just another stage show competing with 1500 other shows in the fringe festival alone" (Hughes 2001). Fourteen years later, this had doubled again: the 2014 NZ at Edinburgh season Fringe shows were appearing against 3,000 other events. The 2019 Fringe, which featured a record number of 29 New Zealand shows at the Fringe, also set a new record for Fringe events: 3,841 events in 322 venues, performed by artists from 63 different countries, "breaking all records for internationalism" (Brooks 2019). Just under 250,000 people attended Fringe events, with ticket sales breaking 3 million for the first time in 2019 (Edinburgh Festival Fringe Society 2019).

For three weeks every August the Fringe overwhelms the city: performances spring up in "every spare stage, school hall, pub back room and alleyway in the Scottish capital" (Kennedy 2014). The Fringe operates as a Darwinian arena: anyone can register, but only the best, as chosen by the marketplace, will survive. Ric Knowles (2004: 181) states that festivals "function primarily as manifestations of a theatrical version of late-capitalist globalisation, postmodern marketplaces for the exchange, not so much of culture as of cultural capital". In the Edinburgh Fringe context, cultural capital accretes over the number of shows you have seen, the strangest or most unexpected performance you experienced, the life-changing show that you discovered. With the overwhelming number of shows and the potential for paralysis of choice, navigation of the Fringe programme is aided by segmentation. There are a multitude of mini-festivals layered within the Fringe Festival that the audience might choose to identify with: the curated programmes of Traverse and Summerhall or the established "super venue" presenters (Assembly, the Gilded Balloon, Underbelly, the Pleasance), the Musicals, the Circus Hub, national showcases (such as Canada Hub), the stand-up comedians, the Free Fringe and so on. Time is made special at the Fringe, the apotheosis of Roland Barthes' (1985) conception that theatre can install another time "which could be experienced not as leisure but as another life [...], by its very duration [...] a saturated time". With the ability to binge on performance throughout the day and night, the over-saturated Fringe operates with a similar logic to contemporary streaming media services: the *Netflix* of live performance (complete with comedy specials), featuring work to cater to all conceivable tastes. The Fringe may also present a "spectre of choice"; critiques of the Fringe contend that its "production values and audience choice are undemocratically determined and standardised by neo-liberal market forces rather than artistic ones" (Harvie 2005: 82).

While the "air of wild improvisation" may be appealing, the monopoly conditions of the Fringe are stacked against the artist. Keren Zaiontz

(2018: 74; 71) describes the Fringe as "inherently exploitative", a simulation of the free market "accomplished through the art and sweat of self-subsidy". The Fringe has been the subject of recent criticism for being an exploitative environment for artists and workers with the launch of a Fair Fringe campaign in 2017 and whistle-blowers exposing illegal labour practice (Livingston 2017; Ferguson 2019). Lyn Gardner's (2017) *The Guardian* expose, headlined "We haven't made a profit for five years", investigated the financial strain experienced by UK companies participating in the Fringe, concluding

> the entire economy of the Edinburgh Fringe is a mirage. The only real beneficiaries are Virgin trains and the city of Edinburgh itself, its hotels and restaurants and shops, those with performance space to rent and the residents who let out their flats for in August.

Producer Sums Selvarajan (2019), who has attended Edinburgh Fringe from 2017 to 2019 with the Modern Māori Quartet and other work, acknowledges that "it's very rare for [...] kiwi works to make bank in the Fringe". A resource created by CNZ for Fringe tourers quotes Karin Williams (who produced Victor Rodger's *Black Faggot* at the 2014 Fringe): "everyone says you won't make money at Edinburgh Fringe and it's true [...] do whatever you can to cut costs. Assume the worst" (Creative New Zealand "Presenting..." 2017: 14). Indeed, the resource provides a sample budget for a four-week Edinburgh Fringe season of a show for two actors. The actual costs column shows expenses of NZ\$58,398.32 and revenue of \$48,261.83 (including a Creative NZ grant of \$21,000), resulting in a loss of \$10,136.49 (16). Companies enter the market with the strong likelihood of losing money, but take the risk in order for their work to be seen and sold on – the 2019 Fringe accredited 1,661 "producers, programmers, bookers, talent agencies, festivals and others from 54 countries" looking to programme, buy or tour work (Edinburgh Festival Fringe Society 2019). For example, Justin Lewis (2016) told me that Indian Ink lost money both times it went to the Fringe, though, with the benefit of hindsight, as detailed in the previous chapter, the tours paid off in the long run for the company, contributing to international touring becoming an economically sustainable activity for Indian Ink.

There is, however, no guarantee that presentation at the Fringe will result in future tour bookings, and the financial model for the Edinburgh marketplace involves considerable risk. Many Fringe venues charge a minimum fee for each performance – if sales are under this target, the company takes the loss. CNZ funding was intended to cover travel and freight and costs incurred within New Zealand in order to counteract, in principle, the tyranny of distance in order for the New Zealand companies to enter the Fringe on a more level-playing field with the UK companies presenting. However, CNZ's funding did not initially cover costs in Edinburgh, including accommodation, venue fees and marketing, contributing to the difficulty for New Zealand companies to even reach breakeven point at the Fringe. Despite income from CNZ funding, ticket sales and private donations, often artists still self-subsidise their seasons and take substantial fee cuts in order for their work to be seen in Edinburgh. The following section analyses the strengths and weaknesses of CNZ's developing strategy for supporting presentation at the Edinburgh Fringe in the lead-up to and aftermath of the 2014 NZ at Edinburgh season.

Creative New Zealand at Edinburgh

The 2014 NZ at Edinburgh season was inspired by an invitation, issued in 2012 by Festivals Edinburgh, for New Zealand to be a country of focus for the various Festivals held annually over August in Edinburgh, which include the Edinburgh International Festival, Edinburgh Festival Fringe, Edinburgh International Book Festival, Royal Edinburgh Military Tattoo and the Edinburgh Art Festival. Being "the largest season of New Zealand arts and culture ever performed across multiple festivals at the same time", it was anticipated that this would support increased media coverage, artist support and relationship building than would typically be possible under a one-off artist presentation model (Ministry of Culture and Heritage 2013). The year 2014 represented an important year for Aotearoa New Zealand to connect with Scotland and the UK: New Zealand sports teams would be travelling to Scotland for the Commonwealth Games held in Glasgow, and the countries were also commemorating the centenary of the outbreak of WWI. CNZ announced additional partnership with Edinburgh Fringe's Assembly Festival, which would present a season of New Zealand work with the intention of building a long-term partnership. As a pilot for what would become the 2014 NZ at Edinburgh branded season, CNZ's International presentation fund financially supported five productions to appear at Assembly Festival's venues during the 2013 Fringe. In addition, CNZ initiated the development programme Momentum New Zealand in partnership with Creative Scotland, British Council Scotland and British Council New Zealand. Momentum supported 16 delegates to attend the 2013 Festivals to build market knowledge and professional relationships; 50% of the Momentum delegates returned to present work for the 2014 Festivals.

CNZ budgeted for NZ$949,862 to deliver the 2014 NZ at Edinburgh season of work. CNZ'S Arts Council Toi Aotearoa directly contributed $745,000, which was topped up by $118, 267 from the chief executive's discretionary "Flexi-fund" (Arts Council 2014). Further funding sources were British Council New Zealand and British Council Scotland, which contributed a combined $39,701 and $110,000 from the government's Cultural Diplomacy International Programme (CDIP) (Arts Council 2014). CDIP is a group steered by the Ministry for Culture and Heritage from MFAT, New Zealand Trade and Enterprise, and Tourism New Zealand with the aim of helping to "establish and/or maintain a New Zealand cultural presence in key overseas regions or countries to boost New Zealand's profile and economic, trade, tourism, diplomatic and cultural interests" (Arts Council "Item 3.11..." 2013).

In addition to the perceived benefits in the participation of New Zealand's artists, CDIP identified the Festivals as a platform for cultural diplomacy and the promotion of New Zealand business. Part of CDIP's funding was allocated towards the development and execution of the Backyard at the Roxy bar, a New Zealand themed garden bar that showcased "the best of New Zealand wine, beer, food and coffee" over the month of August (Ministry of Culture and Heritage 2013).

Described by *The Guardian* as "New Zealand's biggest ever cultural charge to Edinburgh", CNZ's funding supported a total of 240 New Zealand artists from the disciplines of theatre, dance, literature and other art forms to attend festivals held at Edinburgh in 2014 (Brown 2014). Country-specific showcases have become a "staple" in Edinburgh, particularly in the crowded Fringe market (Awde 2017). The Australian High Commission led an Australian performance showcase during the 2006 Fringe, and other national governments – including Finland, China and Canada – have utilised the Fringe in an attempt to promote their country's performance work (the 2019 Fringe featured a record 15 separate country showcases). For Creative New Zealand, the 2014 Fringe represented an opportunity to build the brand recognition for New Zealand theatre, with the potential to generate future exports to other international markets if the work could attract the interest of international presenters attending the Fringe. Economic questions of "what work will sell?" intersect with existential artistic and cultural questions at the heart of New Zealand's anxious conception of national identity: in placing New Zealand performance work together within the context of an international showcase, what kind of image of the nation would be projected to Edinburgh?

Edinburgh Festival Fringe 2014

CNZ opted to fund six theatre works to tour to the 2014 Fringe as part of the NZ at Edinburgh season. For any cosmopolitan audiences who wanted to sample Aotearoa New Zealand theatre that year, they could have attended *The Factory*, prominently billed on Edinburgh posters as "a big hearted Pacific musical". Next, they might have seen the provocatively titled *Black Faggot* (2013) by Victor Rodger, in which two actors presented a series of monologues articulating a contemporary queer New Zealand-Sāmoan perspective; *On the Upside Down of the World* (2011) by Arthur Meek, a solo show from the perspective of a female early colonial settler; *Strange Resting Places* (2007) by Rob Mokaraka and Paolo Rotondo, which centred on the experiences of a Māori Battalion solider in Italy during WWII; and *Duck, Death and the Tulip* (2013), a children's puppetry show, adapted by Peter Wilson from the 2007 book of the same name by German author Wolf Erlburch. If prospective audience members could get a ticket before they were all sold out, they could also have tried *The Generation of Z* (2013) by David Van Horn, Simon London and Benjamin Farry, an immersive and interactive theatre experience where audiences attempted to survive long enough to be evacuated from the

Zombie apocalypse. New Zealand dance was represented by Neil Ieremia's contemporary dance company Black Grace and Te Matatini's *Haka*. The Edinburgh International Festival featured Salā Lemi Ponifasio's *I Am* from MAU company, composer Gareth Farr and pianist Michael Houston. CNZ contracted a Scottish public relations firm to lead an overall publicity campaign for the NZ at Edinburgh season, with the novelty of the season resulting in media coverage and major press reviews which CNZ estimated to be worth £GBP 1,000,000 ($NZ2 million) (Arts Council 2014).

The narrative promoted by this funded curation of work was of an inclusive multicultural nationalism. Prominent Scottish critic Joyce McMillan (2014), previewing the season in *The Scotsman*, identified a nation in transition, on a journey from being the "Britain of the southern seas" to claiming a "powerful identity as a Pacific nation". The NZ at Edinburgh programme offered "a vivid, wide-ranging and revealing glimpse of where New Zealand's post-colonial culture stands now – still mid-journey, still evolving at impressive speed" (McMillan). McMillan (2014) stated that New Zealand was a site of "cultural alchemy" and could offer the world a national story that was "both *unique* and full of *global resonances*" (my emphasis). Arthur Meek, who wrote *On the Upside Down of the World*, echoed McMillan's claims, arguing that the season demonstrated the nation was embracing its identity as "a Pacific country, the largest Pacific island" and expressed his pride in being part of a season that demonstrated "that change so powerfully, and in so many different voices" (McMillan 2014).[3]

Arthur Meek's play, which explored the British settlement of New Zealand, was, ironically, the only entry to articulate New Zealand's majority Pākehā identity. Unlike many other European New Zealand/Pākehā texts that sought to portray a naturalised New Zealand identity, *On the Upside Down of the World* explicitly frames Pākehā as transnational migrants: the play's arc is for the British settler Mary Ann Martin to become an enlightened proto-Pākehā, changed for the better by New Zealand. The Edinburgh season's posters feature actor Laurel Devenie, dressed in white and facing the camera, in a bicultural embrace with a naked Māori warrior, his tattooed buttocks positioned to catch the viewer's eye. Like the imagery of *Toroihi rāua ko Kāhira* that featured in *The Guardian* in 2012, this is exoticised titillation, and potentially misleading, as only Devenie appears in the solo show. Marketing clearly strategised that an Indigenous bottom would get bums on seats in Edinburgh. Meek said:

> It was a surprise bonus for me that a play I'd written for Kiwi audiences could jump the culture divide and appeal to an international crowd. Funnily enough, a story that we consider to be about the birth of the New Zealander translates to them as a story about the difficulties of immigration and assimilation as seen from the counterintuitive perspective of a white English-speaker.
>
> (Auckland Theatre Company 2014)

Gilbert and Lo (2007: 219) rightly point out that "white diasporic populations [...] are rarely labelled as such", and the Edinburgh tour can also be understood as the British diaspora returning to their origins to tell their story of departure.

With the exceptions of Meek's play, the children's theatre adaptation of *Duck, Death and the Tulip* and the Zombie fantasy *The Generation of Z*, the majority of the work in the Fringe and International Festival funded by CNZ – *Black Faggot*, *The Factory*, *Strange Resting Places*, *I AM*, Black Grace and *Haka* – celebrated Māori and Pasifika cultures within New Zealand. This image was not wholly reflective of the theatre environment back in New Zealand. New Zealand's mainstage theatres are dominated by European and Pākehā narratives; between 2011 and 2015 only 6% of productions by main centre theatres recurrently funded by CNZ were of Māori or Pasifika work (Creative New Zealand 2015). The selection of the NZ at Edinburgh programme created other distortions. In addition to the CNZ-supported work appearing at the Fringe, six other New Zealand theatre work self-funded their own seasons (in this, there is something of the spirit of the Fringe's origins – having missed out on CNZ support, these shows turned up to the Fringe anyway). Reflecting the punishing economics of such an endeavour, all six of these works were solo performances: *The Pianist* (2013) by Thomas Monckton (which won the Total Theatre Award for Best Circus Show), *Miss Fletcher Sings the Blues* (2012) by Hayley Sproull, *Echolalia* (2011) by Jen McArthur, *Real Fake White Dirt* (2014) by Jess Holly Bates, *Calypso Nights* (2013) by Barnie Duncan and *The Height of the Eiffel Tower* (2009) by Morgana O'Reilly. Other than a token mention on the NZ at Edinburgh website, these shows were not promoted by CNZ as part of the season, creating two tiers of NZ at Edinburgh Fringe shows: the "official" shows promoting a culturally progressive Polynesian New Zealand at ease with a diverse, multicultural identity, and the unfunded works that did not necessarily support this nationalistic agenda. The tiers also reveal a stark gender disparity around what was valued institutionally, with the official six theatre works written by men and majority of the unfunded shows being created and performed by female artists.

In Creative New Zealand's internal evaluation of the NZ at Edinburgh showcase, provided to me through an Official Information Act request, the Arts Council (2014) reported that the organisation's stated objectives for the project had been met. As supporting evidence for attaining increased awareness of New Zealand arts in Scotland, the UK and internationally, CNZ cited an audience survey conducted with Edinburgh audiences that found 73% of respondents expressing interest to experience more NZ art and culture as a result of the work they had been exposed to. CNZ reported that "overall, the New Zealand work in the Edinburgh season was well attended" (Arts Council 2014). The highest selling New Zealand shows at the Fringe were *The Generation of Z* at 98% capacity across 46 shows (with additional shows added to meet demand) and Black Grace at 56% capacity. However, *The Factory* and

Strange Resting Places both had disastrous seasons, achieving 15% capacity (CNZ advised budgeting for 30% houses). *The Factory* played at the Assembly Hall's Main Hall venue in a prime 7:30pm slot, but the venue's 800-seat capacity proved difficult for the company to fill, despite the high media profile the NZ at Edinburgh season had gained overall. In addition, Kila Kokonut Krew had to cut 20 minutes from *The Factory* to fit the venue's designated running time and, therefore, was unable to present the best version of the show (Manusaute 2015). Despite being promoted as a centrepiece of the 2014 NZ at Edinburgh Fringe season, Kila Kokonut Krew was financially ruined by the Fringe and subsequently liquidated ("Kila Kokonut Krew..." 2014).

A striking outcome of the 2014 NZ at Edinburgh Fringe season, not featured in CNZ's report, was that the two New Zealand theatre shows that gained the most attention from audiences and critics neither focussed on representations of New Zealand cultural identity, nor fit within the projected Pacific-New Zealand national image. The first, *The Generation of Z*, a site-specific work, adapts to its host city; for the Fringe it became a story of a Zombie outbreak in Edinburgh and, therefore, its country of origin was largely irrelevant to Edinburgh audiences. While *The Generation of Z* had received CNZ funding support since its early development in New Zealand, the second show – *Calypso Nights* (2013), a solo show featuring Barnie Duncan as the clown Juan Vesuvius – entered the Fringe without gaining CNZ's NZ at Edinburgh promotional and financial support. As part of a pragmatic strategy to reduce costs and make the most of appearing in Edinburgh, in the afternoons Duncan performed as a cast member in CNZ-funded *Strange Resting Places* to tiny audiences, while in his 10:45pm *Calypso Nights* slot he sold out his final fortnight and won the Fringe Genius Award from entertainment website *The Skinny*. These results indicate the difficulties for funding bodies like CNZ in being able to predict which shows will prove successful in the global market.

As to CNZ's objectives around creating long-term relationships between New Zealand artists and international presenters/venues and strengthening touring capability, half of the theatre shows at the 2014 Fringe went on to book further international tours. Interest from the Edinburgh presentation allowed *The Generation of Z* to perform a three-month season in London in 2015 (the subject of Chapter 9), although a proposed New York season did not eventuate. The picture book adaptation *Duck, Death and the Tulip* has continued to tour, including in China. Ironically, counter to the projection of Pacific-New Zealand identity, both of these works were uninterested in displaying markers of New Zealand national identity. The final show to book a tour after Edinburgh, *Black Faggot*, applied for one-off CNZ funding for a Melbourne season in 2015, but was unable to leverage any other tours through the Edinburgh season.

The 2014 Edinburgh season was used as a political and economic tool, a cultural product to build brand recognition in an overseas market, with the potential for future exports and further visibility back home. Whilst the season gained a great deal of positive press attention and reviews, the season also produced a counter narrative that undermined the season's ideals, including the financial exposure of *The Factory* and *Strange Resting Places*. Lyn Gardner's two-star review of *The Factory* categorised the show and NZ at Edinburgh shows as less than world-class, a repudiation of CNZ's profile-building aims for the season. Viewing the work through a colonialist lens, Gardner stated, "this is the third show I've seen in an invasion of New Zealand work at this year's fringe, and like the other pieces it is heartfelt, likable but theatrically unsophisticated" ("The Factory..." 2014).While CNZ reported that the outcomes for the NZ at Edinburgh season had been met against its own criteria, a fuller evaluation reveals that outcomes from the 2014 season were decidedly mixed, challenging the image that the funded selection of NZ at Edinburgh shows attempted to project to audiences in Edinburgh.

New Zealand at the Edinburgh Fringe 2015–2018

More shows ventured to the Edinburgh Fringe in 2015 and 2016 with investment from CNZ, but without the wrap around branded season support of 2014.[4] *Daffodils* (2014) by Rochelle Bright, a musical love-story-turned tragedy told using popular New Zealand songs, received NZ$50,000 from CNZ to tour to Edinburgh in 2016, where it was recognised with a Fringe First Award. Against this acclaim, critic Michael Billington, who decades before perceptively noted that the Roger Hall's West End adaptation of *Middle-Age Spread* covered something that was "once local and plausible" (1979), gave *Daffodils* two out of five stars. Billington's (2016) view was that *Daffodils* did not "travel well". He suspected that although the show "intended to question the notion of New Zealand as a quiet place in which nothing too sensational ever happens, its final effect is to support rather than subvert the myth". Billington's comments, dismissing the projected identity as a provincial one, speaks to the ongoing problems faced by New Zealand theatre makers desiring overseas performance and anxieties about whether the work will be recognised and understood. *Daffodils* represented the Pākehā-New Zealand culture of the 1950s–1980s, critiquing a dominant strain of masculine repression in society, but in this instance Billington did not strongly connect with the markers of identity in the work.

In 2017 there was a renewed focus by CNZ on the Edinburgh Fringe through a second branded NZ at Edinburgh season. Influenced by the experiences in 2014, there were some distinct changes in strategy for the second incarnation of the season. First, as there were no New Zealand companies invited to perform at the International Festival, the major focus was presentation at the Fringe. CNZ's risk management strategy involved funding work that was smaller in scale than in 2014 and companies that were "more experienced in the Edinburgh context and aware of the financial risk involved" (Arts Council 2016). Rather than making a distinction between the official NZ at Edinburgh and "other" shows as had occurred in the 2014 Fringe, CNZ would "include all New Zealand artists in the overall marketing collateral, irrespective of how they are funded" (Arts Council 2016). CNZ also identified the importance of using the overseas season as a way to build brand recognition and prestige in the domestic market. It was recorded that "staff will also develop a domestic communications plan around the Edinburgh season, sharing the stories of the artists and the importance of New Zealand artists taking their work overseas" (Arts Council 2016).

Of the nine theatrical works that CNZ supported in the NZ at Edinburgh Fringe 2017, only a minority displayed their national origins in their content. Having abandoned the overt Pacific-nation branding focus of the 2014 curation, the press release for the 2017 reflects the difficulty of projecting a coherent national narrative: "Whales, puppetry, breakups, gender equality, rape culture, Caribbean calypso, grief and healing, community and salvation, sexual empowerment, and homage to Māori showbands with a contemporary twist are all features of NZ at Edinburgh 2017" (Creative New Zealand "NZ at Edinburgh" 2017). Binge Culture's outdoor participatory work *Whales* (2013) featured whales migrating from Aotearoa stranding in Edinburgh, and the improvised durational work *Break Up (We Need to Talk)* (2014) saw New Zealanders ending their relationship while travelling in Scotland. In the premiere of *Ancient Shrines and Half Truths*, in which audiences navigated the outdoor area around Summerhall with an audio app, the New Zealand company became local Edinburgh tour guides. *Whales* takes place in a public space, with volunteers in wet suits performing as beached whales, with members of the public guided through a simulated rescue. While the work was "spectacular when it's disrupting the norm", it was less successful in the Fringe context where the automatic response from bystanders was to assume the event was advertising a show, rather than registering that this was the show itself (Baxendale 2019). Binge found few presenters representing Festivals at the Fringe that were seeking the unconventional programming that Binge produced, and the company's only subsequent international engagements to date have been Australian Fringe seasons of *Ancient Shrines* and *Break Up*. In White Face Crew's *La Vie Dans un Marionette* (2013) and Barnie Duncan's premiere of *Juan Vesuvius: I Am Your Deejay* (Duncan's Vesuvius sequel now supported as part of the NZ at Edinburgh programme), the performers also pretended to represent other nationalities.

Producer and Auckland Fringe director Lydia Zanetti, who had attended three previous Edinburgh Fringes as an operator (2014), Momentum Programme delegate (2015) and assistant producer (2016) produced three of the independent works as part of the 2017 NZ at Edinburgh season: *Power Ballad* (2017) by Julia Croft and Nisha Madhan, *Jane Doe* (2015) by Eleanor Bishop and Trick of the Light's puppetry work *The Road That Wasn't There* (2012) by Ralph McCubbin Howell. *The Road That Wasn't There* begins in New Zealand, although it was explicitly written to be performed in Edinburgh (it had in fact premiered at the Edinburgh Fringe in 2012) so the company consciously included a "Scottish element" by giving the protagonist Scottish heritage (Jewell 2017). The final two works, *Jane Doe* and *Power Ballad*, engaged with global debates around contemporary feminism. The majority of the works promoted the country's theatrical innovation, but not its national culture, a distinct departure from the previous branding, with the selection representing the broad artistic interests of contemporary New Zealand theatre makers seeking Edinburgh Fringe presentation. This impacted the Modern Māori Quartet, performing showband revue *That's Us* (2017), who found themselves the default representatives of Aotearoa, which producer Sums Selvarajan (2019) said "took away from the work and also overshadowed the focus of the whole exercise".

Following an evaluation of the 2017 season, CNZ decided it would no longer invest in a "large-scale umbrella marking campaign or present the NZ work as a 'season'" as had occurred in 2014 and 2017 (Congreve 2018). Instead, companies would be supported to deliver their own individual marketing campaign. Signalling the difficulty of telling a coherent New Zealand story at Edinburgh, responsibility was placed on the individual companies to tell their own. CNZ's senior adviser of International Services and Initiatives Eleanor Congreve said that the organisation had concluded, based on feedback from companies, that the "one size fits all" approach was limiting, and it was preferable to allow each company to determine the scope of their marketing campaign (e.g., level of flyering vs postering) based on the needs of their show and venue (Congreve 2019). CNZ also recognised that restricting companies to apply for funding to subsidise the costs of freight, flights and domestic costs was severely impacting the financial viability of touring to Edinburgh (especially with rising accommodation costs), so it amended the International Initiatives Presentation funds to allow companies with an invitation from a major Fringe venue to apply for funding for a maximum of 50% of costs up to $30,000 (Arts Council 2018). Under these revised settings, at the 2018 Fringe eight companies presented nine shows. Returning to the Fringe were Arthur Meek (with *Erewhon*), Modern Māori Quartet (*Two Worlds*) and marking his tenth Fringe, Mika (with *Salon Mika on Bare Feet Street*). New to the Fringe were A Slightly Isolated Dog (*Don Juan*), Tikapa Productions (*Not in Our Neighbourhood, The Moa Show*) by Jamie McCaskill and the Fringe First awardees *Valerie* and *The Basement Tapes*. Thus far only *The Basement Tapes*, Modern Māori Quartet and A Slightly Isolated Dog have achieved further international tours following the 2018 Fringe.

Evaluating the Edinburgh strategy

Creative New Zealand's investment emphasis on the Edinburgh Festival Fringe since 2013 has consolidated the mythos of Fringe as the key market destination for theatre makers' seeking access to touring opportunities in the global theatre marketplace. There have been clear benefits for some shows in being able to leverage interest from international presenters and critical and awards success by booking further international tours. However, the inconsistent record of show's continuing to tour after Edinburgh suggests CNZ needs to adapt its strategy to better support companies following Edinburgh – getting them to the Fringe is not enough. There is also an unfortunate record of Māori and Pasifika work being marketed as a core component of Aotearoa's "point of difference" within the global marketplace, but, in some instances, after being financially exposed at the Fringe, having their capacity to operate domestically in Aotearoa irrevocably affected. Utilising Edinburgh as a nationalistic enterprise has repeatedly come under strain, exposing the challenges of selling a coherent and desirable image of New Zealand to audiences in Edinburgh, signalled by the abandonment of the wrap around "NZ at Edinburgh" marketing model in favour of supporting companies with individualised marketing strategies. Supporting would-be tourers to participate in the Momentum/Edinburgh Intensive programmes prior to bringing their own work to Edinburgh has played a vital role in preparing theatre makers for the pressures of presenting in the Edinburgh context, helping to mitigate the risk of funding artists without prior experience of touring to this market.

Nevertheless, it is my contention that greater institutional and artistic criticality is required in assessing whether the Edinburgh Festival Fringe, with its oversaturated, exploitative and antagonistic market conditions, is necessarily the ideal destination to achieve international presentation aims. UK producer Richard Jordan (2019), who visited New Zealand as part of the Performing Arts Network of New Zealand (PANNZ) Conference in March 2019, has questioned New Zealand's strategic focus on Edinburgh, arguing that while the Fringe "can serve as a valuable and obvious platform for bringing attention to a county's arts industry [...] many works may be served better by linking up with a regional producing theatre or touring to places they connect with". Jordan advised that a show in Edinburgh can easily get lost or overlooked, but, by placing a show "as a stand-alone presentation, its subject matter could have a much more powerful resonance and connection to audiences, especially within its coastal regions where similar issues are being faced, both in the UK and elsewhere" (Jordan 2019). Jordan's comments register with ongoing questions raised by the cases surveyed in this book around how New Zealand theatre makers can enter the global marketplace and have audiences around the world find connections with their work. A myopic focus on Edinburgh risks overlooking other performance opportunities, including New Zealand's potential to be a leader across the Asia-Pacific market in the Southern Hemisphere. In the meantime, the forces of cultural legitimacy and institutional approval continue to platform Edinburgh as an essential rite of passage for New Zealand theatre makers. The powerful pull of Edinburgh on the psyches of New Zealand artists was again evident at the 2019 Fringe, which featured the largest "delegation of artists and performers" to date (Creative New Zealand 2019). New Zealand's involvement in the 2019 Edinburgh Festival Fringe is the subject of the next chapter, analysing audience responses in Edinburgh to five of the Aotearoa New Zealand works playing at the Fringe that year.

Notes

1 Mika's first performance at the Edinburgh Festival Fringe was in 1992. He marked his tenth appearance in 2018.
2 The Fringe was not officially recognised as a Festival until 1958.
3 A precedent for the showcase of New Zealand arts at the 2014 Edinburgh Festivals was the Festival of New Zealand Arts held at London's Southwark Playhouse in 1997. Featured in the Festival was the "Air New Zealand Season of Kiwi Theatre" consisting of productions from Circa Theatre of *Joyful and Triumphant* (1992) by Robert Lord (a domestic drama exploring a Pākehā family over several generations), *C'Mon Black* (1995) by Roger Hall (about a fan touring with the All Blacks in the 1995 World Cup) and Catherine Downes' *The Case of Katherine Mansfield* (1978). Contrasting with the 2014 NZ at Edinburgh selection of theatre, the 1997 Festival projected an almost exclusively New Zealand Pākehā identity to audiences at Southwark.
4 These touring works included Fringe returnees' Trick of the Light with *The Bookbinder* and *Beards! Beards! Beards!* by Ralph McCubbin Howell and Arthur Meek and Geoff Pinfield with *On the Conditions and Possibilities of Hillary Clinton Taking Me as Her Young Lover*. Julia Croft made her Edinburgh Fringe debut with *If There's Not Dancing at the Revolution, I'm Not Coming*.

References

Note: "OIA" indicates the source was received from Creative New Zealand February 2020 as part of an Official Information Act Request.

Abbott, Ian. 2019. "Ian Abbott at the 2019 Edinburgh Festival Fringe – Part 2". *Writing about Dance*. Last modified August 29, 2019. www.writingaboutdance. com/performance/ian-abbott-at-2019-edinburgh-festival-fringe-part-2/
Arts Council. 2013. "Item 3.11: Update on the Development of the New Zealand at Edinburgh Festivals Project". July 10. (OIA)
———— 2014. "Item 4.11: Summary of the Evaluation of New Zealand at Edinburgh Festivals 2014". December 10. (OIA)
———— 2016. "Item 2.5: NZ at Edinburgh 2017". October 26. (OIA)
———— 2018. "Item 2.6: International Initiatives Update". October. (OIA)
Auckland Theatre Company. 2014. *The Trees beneath the Lake* Programme. Auckland.
Awde, Nick. 2017. "Showcasing China at the Edinburgh Fringe". *The Stage*. Last modified August 16, 2017. www.thestage.co.uk/features/2017/showcasing-china-at-the-edinburgh-fringe/
Barthes, Roland. 1985. *The Responsibility of Forms*. Translated by Richard Howard. New York: Hill and Wang.
Baxendale, Joel. 2019. Interviewed by James Wenley. Wellington. October 10.
Billington, Michael. 1979. "Middle Age Spread". *The Guardian*. October 17. (MS-1614/012, Roger Hall Papers, Hocken Collections, University of Otago Library, Dunedin)

———— 2016. "New Zealand Romcom Wilts at the Fringe". *The Guardian*. Last modified August 8, 2016.

Brooks, Libby. 2019. "Edinburgh Festival Fringe to 'Break Records for Internationalism'". Last modified June 5, 2019. www.theguardian.com/culture/2019/jun/05/edinburgh-festival-fringe-to-break-records-for-internationalism

Brown, Mark. 2014. "New Zealand Launches Biggest Ever Cultural Charge to Edinburgh Festival". *The Guardian*. Last modified August 4, 2014. www.theguardian.com/stage/2014/aug/04/new-zealand-edinburgh-festival-biggest-ever-cultural-charge

Congreve, Eleanor. 2018. "Project Control Document: NZ at Edinburgh". May. (OIA)

———— 2019. Interviewed by James Wenley. Video Conference (Auckland/Wellington). December 19.

Creative New Zealand. 2015. "Review of Theatre: Final Report". *Creative New Zealand*. Last modified January 11, 2020. http://web.archive.org/web/20160124065146/http://www.creativenz.govt.nz/assets/paperclip/publication_documents/documents/470/original/final_report_2015_review_of_theatre.pdf?1448404948

———— 2017. "NZ at Edinburgh 2017". *Scoop*. Last modified May 29, 2017. www.scoop.co.nz/stories/CU1705/S00459/nz-at-edinburgh-2017.htm

———— 2017. "Presenting at the Edinburgh Festival Fringe". *Creative New Zealand*. Last modified January 11, 2020. www.creativenz.govt.nz/assets/paperclip/publication_documents/documents/529/original/guide_to_presenting_at_the_edinburgh_festival_fringe.pdf?1489453593

————2019. "Largest Delegation of Artists and Performers to Represent New Zealand in Edinburgh". *Creative New Zealand*. Last modified July 26, 2019. www.creativenz.govt.nz/news/largest-delegation-of-artists-and-performers-to-represent-new-zealand-in-edinburgh

Edinburgh Festival Fringe Society. 2019. "Record Edinburgh Audiences as Fringe Comes to a Close". *Ed Fringe*. Last modified August 26, 2019. www.edfringe.com/learn/news-and-events/record-edinburgh-audiences-as-fringe-comes-to-a-close

Ferguson, Brian. 2019. "'Terrible' and 'Shameful' Edinburgh Festival Fringe Work Practices Revealed". *The Scotsman*. Last modified July 29, 2019. www.scotsman.com/arts-and-culture/edinburgh-festivals/terrible-and-shameful-edinburgh-festival-fringe-work-practices-revealed-1-4972566

Gardner, Lyn. 2014. "The Factory – High School Musical with Polynesian Vibes". *The Guardian*. Last modified August 20, 2014. www.theguardian.com/stage/2014/aug/20/the-factory-review-assembly-hall-edinburgh-fringe

———— 2017. "'We Haven't Made a Profit for Five Years': Risky Business at Edinburgh Fringe". *The Guardian*. Last modified July 19, 2017. www.theguardian.com/stage/2017/jul/19/risky-business-edinburgh-fringe-hidden-costs-of-theatres

Gilbert, Helen and Jacqueline Lo. 2007. *Performance and Cosmopolitics: Cross-Cultural Transactions in Australasia*. Hampshire: Palgrave Macmillan.

Harvie, Jen. 2005. *Staging the UK*. Manchester: Manchester University Press.

Hughes, Ian. 2001. "'Bare' Facts about Touring". *NZ Herald*. March 19. (Client File: Toa Fraser, Playmarket, Wellington)

Jamieson, Kirstie. 2004. "The Festival Gaze and Its Boundaries". *Space & Culture*, 7 (1): 64–75.

Jewell, Stephen. 2017. "Kiwis Take Edinburgh by Storm". *NZ Herald*. Last modified August 25, 2017. www.nzherald.co.nz/entertainment/news/article.cfm?c_id=1501119&objectid=11910102

Jordan, Richard. 2019. "Producers Shouldn't Worry about Distances and Always Look to Expand Their Horizons". *The Stage*. Last modified March 21, 2019. www.thestage.co.uk/opinion/2019/richard-jordan-producers-need-to-look-beyond-distance-to-expand-their-horizons-new-zealand-australia/

Kennedy, Maev. 2014. "Edinburgh Festival Fringe 2014 Set to Be the Biggest in Its History". *The Guardian*. Last modified June 5. www.theguardian.com/culture/2014/jun/05/edinburgh-festival-fringe-2014-biggest-history

"Kila Kokonut Krew Entertainment Limited (in Liquidation)". 2014. *Gazette*. Last modified January 8, 2015. www.gazette.govt.nz/notice/id/2015-al60

Knowles, Ric. 2004. *Reading the Material Theatre*. Cambridge: Cambridge University Press.

Last Tapes Theatre Company. 2018. "Valerie". *Boosted*. Page no longer available. Last modified July 2019. www.boosted.org.nz/projects/valerie-goes-to-edinburgh

Lewis, Justin. 2016. Interviewed by James Wenley. Auckland. November 16.

Livingston, Eve. 2017. "The Secret Exploitation at the Edinburgh Fringe". *Vice*. Last modified August 16, 2017. www.vice.com/en_nz/article/a33v3k/the-secret-exploitation-at-the-edinburgh-fringe

Manusaute, Vela. 2015. Interviewed by James Wenley. Auckland. September 12.

Mason, Bruce. 1963. "Edinburgh 1963". *NZ Listener*. November 1.

Mazer, Sharon. 2018. *I Have Loved Me a Man: The Life and Times of Mika*. Auckland: Auckland University Press.

McMillan, Joyce. 2014. "Here Come the Kiwis: New Zealand Culture at the Fringe". *The Scotsman*. Last modified August 24, 2014. www.wow247.co.uk/2014/08/02/here-come-the-kiwis-new-zealand-culture-at-the-fringe

Ministry of Culture and Heritage. 2013. "Creative New Zealand Briefing to the Minister, Culture and Heritage". May. (OIA)

Selvarajan, Sums. 2019. Interviewed by James Wenley. Edinburgh. August 22.

Wayne, Emma. 2018. "Perth's Fringe Festival Grows to Third Biggest in the World in Just Seven Years". *ABC News*. Last modified January 26, 2018. www.abc.net.au/news/2018-01-26/perth-fringe-festival-grows-to-be-third-biggest-world/9357046

Zaiontz, Keren. 2018. *Theatre & Festivals*. London: Palgrave Macmillan.

8   Making meaning

Responses to Aotearoa New Zealand at the Edinburgh Festival Fringe 2019

Having followed from afar the Aotearoa New Zealand work travelling to Edinburgh over the past few years, I finally made my own journey to Edinburgh as a researcher during the final week of the 2019 Edinburgh Festival Fringe. My project was to gather data on audiences attending New Zealand work at Edinburgh to learn more about *who* was going to work which had toured from New Zealand, and what factors influenced decisions to attend. As individual shows receive few demographic details from the Fringe about their ticket buyers, I wanted to discover whether I could find any evidence that Creative New Zealand's multi-year investment in touring theatre to the Edinburgh Fringe market, as discussed in the previous chapter, was having a discernible impact on influencing audience to attend multiple New Zealand works at the Fringe. The research also enabled me to gather an expanded range of responses to New Zealand work overseas, beyond the traces of responses recorded in the critical archive in order to better understand the "wider process of sense-making" involved when encountering live performance (Sedgman 2019: 474). A qualitative audience survey allows me to assess a wider range of possible meanings and identifications that individual audience members might produce in relationship to a New Zealand work playing at Edinburgh.

Building on New Zealand's artistic and financial investment in Edinburgh over the previous six years, the 2019 Edinburgh Festival Fringe featured the largest number of individual shows from New Zealand artists to date, with 29 different shows listed in a 2019 New Zealand at the Edinburgh Festivals booklet cataloguing the works.[1] Creative New Zealand directly invested in nine theatrical works to attend the 2019 Edinburgh Fringe via the International Presentation Fund and General Arts Grant fund: *Jekyll and Hyde* (2016) from A Slightly Isolated Dog; *My Best Dead Friend* (2016) by Anya-Tate Manning and Isobel MacKinnon; *Aunty* (2017) by Johanna Cosgrove; *Working on My Night Moves* (2019) by Julia Croft and Nisha Madhan (all three produced by Zanetti Productions); *Tröll* (2019) by Ralph McCubbin Howell (Trick of the Light, in partnership with Zanetti Productions); two shows from the Modern Māori Quartet – *Two Worlds* (2018) and *Garage Party* (2019) – *Super Hugh-Man* (2017) by Rutene Spooner (all three produced by SquareSums&Co); *Two*

Hearts: The Comeback Tour (2019) by Laura Daniel and Joseph Moore; and in the wake of comedian Rose Matafeo's success the previous year, CNZ also funded two stand-up comics: Chris Parker and Eli Matthewson. Of these, I selected five focus shows to survey audiences for: *Two Worlds, Super Hugh-Man, Aunty, My Best Dead Friend* and *Working on My Night Moves*. The first four shows consciously represented markers of Aotearoa New Zealand identity in their content, whereas *Working on My Night Moves* was chosen as a counter example of a work that did not attempt to display national identity, allowing me to assess whether I could discern any noticeable differences in the pattern of responses.

I conducted my research in the final week of the Fringe when attention is generally concerned with whether a show has momentum: is it on a streak of selling out? Are there a string of five-star reviews that can be pasted on show posters around the city? An English bank holiday and British Council show-case meant the final week also attracted a number of visitors from England. With audiences often racing to the next show at the end of each performance, gathering research participants willing to share their responses is challenging in the Fringe environment. My strategy was to leverage the Fringe culture of lining up before shows to recruit audience members prior to their entry into each venue. Wearing a customised t-shirt with a message on the front stating, "Kia ora, I'm a NZ theatre researcher. What's your response to the show?", I introduced myself and my research project; if an attendee was willing to participate, I asked them to supply their email address, and after the performance I sent them a link to an online survey to complete at their leisure. I recruited participants at each performance of each of the five shows over six days (August 19–25), and the final number of respondents who completed the online survey was 115. The bulk of responses were received from attendees of *Two Worlds* (43) and *Working on My Night Moves* (34), a reflection of the greater audience numbers these works consistently achieved in the final week, compared with the other works which were struggling to attract audiences, thereby making it more difficult to recruit participants due to the smaller pool of potential participants. The survey gathered demographic data (age, gender identity, place of residence) and asked whether participants had at any stage lived in or visited Aotearoa New Zealand, the number of shows they had attended at the 2019 Fringe at the time of the survey, whether they had seen any other New Zealand works at the 2019 Fringe or previous Fringes, how they had found out about the particular show I was surveying and what made them decide to attend.

As highlighted in Figure 8.1, 44% of respondents lived in Scotland (56% of whom were Edinburgh locals) and 45% lived elsewhere in the UK (making a total UK figure of 89%).[2] Gaining such granular demographic detail builds a more complex impression of a heterogeneous audience attending a performance event beyond the flattening binary of local versus non-local that I have by necessity employed elsewhere in this book. While I cannot trace a direct causality between direct experience of New Zealand and a decision to

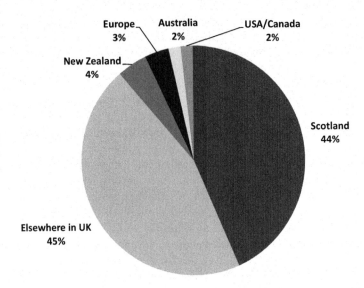

Figure 8.1 Place of residence (survey data collected at Edinburgh Festival Fringe 2019)

attend an Aotearoa New Zealand work in Edinburgh, it is notable that, per Figure 8.2, 29% of attendees had either visited, previously lived or currently live in New Zealand, contributing to the "horizon of expectations", to use Susan Bennett's framework, that potentially influences their personal engagement with a work from New Zealand. For the 71% of respondents who had never been to New Zealand, there is the possibility of a cosmopolitan engagement with work that specifically references New Zealand locality (*Working on My Night Moves* being the exception in my surveyed works), allowing the audience to gain (or at least, offer a perception of gaining) greater familiarity with place, people and worldviews that may be "outside one's local or national settings" (Kendall, Woodward and Skrbiš 2009: 113).

Although I cannot make any claims for the representativeness of my data in relation to the overall demographic profile of the attendees of the full Edinburgh seasons of these five focus works, the survey offers a snapshot of individual receptions to the productions, counteracting what Helen Freshwater (2009: 13) has identified as "the continuing absence" in performance scholarship "of the voices and opinions of 'ordinary' audience members who have no professional links to theatre". Kirsty Sedgman (2019: 465) is a strong advocate for rigorous research involving theatre audiences, arguing that a failure "to listen to how audiences themselves articulate their own experiences is to shirk the urgent responsibility of understanding the ways differing individuals imagine and make sense of our shared social word". In line with the importance of allowing audience to articulate their own experiences, in my

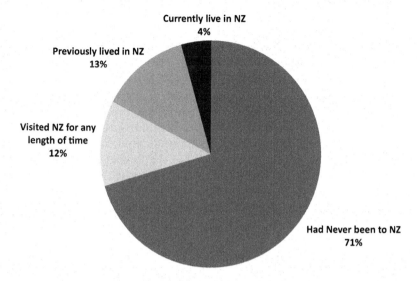

Figure 8.2 Survey respondents – previously lived or visited NZ (survey data collected at Edinburgh Festival Fringe 2019)

survey I asked the following open-ended questions to prompt participants' individual responses to the work itself:

1. Can you describe your experience of viewing this show?
2. What, if anything, did you personally connect with or identify with in this show?
3. What impressions of Aotearoa New Zealand has viewing this given you, if any?

Sedgman explains that qualitative research "can offer the tools to understand how actual audiences work to fill up a text with meaning: how people go about telling stories about the stories they are told", but also stresses the need to be conscious of its limitations and the speculative nature of interpreting audience responses (470–471). I take the cue from Sedgman that the responses from my survey cannot be presented as "verifiable slices of experience, able to transmit the reality of audience response from spectator to researcher to reader", but instead represent "a complex interplay between research context and analytical approach" (465). My survey questions potentially prompt participants to form and articulate thoughts that they may not otherwise have consciously made. Even my preshow interaction with would-be participants, introducing the prospect of responding in some way to the performance, provided a frame to the performance event that would not otherwise have been present. Therefore, I would categorise the responses that I collected in Edinburgh as traces of subjective meaning produced by both the performance and research contexts.

A key question for Sedgman in audience research is "why certain people are prompted to think and feel in particular ways, while others take away such different kinds of experience" (474). My particular agenda in collecting and assessing responses to New Zealand work at Edinburgh was to discover to what extent, if any, that national familiarity and proximity (e.g., whether a respondent had previously lived in New Zealand) was a discernible influence on participants' self-reported motivations for attending the performance or their interpretations of the performance. Throughout this book I have used the framework of the feedback loop to investigate the processes of production and reception in relation to national identity in theatrical works. My premise is that some markers of identity may be recognised by audiences that reinforce existing conceptions of a particular New Zealand identity or context, but some markers may be deemphasised or read differently when a work is viewed outside of its "home" context. Conducting this survey was an opportunity to examine the feedback loop process by collecting a range of individual responses in order to assess what markers and features of the work people chose to emphasise in responding to my prompts, and what kind of "common" individuals might perceive that they share with a work.

Keeping in mind the caveats that my survey was a non-representative sample of participants who attended New Zealand work in the final week of the Fringe, and responses are necessarily subjective and incomplete, I wanted to see what patterns and divergences I could discern based on what individual respondents identified in their survey responses. In the next section I present an overview of the five shows and survey findings, followed by a deeper analysis of what the responses reveal about the Creative New Zealand's Edinburgh strategy and the processes of meaning making involved in the placement of these works in Edinburgh.

The focus shows

Modern Māori Quartet: Two Worlds

Touring for a third time in a row to the Edinburgh Fringe, the Modern Māori Quartet performed two distinct shows. At 3:30pm in Assembly George Square Studios Three (a lecture theatre room), the Quartet presented *Two Worlds*, which had debuted at the Fringe the year before. Departing from their usual showband-style variety show, *Two Worlds* involves a theatrical frame featuring characters stuck in limbo after death, the drama leading them to revelation and release. Five hours later, at 8:35pm in Underbelly's Bistro Square Ermintrude, the Quartet performed the more free-form *Garage Party*, evoking the New Zealand social tradition in which friends and family gather in a host's garage and "share food and drink and sing at the top of our lungs till the wee hours" (Edinburgh Team 2019). I opted to research *Two Worlds* due to its dramatic narrative and representation of Aotearoa history for audiences in Edinburgh.

Two Worlds was designed specifically for an international market with the assumption that audiences may have little if any knowledge of the Indigenous and colonial history of Aotearoa, dramatising issues that producer Sums Selvarajan (2019) describes as "universal for most indigenous people". The four characters demonstrate how colonialism has impacted generations of Māori men. Prior to his arrival in limbo, Big Bro (Rutene Spooner) struggled with romantic relationships. Koro (Matutaera Ngaropo), a member of the Māori battalion during WWII, was afflicted with Post Traumatic Stress Disorder as a result of his war experience. Uncle (Francis Kora) was punished in school for speaking Te Reo, and during the course of the performance has to confront his own internalised racism and self-hatred. Bub (Matariki Whatarau) had hopes of being the "first Māori Prime Minister of New Zealand", but struggled with the pressure of medical school and took his own life, registering with the high suicide rate of young Māori men in Aotearoa. Each sings a waiata (song) reflecting their journey, and Bub performs a haka, described by Edinburgh reviewer Gareth K. Vile ("Modern Maori Quartet..." 2019) as "brutal", capturing the "pressures of modern life [...] simultaneously a reworking of indigenous dance and a thrilling commentary on psychological anguish".

My survey of *Two Worlds* audiences revealed that the Quartet's previous engagements had created fans that were returning for a "repeat prescription" [59, Male, Edinburgh resident], with ten respondents indicating they had previously attended Modern Māori Quartet shows in 2017 and/or 2018. Twelve respondents referenced interest in the show's connection with New Zealand and Māori culture as a primary reason for attending, for instance: "I am very interested in NZ and the Māori and Polynesian people during the Fringe it is a great chance to hear music from all over the world" [64, F, Melrose, Scotland]. *Two Worlds* could be used by audiences to imaginatively transport themselves to a country and cultural context they had not necessarily experienced in person: 63% of the *Two Worlds* respondents had never been to New Zealand. 27% of respondents lived in Edinburgh, with a further 30% from elsewhere in Scotland, while 41% resided in other parts of the UK, mostly England (2% resided in New Zealand).

In responding to the prompt to describe their experience of viewing the show, the majority of comments were highly positive, with one person claiming it as "one of my favourite shows of the festival" [37, F, London]. Despite the show's critical representation of the effects of colonialism in Aotearoa, audiences expressed they had gained a positive impression of New Zealand and desired to "visit and/or find out more about this part of NZ" [64, F, Melrose], "learn more about Māori culture, language and potentially visit New Zealand [30, F, Edinburgh]. Supporting a reviewer's sentiment that they "learned more than I ever did before about Māori culture and its place in modern New Zealand" (Brownlee 2019), audiences commented on their gratitude of learning more about Māori culture and how the ritual at the end of the show of sprinkling water (a tikanga Māori practice to restore noa or balance after an encounter with death) was a new experience [69, F, Port Glasgow]. One respondent provided an anecdote about once being asked if Māori were in the same position as Aboriginal peoples of Australia and had replied that they "didn't think so as they are very proud and were stronger". However, Uncle's storyline gave this audience member new "information that this may not have been true" [67, F, Markinch]. These comments register *Two World*'s potential to inform audiences in Edinburgh about unfamiliar aspects of Māori history and tikanga, although the comment from the Markinch resident still reveals a degree of uncertainty. The emphasis in responses on the desirability of Aotearoa as a tourist destination, promising further direct engagement with Māori culture, illustrates the tension within *Two Worlds'* emplacement in Edinburgh in that the Quartet is perceived as a positive ambassador of New Zealand culture, despite the Quartet critiquing ongoing injustice faced by Māori within New Zealand.

Super Hugh-Man

Like *Two Worlds*, *Super Hugh-Man* by Rutene Spooner had the potential to provide an educational value for audiences, with Spooner consciously designing an "international version" of his autobiographical cabaret show. Narrating his journey towards becoming an actor in musical theatre, Spooner details his experiences growing up in Gisborne, emphasising its isolation as a "little village on the edge of the world", and taking part in kapa haka competitions (as an example of providing cultural context for international audiences, Spooner breaks down kapa haka's structure and conventions). As a child Spooner had worshipped Australian actor Hugh Jackman's screen performance as Marvel comic hero Wolverine, but it was only when Spooner attended the National Academy of Singing and Dramatic Art (NASDA) in Christchurch, which offers a bachelor of performing art's degree with a specialisation in musical theatre, that Spooner learned that Jackman also had a musical theatre career; Jackman's dual ability to represent hyper-masculine Wolverine and camp Australian singer/songwriter Peter Allen eases Spooner's own masculine anxieties. Spooner recreates Jackman's performance of Allen in the musical *The Boy from Oz* (1998) and merges the binaries of Jackman's performance styles in Spooner's own "Wolverine: The Musical" medley for the climax of the show. Spooner's Māori identity provides a specific cultural context for the show, as reviewer Gareth K. Vile ("Maori Musical..." 2019) observed,

> the tension between Māori identity and triple-threat training provides a poignant depth to the comedy [...] reasserting the notion of appropriation as a strategy not to steal from colonised cultures but to subvert

expectations and toy with a dominant culture's aesthetics, it works as both entertaining, witty cabaret and an exercise in post-colonial cabaret.

While Spooner was covering the role of Big Bro in *Two Worlds* after the original performer fell ill shortly before the Fringe season, according to the survey data Spooner's appearance with the Quartet (plugging his solo show at the conclusion of each performance) was not observably driving audiences to *Super Hugh-Man* (which played at 12:50 PM in the same Assembly Three venue as *Two Worlds*). As with the responses to *Two Worlds*, *Super Hugh-Man*'s New Zealand connection appealed, with audiences explaining their reasons for attending as: "wanting to support NZers" [41, F, London]; "Love of NZ and it looked amusing" [72, F, Stratford-upon-Avon], "Wanted to support Māori in performing arts" [22, F, London]. *Super Hugh-Man*'s content offered a range of access points that different audience could connect to in the show (Marvel fandom, musical theatre, Māori culture), although for some audience this could also be exclusionary: "didn't know anything about Hugh Jackman or Wolverine so couldn't completely connect. Wished I'd seen the films so I could appreciate the references"; however, they had been "able to identity with much of his story as I am a NZer" [69, F, Edinburgh].

My Best Dead Friend *and* Aunty

Both *My Best Dead Friend* (5:15pm, Summerhall – Old Lab) and *Aunty* (6:45pm, Assembly George Square – The Box) were solos from female performers, and foregrounded markers of Pākehā–New Zealand identity. *Aunty*, written and performed by Johanna Cosgrove, is an interactive comedy in which the audiences are cast as the relations of the "very anarchic, very New Zealand Aunty" (Ralph 2019). For the Edinburgh season Aunty has flown to Edinburgh for a reunion with the Scottish side of her family, and she asks us to pour her wine, eat and dance as she recounts stories from her life in New Zealand. In *My Best Dead Friend*, directed by co-writer Isobel MacKinnon, performer and co-writer Anya Tate-Manning recounts her coming-of-age story as a 17-year-old living in Dunedin in 1998, a time and place where "rugby is King" and Tate-Manning is in love with singer Nick Carter from boyband the Backstreet Boys. Like Spooner's description of Gisborne, Tate-Manning evokes Dunedin as globally isolated, at "the bottom of New Zealand, bottom of the world". "Anyone from Dunedin?", she asks her audience, and at my performance two people put up their hands, contrasting perceived isolation with the potential for global connections. Dunedin had particular resonance in an Edinburgh context as the New Zealand city was modelled off of Edinburgh when founded by settlers. As one reviewer commented, "Dunedin is a city that exercises a fascination from afar for Scots. Founded by Scottish Presbyterians, its very name is from the Gaelic for Edinburgh, with a George Street and Princes Street and a Portobello" (Cornwell 2019). A key event in *My Best Dead Friend* is when Tate-Manning and her best friends chalk the streets of Dunedin with poems and lyrics; Tate-Manning re-enacts this, chalking the set with references to New Zealand poets Hone Tuwhare, Allen Curnow, James K. Baxter, Denis Glover (quoting the same Glover poem Gary Henderson used as the basis of *Skin Tight*), as well as Canadian singer-songwriter Leonard Cohen. Reflected in Allen Curnow's famous quote, to "learn the trick of standing upright here" (from *The Skeleton of the Great Moa*, 1943), chalking New Zealand literary references on streets designed to replicate Edinburgh represents a charged act of cultural definition and Pākehā belonging, learning to stand up right as both young adults and New Zealanders. However, the chalk is impermanent, quickly and violently removed by the street cleaners, leaving only Tate-Manning's chalked tribute to the Backstreet Boys, "as long as you love me". Tate-Manning's work has a clear seriousness of purpose, intersecting the teenage story of developing individual and national identity with the death of her friend Ali a number of years later.

My Best Dead Friend had a clear appeal for audience members with personal connections to New Zealand, with 39% of respondents currently living or having previously lived in New Zealand, and a further 15% who had visited (in contrast, the majority of *Aunty* respondents at 64% had never been to New Zealand). One *My Best Dead Friend* attendee, who was born in New Zealand and lived there for three decades, described an initial worry based on the opening of the show that it would feature a

> superficial NZ humour, but within 10 minutes it was clear it was so much more than that, I laughed and cried, so touching at times [...] I left completely amazed and touched and tearful and thinking what a country NZ is, what people.
>
> [68, F, Edinburgh]

A respondent to *Aunty* who had lived in New Zealand most of their life described their experience of being the "only New Zealander in the audience and the only person to get the Michael Hill Jeweller jokes" [28, M, London].[3] The London resident became aware that there were Australians and Scottish people in the audience as Cosgrove "wove their nationalities into the narrative" and felt "proud that the audience was appreciating a New Zealand work". The potential divisions in the audience between those who did and did not recognise New Zealand allusions and identity markers within the feedback loop was highlighted by Edinburgh reviewers. Apparently having attended a performance with a higher contingent of New Zealanders than the previous respondent, one reviewer commented that "Cosgrove has friends from home in and they hoot with glee at every obscure New Zealand reference included for their benefit", concluding negatively that "something seems to have been lost in translation here" (Porteous 2019). Upon returning from Edinburgh, Cosgrove told a New Zealand journalist that "she realised this show was best saved for audiences back home [...] the international crowds in Edinburgh appreciated the show and laughed at its humour, but there were some elements only Kiwis would appreciate thoroughly" (Brooker 2019). Relying on the subjectivities of comedy, humour and allusions that might stimulate a New Zealander's feedback loop could exclude audiences who did not have this context and affect the show's portability in the Edinburgh context.

Working on My Night Moves

In contrast, *Working on My Night Moves*, the final show I surveyed, does not consciously attempt to represent New Zealand identity and allusions. The absence of a visible connection to New Zealand within the work is reflected in the geographic profile of respondents, with 97% recording they had never been to Aotearoa New Zealand, and 97% had not seen any other New Zealand shows at the 2019 Fringe (53% of the respondents resided in England, 23% in Edinburgh, 12% elsewhere in Scotland, with 3% each from Wales, Belgium, Germany and Italy). However, the survey did record that 21% of respondents had been to New Zealand shows performed in Edinburgh in previous years, with Julia Croft's *If There's Not Dancing at the Revolution, I'm Not Coming* and *Power Ballad* listed, as well as the Binge Culture company and *The Basement Tapes*, all of which had been previously performed at Summerhall. Like Modern Māori Quartet, Croft had built a following through repeated tours to Edinburgh, with six respondents reporting they came to *Night Moves* on the strength of Croft's previous work. Other reasons that were cited for attending included the show's recommendation by critic Lyn Gardner and *Night Moves'* inclusion in the Total Theatre shortlist, demonstrating the influence of "expert" validation in selecting shows (*Night Moves* went on to win the 2019 Total Theatre award for Best Physical & Visual Theatre).

Croft began developing *Working on My Night Moves* during Rough Mix NZ in May 2018, with Creative New Zealand funding artists and Scottish company Magnetic North to deliver an Auckland version of the artist development programme. Development continued during a week's residency at Battersea Arts Centre in London, where Croft was also performing a season of *Power Ballad* in June 2018. Influenced by "The 13 Tenants of Future Feminism" (conceived by Anohni, Kembra Pfahler, Johanna Constantine, Bianca Casady, Sierra Casady for the Future Feminism exhibition in Aarhus, Denmark 2017), Croft, director Nisha Madhan and scenographer Meg Rollandi sought to explore how power could be alternatively conceived through feminist futurism, by "taking the traditional world of theatre and building new worlds out of what's already in the space" (Brooks 2019). For *Working on My Night Moves'* debut at Auckland's Basement Theatre in March 2019, the show was performed without a seating block, meaning the audience was able to move about the room as Croft (de)constructed the space, rigging and focusing lights, moving technical equipment and suspending objects from a ceiling, "a method for dispersing power in the room" (Essuah 2019). The negotiation of space between Croft and the audience, and audience and audience, offered a potent layer of meaning to the work; as Auckland reviewer India Essuah (2019) commented, "even as Croft is actively deconstructing the hierarchy in the room, we're inadvertently propping it up". This element had to be compromised for the Edinburgh season, as Summerhall was unable to programme the work in a space in which these proximal conditions could be achieved. As a technically challenging show *Night Moves* could not easily be set up and struck under typical Fringe timeframes, and *Night Moves* was given the final timeslot of 9:55pm in the Old Lab to accommodate a lengthier pack down.

A trace of the audience configuration from *Night Moves'* Auckland season remains in the Edinburgh version, with audience initially standing behind a star cloth in the corner of the room; the cloth drops and Croft swings a light in time to Bob Segar's song "Night Moves".[4] A lighting cue indicates when the audience can enter the Old Lab seating block, and we remain in these seats for the remainder of the performance. *Night Moves'* dramaturgy is structured around Croft (at times joined by operator Anna Bennington), resetting the space and lighting rig for each section of the work, drawing attention to the often unseen labour of production. Edinburgh reviewer Ian Abbott (2016) gives an account of the show's various images:

> dangling seats (on a safety chain) above the audience, tailoring suits made of tinfoil, dropping parcans from the lighting rig dangling just above the floor and invoking some sort of poetic fever dream of Judy Garland's Dorothy from *The Wizard of Oz*.

Participants recorded responses to their experience of the work which ranged from "very positive" [25, M, Edinburgh] to "disconnected, excluded and bored" [57, F, UK]. I would categorise 8 of the responses as more negative than positive, with 24 more positive than negative (a pronounced division compared to the generally positive responses for the other 4 surveyed works). Audiences who answered positively appreciated the "suspension of the need of understanding and sudden meanings filling my own version of it" [32, M, Milan] and saw the work as an "engaging and compelling invitation to feel out chaos and non-hierarchical structures of meaning" [33, F, Leeds]. A respondent who reported a negative experience described feeling

> a bit lost, frustrated, I was trying to like it because I care about work that deconstructs the act of performance, and I think the artist has made bold choices which are exciting but I was ultimately confused and bored sadly.
> [38, M, Bristol]

It is interesting to note the criteria used here to judge the performance, with the feelings of confusion and boredom experienced during the performance contributing to the negative appraisal. Another expressed, "I didn't understand what was happening throughout, there was too little information to give an impression of the meaning" [23, F, Birmingham], contrasting with the positive response that valued the show precisely because it suspended the need for understanding. Performed without any dialogue from Croft, it is understandable that the meanings and intentions of the work can remain opaque in performance, as captured in some of the survey responses; it is possible that if a programme had been provided, audience could have been guided towards a clearer interpretative frame of reference for the work as an expression of feminist utopia, which may have settled some anxiety around interpreting the work.

The survey's final question, asking respondents to consider what impressions, if any, of Aotearoa New Zealand, that they directly associated with the work, was particularly leading in relation to *Night Moves*, as many audience members "had no idea it was a NZ show" [32, Did not say, Manchester] and if it were not for the intervention represented by my research, may have left the performance without this knowledge. A number of respondents recorded "no impression" [76, F, Wigan] and that they "didn't place it anywhere geographically" [31, F, Edinburgh]. My survey question did prompt some respondents to suggest they had gained an impression of New Zealand as a place where "interesting experimental theatre" is being created [26, F, Manchester] and would be "interested to keep seeing work from Aotearoa/NZ in the future, and particularly from these makers" [28, F, Edinburgh]. Another responded that "I didn't know that the show was from here so at the time nothing, but now I know I think it's great they are supporting artists to take the work to the Fringe" [45, F, Brighton]. While the work's New Zealand origins was not a perceptible influence on motivating audience to attend the work, and none of the respondents perceived the work to be directly about New Zealand, drawing attention to the work's place of creation through the survey did result in some audience suggesting their impression of New Zealand had been enhanced. This appears to have been influenced by the respondents valuing the experimental/live art performance represented by *Night Moves*, connecting New Zealand with positive attributes for supporting the creation of such work. Conversely, a respondent who had a negative impression of *Night Moves* reported gaining a negative impression of New Zealand as a country that produces shows that are "fairly inaccessible to all except those with some degree of literacy in art" [26, M, Edinburgh].

Making sense of the survey

Evaluating the overall survey data suggests there is evidence that Creative New Zealand's repeated investment in supporting tours to the Edinburgh Festival Fringe has resulted in Aotearoa New Zealand's theatre being associated in Edinburgh with the values of quality and innovation, with some audience specifically seeking out work originating from the country. An audience member who attended *My Best Dead Friend* commented that "for the last couple of years, I have been specifically looking out for New

Zealand acts at the Fringe as I have had a consistently good experience of watching theatre and comedy from New Zealand" [27, F, Edinburgh], and a viewer of *Two Worlds* who grew up in New Zealand said he always looked for New Zealand shows in the Fringe brochure [76, M, Glasgow]. Overall, a quarter of respondents (24.35%) reported attending other New Zealand shows at the 2019 Edinburgh Fringe, with a similar number having attended New Zealand shows at previous Fringes (26.95%). A Slightly Isolated Dog's *Jekyll and Hyde* was cited the most times attended by a quarter of those who affirmed they had been to other New Zealand works in 2019. Performing at the Piccolo at Assembly George Square Gardens, A Slightly Isolated Dog doubled their audience numbers in 2019 compared to their Edinburgh Fringe debut at 2018, selling 3,000 tickets (Peters 2019). It is possible that A Slightly Isolated Dog's high citation in my data is partly due to the company distributing the booklet listing the New Zealand shows at Edinburgh at the end of each of performance (with the cast adopting French accents, the company's New Zealand identity is otherwise invisible). While Creative New Zealand's strategy of supporting and promoting a cluster of New Zealand works to tour to Fringe appears to have had only a minor impact on encouraging audiences in Edinburgh to attend multiple New Zealand works each year, I observed that the large contingent of New Zealand artists at the 2019 Fringe created a support network, with offstage socialising and solidarity with fellow New Zealanders an important feature of the experience for the artists. The abandonment of the NZ at Edinburgh model in favour of investing money for individual companies to develop their own brand in the market, as discussed in the previous chapter, appears to be working for theatre makers attending multiple Fringes for whom the Aotearoa New Zealand context is irrelevant (A Slightly Isolated Dog, Julia Croft) as well as those for whom it is central to the marketing of the show (Modern Māori Quartet).

A final question that I had regarding the survey data was how the audience would self-report the ways that they personally connected or identified with each show. What insights could I gleam regarding the meanings that could be produced when these shows were placed in the Edinburgh context and made available within the common space? A minority reported they did not find a connection with the work. A respondent to *My Best Dead Friend* explained that "unfortunately I didn't feel I connected particularly, and wondered maybe If I was the wrong age to understand some of the references"; however, the same respondent said that they did revisit their 17-year-old experience [55, F, Edinburgh]. This suggests that one way of receiving Tate-Manning's story was to parallel and contrast the audience member's memories of experiences at the same age, but this also confronted the audience with cultural and generational differences. A few of the *Working on My Night Moves* responses were in the vein of "the show felt too vague to connect with, I have no idea what happened" [23, F, Birmingham], but the survey prompts also generated some very personal reflections: "The scene with the pile of chairs [...] reminded me of feelings I have had of frustration verging on madness" [26, M, Edinburgh];

"it reminded me of myself when I'm in a slow, creative, destructive, playful, day dreamy mood in my house when I move furniture around/edit clothes/ listen to music, when I am both flippant and diligent, spontaneous and specific" [26, F, Manchester].

The patterns of responses add further nuance to the argument I have pursued in this book that when a production is placed in a non-local context there is a tendency for audiences to interpret the work based on perceptions of what is shared in common, generalising the cultural specificities of the performance representations to apply to their own context. Many of the responses from *Two Worlds* audience members about what they personally connected or identified with generalised the themes of the work without reference to the specificity of the Aotearoa cultural context: "stories of missed opportunities and regrets, not telling our loved ones how we feel, not acting before it's too late" [37, F, London]; "the show was more about the universal human experience of life and death" [51, F, Edinburgh]. Similarly, responses to *Super Hugh-Man* demonstrated some in the audience were transferring the specificities of the work to their own contexts: "my husband is a big man (used to pull fire engines) who went to drama school and had an argument over ballet!" [48, M, London]. None of *Aunty*'s respondents specifically referenced New Zealand when answering the connection/identification prompt, but mentioned finding equivalence with their own family relationships, which made "the performance very relatable and nostalgic" [25, M, Utrecht]. Respondents to *My Best Dead Friend* connected to the play's depiction of loss and grief and "feeling on the outside while being part of a close friend group" [27, F, Edinburgh]. Tate-Manning herself reported that she would often get audience commenting that they felt like she was talking about their own town: "there's something quite universal about the experience of being young and bursting to get out and be free" (Blake 2019). This is supported by a respondent who answered in detail:

A few years ago, I briefly toyed with the idea of coming to study in New Zealand, specifically in Otago. So having the town described so specifically to me was quite surreal as in a way it gave me the opportunity to imagine that alternative pathway I didn't end up choosing to take. I personally connected with the description of the character's close friendship group as I had a similarly close group of friends growing up who were always round at each other's houses. [...] I'm fortunate not to have gone through the death of a friend in the way the main character has, but I nevertheless still personally connected with this and empathised with the sadness expressed by the narrator in the description of her experience.
[27, F, Edinburgh]

These responses reflect an interpretative process in which the Aotearoa New Zealand context is necessarily deemphasised as individuals accommodate their own frames of reference and meaning making, the specificity and detailed description of Dunedin in the show potentially making it sound as familiar as the audience's own town. Focusing on the process of identification at an individual level reinforces that this process of transference, in which perceived similarity is privileged over difference, is only a general principle.

One *Two Worlds* respondent gave a detailed account of the specific connection that she perceived her family had with the show, explaining that since she lived in Scotland, her two Māori sons had "very limited opportunity to experience Māori culture and language". The respondent wrote:

> The show was fantastic – so artfully combining humour, musical performance, and such powerful messages to portray the devastating impact of colonisation and ongoing coloniality on the health and well-being of Māori over successive generations. [...] the wee one didn't totally understand the stories that were told; however, he still felt the compelling emotions through the music and waiata. My older boy understood more and it has made a strong impact on him, reinforcing the histories he has been told and has seen unfold within his own whakapapa and living whānau. [...] We identified 100% with all the stories the 'wairua' told within members of our own whānau who died for these exact same reasons – it could not have been more personally meaningful and left us much to discuss as a family after the show.
>
> [44, F, Scotland]

Two Worlds is valued for providing a means for young Māori living overseas to connect with and reinforce markers of cultural identity. Influenced by the life history of these viewers, this is an intensely personalised example of meaning making that experiencing *Two Worlds* generated for these particular audience members. The specificity of such responses provide a counter narrative to the market-driven outcomes often privileged in the Edinburgh context of box office, critical reception and interest from presenters and programmers. Instead, the value of an international tour could – and should – ultimately be placed in the highly individualised ways a production can resonate for audiences.

Notes

1 Although CNZ no longer pursued the unified marketing and promotion of the NZ at Edinburgh seasons in 2014 and 2017, it has continued to produce and distribute the collateral that showcases all the New Zealand work performing at the Fringe every year.
2 Compared with data from the 2018 Edinburgh Festival Fringe that recorded that 58% of overall attendees lived in Scotland, my survey recorded a higher proportion of respondents who had come from outside of Scotland (The City of Edinburgh Council 2019).
3 Cosgrove retained many idiosyncratic New Zealand references in the show for the Edinburgh season, including gym chain Les Mills and Michael Hill Jeweller.
4 A number of survey respondents mentioned their frustrations of being unable to see this section.

References

Blake, Elissa. 2019. "My Best Dead Friend: Chalkin' about a Revolution". *Audrey Journal*. Last modified September 23, 2019. www.audreyjournal.com.au/arts/my-best-dead-friend-riverside-parramatta-preview/

Brooker, Sally. 2019. "'Aunty' Gets Ready for Retirement". *Oamaru Mail*. Last modified October 4, 2019. www.oamarumail.co.nz/whats-on/aunty-gets-ready-for-retirement/

Brooks, Sam. 2019. "What a Feminist Future Could Look Like: Julia Croft on Working on Her Night Moves". *The Spinoff*. Last modified March 7, 2019. http://thespinoff.co.nz/society/07-03-2019/what-a-feminist-future-could-look-like-julia-croft-on-working-on-her-night-moves/

Brownlee, Irene. 2019. "Modern Māori Quartet Two Worlds". *Radio Summerhall Reviews*. Last modified August 18, 2019. https://radiosummerhallreviews.wordpress.com/2019/08/18/modern-maori-quartet-two-worlds/

The City of Edinburgh Council. 2019. "Edinburgh by Numbers". *Edinburgh*. Last modified January 18, 2020. www.edinburgh.gov.uk/downloads/file/25200/edinburgh-by-numbers-2019

Cornwell, Tim. 2019. "Theatre Review: My Dead Best Friend". *The Scotsman*. Last modified August 21, 2019. www.scotsman.com/arts-and-culture/edinburgh-festivals/theatre-review-my-dead-best-friend-summerhall-edinburgh-1-4988368

Edinburgh Team. 2019. "Edinburgh 2019: Modern Māori Quartet on Inviting You into Their Garage Gig Memories". *theXreport*. Last modified July 30, 2019. http://thexreport.org/2019/07/30/edinburgh-2019-modern-maori-quartet-on-inviting-you-into-their-garage-gig-memories/

Essuah, India. 2019. "Feminist Futures: A Review of *Working on My Night Moves*". *The Pantograph Punch*. Last modified March 13, 2019. www.pantograph-punch.com/post/review-working-on-my-night-moves

Freshwater, Helen. 2009. *Theatre & Audience*. London: Red Globe Press.

Kendall, Gavin, Ian Woodward and Zlatko Skrbiš. 2009. *The Sociology of Cosmopolitanism: Globalization, Identity, Culture and Government*. Hampshire: Palgrave Macmillan.

Peters, Leo Gene. 2019. Interviewed by James Wenley. Wellington. December 3.

Porteous, Lewis. 2019. "Review: Aunty". Last modified August 1, 2019. www.festmag.com/edinburgh/comedy/review-aunty

Ralph, Charlie. 2019. "Aunty @ Assembly George Square". *The Skinny*. Last modified August 19, 2019. www.theskinny.co.uk/festivals/edinburgh-fringe/comedy/aunty-assembly-george-square

Sedgman, Kirsty. 2019. "On Rigour in Theatre Audience Research". *Contemporary Theatre Review*, 29 (4): 462–479.

Selvarajan, Sums. 2019. Interviewed by James Wenley. Edinburgh. August 22.

Vile, Gareth K. 2019. "Māori Musical Theatre Magic". *The List*. Last modified August 19, 2019. http://edinburghfestival.list.co.uk/article/110836-super-hugh-man/

——— 2019. "Modern Māori Quartet: Two Worlds". *The List*. Last modified August 25, 2019. http://edinburghfestival.list.co.uk/article/111084-modern-maori-quartet-two-worlds/

9   Cultural apocalypse

The Generation of Z: Apocalypse in London

In July 2015 I travelled to London to research and experience *The Generation of Z: Apocalypse*, the immersive theatre show which invites participants to imagine themselves as survivors of a Zombie apocalypse. The show was described to potential London audience members thus:

> It is 2015. London has fallen. The deadly Z virus is transforming the global population into a rabid horde of the infected [...]. *The Generation of Z: Apocalypse* is the immersive live experience that puts you squarely into the dark heart of a zombie massacre. With chaos unfolding around you, prepare to be thrust into your very own action movie, where your choices directly influence the show's narrative and outcome.
>
> ("The Show" 2015)

In this version of immersive theatre, the audiences become spectator-participants within the story, acting as supporting characters.. The story revolves around the audience as the group that the Armed Rescue Coalition (ARC) soldiers must keep alive long enough to rescue and complete their mission.

From the outside, *The Generation of Z*'s location, Dept. W, looked like any other building on the busy commercial street in Whitechapel – the doorway was neighboured by a Tesco Mart and a bar. Inside, the art department converted the venue into an abandoned military base over two levels. Before entry we were briefed to "make our voices heard", and then we entered a large basement.[1] On the walls were multiple posters with the faces of missing persons, some posters featuring handprints in blood. When all the audience had arrived, a steel gate was loudly slammed shut by an usher. An audience member (in actuality an actor planted in the audience) began coughing up blood, and nearby spectators screamed. Each time I observed the show in London (four performances in total), the audience reacted by moving back to the corners of the room, isolating the audience plant in the centre of the space. Then the ARC team arrived: Sarge, their leader; the callow rookie soldier; Moose, the gung-ho would-be hero; Frosty, the female soldier; and Link, the communications expert. When a horde of Zombies arrived and began shaking the gate, the soldiers ordered the audience deeper into the complex. This split the audience into two groups, which were split again soon after. This meant an audience member experienced one of four possible storylines per performance: a quest to find the medical bay to save the injured rookie soldier; an encounter with the base's scientist, who purports to have a cure for the Zombie virus; the rescue of a military officer from the base's prison; and the dilemma surrounding what to do about a pregnant woman, infected with the virus, who is about to give birth.

The Generation of Z: Apocalypse was a strange experience. There I was in London, participating in an imagined-Zombie apocalypse, produced by a company from New Zealand. A number of the actors were New Zealand locals, but there was no explicit acknowledgement of the show's national origins. *The Generation of Z* has been localised for each host city it plays in, and hybridises the popular culture zeitgeist of Zombie media, for example, US drama *The Walking Dead* (2010–), with a *Resident Evil* (1996–) video game format. Reflecting global trends, the colonial imposition of British culture in New Zealand has been superseded by American popular culture, which *The Generation of Z*'s use of Zombie media represents. *The Generation of Z* is both New Zealand intellectual property and a consciously Western-global theatre product that does not want to be limited by national borders. Aotearoa New Zealand identity has been placed at the margin in the hopes of gaining lucrative access to the overseas market by engaging with globally popular entertainment forms and stories.

The Generation of Z: Apocalypse is one manifestation of a wider contemporary trend in New Zealand theatre toured globally that does not engage with the cultural work of representing the nation within its content. In Chapter 6 we observed this with Indian Ink Theatre Company, which creates transnational theatre orientated towards the global market. While its first three plays were primarily made with a local New Zealand audience in mind, and the New Zealand context was, therefore, emphasised, in subsequent works toured to overseas markets, the conscious exploration of the New Zealand context is largely absent. Co-founder Justin Lewis (2016) says that "for us the New Zealand component is not essential". In Chapter 7 we have also seen a number of cases of New Zealand-originated work toured to the Edinburgh Fringe that are uninterested in displaying markers of New Zealand society, complicating curational attempts at branding and projecting a coherent image of cultural identity and nationhood as a means of gaining exposure and attention within this marketplace. At the 2014 Fringe, Barnie Duncan's *Calypso Nights* countered the NZ at Edinburgh season and Duncan rejected the premise of CNZ's project:

I'm not interested in making works that are specific to New Zealand so I didn't want to create a character that traded off that whole

'New Zealand in Edinburgh' thing [...]. I also tour outside New Zealand quite a lot and I like doing stuff for people who don't know who I am because then you get a more honest response.

(Jewell 2014)

Duncan expresses a desire to avoid cultural expectations that an audience might bring into a work billed as a New Zealand show. As noted in Chapter 7, the majority of works showcased during the 2017 NZ at Edinburgh Fringe season promoted the country's theatrical innovation rather than cultural identities. Binge Culture created *Ancient Shrines and Half Truths* to premiere in Edinburgh, relying on Google Maps to remotely plan the route surrounding Summerhall that audiences would be guided around as part of an app-based experience. Exploring how "places promote themselves as tourist destinations", Binge Culture wanted to design a work "that could be adapted and made specific to a place", becoming local tour guides in Edinburgh (Baxendale 2019). In addition, Barnie Duncan returned to Edinburgh with his premiere of *Juan Vesuvius: I Am Your Deejay*, and the performers of *La Vie Dans un Marionette* (2013) adopted faux-French accents.

Julia Croft (2019) – who toured as a performer and co-creator of *If There's Not Dancing at the Revolution, I'm Not Coming* (2015), *Power Ballad* (2016) and *Working on My Night Moves* (2019) to the Edinburgh Festival Fringe in 2016, 2017 and 2019 respectively – states that the work that she makes is "very consciously not for New Zealand". Engaged with feminist and queer politics, resisting patriarchal and capitalist systems of oppression, Croft (2019) is motivated to speak to global discursive contexts rather than "speaking to New Zealand" or a "specific place or culture". Croft explained to me that she feels valued overseas "as an artist in a way that I don't in New Zealand", contrasting enthusiastic responses from UK audiences with a "lukewarm" reception to her work in New Zealand, compounded by what she identifies as the country's anti-intellectualism (Croft). Producer Lydia Zanetti (2019) agrees that there is a context, history and lens for live art/performance art in the UK that does not exist in New Zealand. While Croft (2019) continues to develop work in New Zealand, she perceives that for her own sustainability she needs to create work for an internationalist discourse, untied to place, that will find a constituency in the global market.[2] Croft (2019) says that she does not front or talk about her New Zealandness in any interviews that she gives overseas and does not perceive her national origins to be a draw for any audience. As discussed in the previous chapter, this is supported by the data I collected from those attending *Working on My Night Moves* in Edinburgh, with many ticket holders unaware of Croft's New Zealand connection until I surveyed them. Croft's New Zealand invisibility is reflected in published reviews of the season, with only 2 out of 14 reviews referencing Croft's nationality. Conceived as live art, *Working on My Night Moves* "cannot be held in any singular cultural boundary or place, but occupies many" (Keidan 2006: 9). The New Zealand incubated context of *Working on My Night Moves* is seen as irrelevant to the framing, interpretation or reception of the show internationally: Croft's work travels as a simulacrum without an identifiable origin.

A Slightly Isolated Dog also chooses not to foreground New Zealand national origin when touring. In *Don Juan* (2015) and *Jekyll and Hyde* (2016), which toured to the Edinburgh Fringe in 2018 and 2019 respectively, the company announced itself to audiences as a "really famous French theatre troupe", employing "a specific stereotype that the English-speaking world has of the French" (Peters 2019). While anecdotally some audience members have believed the company to really consist of French nationals, the Gaulier Le Jeau style gag is that the troupe is consciously projecting inauthenticity (the actors are not permitted to speak any French language); however, the troupe's originating New Zealand context remains invisible (Peters). I witnessed this first hand as I waited in line to see *Jekyll and Hyde* in Edinburgh, with the ticket holders in front of me furiously debating where the troupe actually travelled from, with one person convinced they were from Ireland. Influenced by the highly interactive nature of their work, location-specific material is added for each geographic location the troupe perform in, localising their versions of the Western canonical narratives *Don Juan* and *Jekyll and Hyde*. Director Leo Gene Peters (2019) explains that they "just try to play with the local [...] it's important for the work that it exists in this moment, right now, with us here".[3] As with the work of Julia Croft, A Slightly Isolated Dog's New Zealand origin is immaterial to its portability within the global marketplace.

Dramaturge Fiona Graham (2013: 251) suggests that theatre makers "will want to make work that moves beyond the familiar and national frontiers. New Zealand practitioners have fought hard to tell their own stories but now [that] this work is established they can look outwards and make new connections". The works discussed above signal a potential maturation in Aotearoa New Zealand theatre's overseas experience with theatre makers adopting a global outlook, without the need to represent and present New Zealand-specific cultural identities to international audiences in order to have that culture affirmed (or, at least, signals a continuation of the internationalist interests pursued by Red Mole Enterprises in the USA during the 1980s). However, embodied by the international production history of *The Generation of Z: Apocalypse*, the focus of this chapter, this trend also signals the possibility of a kind of *cultural* apocalypse, in which Aotearoa New Zealand identity in theatre is increasingly homogenised or devalued as productions pursue globality as a means to enter the global marketplace. I begin with an overview of *The Generation of Z*'s development as it moved from Auckland, Christchurch, Edinburgh and London. I then discuss the relevance or otherwise of the show's originating New Zealand context when it was performed in London, and conclude with an analysis, based on my multiple experiences of the show, of the positionality of the audience in relation to the work's immersive form – are we active agents, or globalised Zombie consumers?

Case study: *The Generation of Z: Apocalypse*

Unleashing the virus

The Generation of Z producer Charlie McDermott's interest in developing a work utilising an immersive form was influenced by experiencing two works: *Apollo 13: Mission Control* (2008), created by New Zealanders Kip Chapman and Brad Knewstubb, and *Sleep No More* (2003), created by British company Punchdrunk Theatre, which has been running in New York City since 2011. Immersive theatre is a porous concept, used to describe "diverse events that assimilate a variety of art forms and seek to exploit all that is experiential in performance" (Machon 2013: 22). Generally, the term is used to describe theatre that involves high levels of audience interactivity, mobility and involvement, with events happening around them and to them. In *Apollo 13*, the audience is cast as Mission Control during the historical space mission of April 1970 and are given tasks to assist the actors to help bring the space shuttle and crew safely back to earth after an explosion damages the ship's service module.[4] These participatory immersive principles are not new and can be traced back through Grotowski, Artaud or even further back to the Medieval Mystery Cycles and so on. What is of significance is how companies like Punchdrunk have commodified the form as a genre and marketed the interactivity for contemporary audiences. In Punchdrunk's productions the audiences are free to roam in detailed and tactile spaces; in *Sleep No More* the audience find themselves in a 1930s hotel-like environment built over a number of levels. Audience members are required to wear a beak-shaped mask, which can be emboldening, giving a feeling of anonymity as performers and other audience members are prevented from scrutinising your facial responses. Punchdrunk has been criticised for privileging the experiential over the narrative, a dissatisfaction shared by McDermott. His goal was to combine the immersive form with a Hollywood plot structure, which he believed would result in a more fulfilling experience. Like the New Zealand theatre makers of *Apollo 13*, who used American culture as their subject, the creators of *The Generation of Z* did not seek to tell a New Zealand story.

Writers, David Van Horn and Simon London, and producers, Charlie McDermott and Beth Allen, debuted the first incarnation of the show under the title *Apocalypse Z* in Auckland's Aotea Square in 2013 (Benjamin Farry later joined the writing team from the Edinburgh season onwards). Despite its promise of interactivity, most of the show took place in a large shipping container with the traditional separation of the audience/performer relationship intact. For a 2014 Christchurch season (under the title *Zombie: Red Zone*, referencing the Central Business District exclusion zone put in place after the 2011 Christchurch Earthquake) the producers secured an abandoned warehouse and developed a new site-specific version of the show. The show's box office potential is limited by the use of the immersive form. As the size of the audience who participate in the event increases, the more an individual audience member's experience of the work will be diluted because there are fewer opportunities for interactivity. For the Christchurch season the creators experimented with splitting audiences across two simultaneous storylines in order to have a larger capacity while maintaining an intimate interactive experience. The company continued with the two-storyline approach during their three-week season at the 2014 Edinburgh Festival Fringe, redeveloping their show for Edinburgh around a carpark performance space run by Assembly Festival. As noted in Chapter 7, *The Generation of Z* gained the highest audience numbers of the NZ at Edinburgh Fringe shows, adding extra performances and playing to 98% capacity, a notable achievement within the bloated Edinburgh Fringe market.

The Generation of Z's subsequent London season in 2015 was the first time the show was produced under a purely commercial model, without subsidy from Creative NZ. The company was offered a sponsorship deal in which they could use the Whitechapel venue for free for nine months; while this was a considerable saving of £200,000 from the company's half a million cap-italisation, as a venue it presented some crucial disadvantages (McDermott 2015). The East London location, outside of Zone 1 transport area, was a geographic deterrent for potential audiences. The Dept. W venue's lack of an outdoor area meant that budgeted stunts, which included setting a performer on fire, had to be cut, and the creators were forced to substantially reduce the length of the "Zombie Run" in which audience are chased during a dash to safety (McDermott). The reduction of both of these elements impacted the uniqueness of the audience experience and the potential to generate word of mouth and media attention within a competitive market for immer-sive theatre experiences. During the four-month London run, the company performed 200 shows to 17,000 audience members and broke even; in pre-vious seasons, 30% of the audience returned to experience the show again; however, in London, despite there being four different storylines on offer, only 15% returned (McDermott). *The Generation of Z: Apocalypse* was artistically and commercially compromised in its Whitechapel location.

The Generation of NZ?

The Generation of Z was developed with a conscious intention of bringing the show to a global market. As indicated in the Introduction to this book, this was partly motivated by a disillusionment with the New Zealand's arts market, which McDermott (2015) called a "tiny, tiny, tiny speck of an industry in a market where your audience, the general population of New Zealand, do not value the arts in our culture". This echoed the sentiments by Bill Pearson (1952: 212), who, six decades previously, had written that New Zealanders were unwilling to "co-operate" or "speculate about themselves" through the arts, as well as Julia Croft's comments quoted earlier in this chapter. *The Generation of Z* attempted to be freed from the perceived constraints of locality, targeting global performance opportunities and rejecting New Zealand locality in the content of the show. The show was an exportable theatrical product seeking an overseas paradise, where an endless horde of Zombie fans await.

The Generation of Z adapts to place and cultural context as a site-specific work. McDermott (2015) talked about immersing themselves in a place: "The way you market, the way you get volunteers from the community. The show needs to be localised". In Edinburgh, the company created the conceit that they were a New Zealand contingent of soldiers working during an outbreak of the virus in the Scottish city, but from London onwards the decision was made to completely re-localise the show for the host city and, therefore, the actors became British soldiers. Unlike at the 2014 NZ at Edinburgh season, in London the New Zealand connection was downplayed and mostly non-existent in marketing and PR (see Image 9.1).

Emplaced in London, *The Generation of Z* was a New Zealand show only in origin; the show mutates to the conditions of its host body, killing New Zealand locality. In immersive theatre who the audience are, where they come from, and the cultural reference points they bring with them all have an even greater potential to shape the meanings of the work from performance to performance (as evidenced with Indian Ink's *Mrs Krishnan's Party*, as discussed in Chapter 6). Therefore, it is the audience members, even more so than the team's alterations of the story for London, who localise the production by imagining a scenario in which they are trying to survive a Zombie apocalypse

Image 9.1 Promotional image for *The Generation of Z: Apocalypse*, London, UK, 2015. Credit: Oliver Rosser

taking place in Whitechapel. The appeal to a global entertainment culture, represented by the Hollywood and gaming Zombie genre, also denationalises the show. Tom Millward (2015) recalled his "teenage obsession" playing the video game *Resident Evil*: "As I wasted the days and nights away, spending far too many an hour bashing buttons on my PlayStation controller, I wondered what it would be like to actually be in that video game... and now I know!" Audience responses on Twitter mirrored these experiences, such as "Taking part – and I use that expression intentionally – in @GenerationOfZ will be the closest I ever come to appearing in *The Walking Dead*" and "spent my night surviving a Zombie apocalypse, honestly forgot about my own life".[5] Audience members framed their experience in comparison with video game and television media, and the show fulfilled role-play fantasies for its target audience.

Behind the scenes, employing New Zealand actors for the show remained an important goal for the production, although this came under strain with visa rules and local employment requirements (McDermott 2015). With *The Generation of Z* set up as a business in London, rather than as a touring show, the company was obligated to employ local actors, with the London cast made up of a mixture of British and New Zealand actors. Creator-performers David Van Horn, Simon London and Benjamin Farry all had British passports or hereditary visas. Director Michael Hurst had a British passport. Producer Charlie McDermott and Beth Allen acquired entrepreneur visas. The company paid the visa for actor Matthew Sutherland, but could not afford further visas (McDermott). The desire to continue to employ New Zealand actors alongside British actors upheld *The Generation of Z* as a nationalistic enterprise, but the show did not seek to communicate something about New Zealand identity to its audiences. The New Zealand identity was made consciously invisible, and the audience's own individual experience made paramount.

The Zombie audience

Why is the figure of the Zombie so resonant in contemporary global culture as a millennial monster? While the Zombie creature can be traced to Haiti and colonial slavery, by the late 20th century, Marina Warner (2006: 359) argues, it had become "an existential term, about mental and physical enslavement". Eric Hamako (2011: 109) identifies the 2001 film *28 Days Later* as being one of the first to "reimagine Zombies as angry [...], infected with a virus, they are motivated by uncontrollable, animalistic rage", the type that *The Generation of Z* took its cue from in its depiction. Hamako argues this shift was "in part, influenced by contemporary Orientalism", in that "Zombie stories offer audience an opportunity to indulge in these Orientalist narratives without having to recognise the connection to real-life fears of a current Orientalised villain: Muslims" (109–110). As the London production was situated in Whitechapel, with a large Muslim population (a highly visible demographic as I walked to the performance location), there was some potential resonance with anxieties around home-grown Islamic terrorism – anyone could be infected with the Zombie virus, or radical extremism. This was a meaning and fear, however unwarranted, that the particular site made available, but is not one that would necessarily transfer to other locations, and was not a feature of the New Zealand seasons.

The use of the Zombie within immersive theatre further complicates the tension between audience agency and passivity inherent in the format. The liveness of immersive theatre has been conceptualised as a significant appeal to audiences as "the alienation from real intimacy in our workday lives [...] can be addressed by immersive practice, which demands bodily engagement, sensually stimulates the imagination, requires tactility" (Machon 2013: 26). In promoting active engagement within the work, the immersive contract between the performers and audience is one where the audience hold, in theory, heightened agency. Unlike Zombies, our selfhood is acknowledged. Warner (2006: 357) says a Zombie "is a body which has been hollowed out, emptied of selfhood". During the plot line where a father was anxious about having been separated from his daughter, I overheard audience members saying: "We'll get rid of him first". When the father brings his daughter, who had become infected with the virus, back to the group, there were shouts of "kill them!" from the audience. Some participants also clapped when the father eventually killed his Zombie daughter. Representing expendable life, Zombies can reveal desensitisation, with some in the audience quick to call for Zombie deaths to "save" themselves. These audience members engaged with the show as a live version of a video game where you kill to survive, and played along with the genre conventions of the simulation.

In this example, *The Generation of Z* revealed a fear and dehumanisation of the other, promoting the neoliberal ideology of individual self-interest over collective responsibility and, therefore, removal of the cosmopolitan encounter – Zombie lives do not matter. Adam Alston (2013: 3) argues that "immersive theatre is particularly susceptible to co-optation by a neoliberal market given its compatibility with the growing experience industry". Alston says "immersive theatre resembles adventure companies who remove the component of danger from what might otherwise be considered risky activity in order to render it marketable" (13). *The Generation of Z* enacted a fantasy video game experience, simulating violence and fear of terrorist-style attack, but packaging this risk-taking in a safe format. Immersive theatre suggests real tactile experience, but its appeal, especially in *The Generation of Z*, is also its non-realness, that this would never happen in real life. At the end of the show "Zelfies" were encouraged, in which audience members took a photo with a Zombie actor, to post on social media as proof of their experience. On Twitter, attendees boasted about almost dying of "heart failure", or doing a "little panic weewee during the final zombie run!"[6]

Theatre critic Matt Trueman states that the:

> desire to experience more fully is at the heart of immersive theatre, which can place us in situations that we are unlikely to encounter in our everyday

lives [...]. It stands to reason, then, that immersive theatre might be well-suited to tackle the extremities of human experience.

(Machon 2013: 26)

Although a Zombie apocalypse is a fantasy scape, the concept opens reflections of what the individual might be capable of if attempting to survive a social breakdown. The Zombie apocalypse works well within the immersive form when it presents the audience with moral choices. The show featured a moment where the cast exit and the audience believe they are alone, and respond to their apparent moment of agency by calling for death. In this storyline, a "pregnant" actor planted in the audience has her waters break. We learn that she is infected with the Zombie virus, meaning her baby will also be infected. Our solider-protector handed his gun to a hapless audience member and then left the room. "Do I kill her?" the gun holder asked, which set off a rather charged debate amongst the participants, with many advocating for this action. As the pregnant character had been interacting with us as an assumed member up until that point, it was not necessarily obvious initially that they were an actor "plant". Charlie McDermott (2015) recounted an instance in which an audience member was so convinced that the woman was having a miscarriage that the audience member called the emergency services, and the actors had to explain it was not real. Actors during the season also reported witnessing audience members losing control of their bladder and vomiting on the floor. These were extreme cases where the hyper-real immersive environment caused a physiological effect, but on a lesser scale I observed this multiple times during a performance where the audience screamed or rushed to get away from Zombie attacks.

Conversely, a paradox of the immersive form is that it can often be more difficult to get immersed in the story than in a traditional theatre venue because of a heightened awareness of the contrivance of the theatrical event. When the rookie soldier died, some audience members responded with the pantomimic call, "he's still breathing!" Reviewer Jacob Stolworthy (2015) was dissatisfied with the "sporadic sniggers and bursts of unwarranted applause from the faceless mob [that] threatened to derail the performance I saw – a shame considering there were moments I'd genuinely felt as badass as Rick Grimes (minus the sheriff's hat)". Here other audience members had encroached on his fantasy role-play as *The Walking Dead's* hero. Rather than immersing an audience, the show can do the opposite, disrupting any suspension of disbelief. Another potential issue with the form is the extent that the audiences are allowed to influence the narrative. There is potential for the audiences to become Zombie audiences themselves, acting under the illusion of agency, while the actual narratives are tightly scripted and controlled. Despite claims that our choices can influence the show's outcome, when the four audience groups were reunited at the end of the show, the same sequence of events played out each time. One critic complained that it was not "a particularly interactive show" as "for the most part you're ushered through the scenario like a theme park ride" (Nights 2015). Rather than empowering audience agency, the form can produce uncritical Zombie audiences, going through the motions of what the creators expect of them.

During the final sequence of the show, participants were positioned as disposable bodies, Zombie-like, when Link and Frosty turned their guns on us, having decided to terminate us rather than risk our group becoming infected (we were saved from being "shot" just in time by an evacuation team). While audience members had been calling for Zombie deaths throughout the show, now we are dehumanised. This was not the desensitisation of a video game, but a moment of simulation with the potential for critical thought: how would we really behave in such a scenario? Would we close our eyes and wait, or would we surge forward and attack? The irony is that the show ultimately devalued audience members as disposable consumer bodies. We were not individual agents, but passive Zombie consumers of the same globalised cultural product. The familiarity of the Zombie genre was a key part of the show's marketing strategy and appeal, offering a live way to experience the Zombie media popular with the target. The Zombies of *The Generation of Z* resonated as metaphors for terrorist anxieties, entertainment desensitisation and Zombification of millennials, and ultimately of homogenising globalisation, where the same product is consumed everywhere and global sameness is emphasised over national distinctiveness.

The Generation of Z: Apocalypse represents an attempt by New Zealand theatre makers to free themselves from the restraints of locality in order to pursue the experiential economy and a global market for Zombie media products. Any external appeal to New Zealand identity in the London show was cauterised as irrelevant or even a hindrance due to a lingering colonial stereotype of New Zealand being perceived as lesser than compared to Britain. Although I have argued that *The Generation of Z* is uninterested in national culture, it is still worth considering what sort of national culture it does represent – what *kind* of New Zealand play is it? The work fits within a New Zealand identity that is largely associated in the global consciousness with Peter Jackson's *Lord of the Rings* and *The Hobbit* film trilogies, emphasising spectacle and technological (or theatrical) innovation over local culture. If *The Generation of Z* does display a New Zealand identity, it is one that is culture-less, history-less, a blank, a willing participant in the synthesising power of globalisation.

Notes

1 My description of *The Generation of Z: Apocalypse* is based on my notes from watching four performances of the show in July 2015.
2 In addition to Scotland and Ireland, Julia Croft's work has toured to England, Canada, Australia and Singapore.
3 A Slightly Isolated Dog has also licensed a Mandarin version of *Don Juan* for a company in China after producers saw the work in Edinburgh in 2018.

4 *Apollo 13: Mission Control* was toured to Australia in 2011 and to three locations in the USA in 2012/2013 to test the work's viability in the global market. To date, there have been no subsequent seasons.
5 Dan Essex (_danessex). Twitter post. June 27, 2015; Kayleigh (sickperalta). Twitter post. July 2, 2015.
6 Rhian (WONHOJW). Twitter post. July 2, 2015; Dan Robles (ripplepuss). Twitter post. June 29, 2015.

References

Alston, Adam. 2013. "Audience Participation and Neoliberal Value: Risk, Agency and Responsibility in Immersive Theatre". *Performance Research*, 18 (2): 128–138.
Baxendale, Joel. 2019. Interviewed by James Wenley. Wellington. October 10.
Croft, Julia. 2019. Interviewed by James Wenley. Edinburgh. August 21.
Graham, Fiona. 2013. "Catalyst for Change: The Dramaturge and Performance Development in New Zealand". PhD Thesis. University of Auckland.
Hamako, Eric. 2011. "Zombie Orientals Ate My Brain! Orientalism in Contemporary Zombie Stories" in *Race, Oppression and the Zombie*, edited by Christoper M. Moreman and Cory James Rushton. Jefferson, NC: McFarland: 107–123.
Jewell, Stephen. 2014. "Vesuvius Blows His Top in Edinburgh". *NZ Herald*. August 30.
Keidan, Lois. 2006. "This Must Be the Place: Thoughts on Place, Placelessness and Live Art since the 1980s" in *Performance and Place*, edited by Leslie Hill and Helen Paris. Hampshire: Palgrave Macmillan: 8–16.
Lewis, Justin. 2016. Interviewed by James Wenley. Auckland. November 16.
Machon, Josephine. 2013. *Immersive Theatres*. Hampshire: Palgrave Macmillan.
McDermott, Charlie. 2015. Interviewed by James Wenley. London. July 14.
Millward, Tom. 2015. "*The Generation of Z: Apocalypse*". *London Theatre*. Last modified April 27, 2015. www.londontheatre.co.uk/reviews/the-generation-of-z-apocalypse
Nights, Ed. 2015. "The Generation of Z @ Dept W". Last modified May 21, 2015. www.thegizzlereview.com/2015/05/the-generation-of-z-dept-w.html?spref=tw
Pearson, Bill. 1952. "Fretful Sleepers – A Sketch of New Zealand Behaviour and Its Implications for the Artist". Republished in *Fretful Sleepers and Other Essays*. Auckland: Heinemann Educational Books, 1974: 1–30.
Peters, Leo Gene. 2019. Interviewed by James Wenley. Wellington. December 3.
Rebellato, Dan. 2010. *Theatre & Globalization*. Hampshire: Palgrave Macmillan.
"The Show". 2015. *The Generation of Z*. Last modified January 9, 2020. http://web.archive.org/web/20150507080405/http://www.thegenerationofz.com/
Stolworthy, Jacob. 2015. "What to Do in London This Week: *The Generation of Z*". *Esquire*. Last modified January 9, 2020. http://web.archive.org/web/20150529034616/http://www.esquire.co.uk/culture/article/8361/would-you-survive-a-zombie-apocalypse/
Warner, Marina. 2006. *Phantasmagoria*. New York: Oxford University Press.
Zanetti, Lydia. 2019. Interviewed by James Wenley. Auckland. December 1.

Conclusion
Departure, arrival, return

In this book I have tracked the journeys of a range of plays and productions, exploring the potentialities of the cultural meanings that can be produced and generated when a theatrical work – in this case, originating from Aotearoa New Zealand – travels and circulates across social, geographic and market space. Some markers of identity and meaning may travel as a work moves beyond a "home" audience, but the work is always reshaped in the performative encounter with each audience, contracting and expanding meaning and the extent that markers of New Zealandness can be read into and out of a text. The responses that I gathered to the Aotearoa work performed at the 2019 Edinburgh Festival Fringe, highlighted in Chapter 8, provided glimpses into this process, revealing a range of self-reported individual resonances and emphases as spectators reflected on their experience of the event, the extent that they personally connected and identified with the work and any associations that the performance generated that they might link specifically with Aotearoa New Zealand. My personal experience of attending the Aotearoa touring works in Edinburgh was entangled with my own position as a touring researcher from the same country. While theatre may offer an invitation to imaginatively transport us into the fictional or dramatic space, I could not separate these performances from the materiality of their location and placement within Edinburgh. I experienced immense pride in seeing artists that I admired performing there, heightened by the uncanny comparative memory of having viewed two of the works (*Aunty* and *Super Hugh-Man*) previously in New Zealand. What did they mean for *me, now, here*, in Edinburgh?

Having explored in the preceding chapters the meanings that have been implied as various theatrical works have moved across international locations, I am compelled to engage with my own individual reading of *Working on My Night Moves* (2019) by Julia Croft and Nisha Madhan. I have referenced how the production is unconcerned with representing markers of New Zealand identity; Croft (2019) told me that *Night Moves* is "not speaking to New Zealand, a specific place or culture" and "could have been made in Australia or London and been roughly the same". *Night Moves* travelled to Edinburgh with a degree of national invisibility, its New Zealand origins unknown to many of its audiences and unremarked upon in most reviews.

The performance would appear to have constructed a kind of nowhere place, a universal place, a utopic place; in attempting to explore how we might differently conceive social structures and relations, Awam Amkpa's (2004: 2) conception of theatre is well matched to the work's intent, "reflecting a desiring process through which we imagine and live alternative universes". But, when I gazed into the theatrical mirror of *Working on My Night Moves*, what I personally saw reflected back was an identifiably *New Zealand* place.

Within the feedback loop operating between me and *Night Moves*, I perceived markers of New Zealand practice and identity. This was an interpretation that may very well have only been open to me, but nevertheless, was open precisely because of the work's emplacement in Edinburgh in relationship to my own positionality. Croft's performance of technical labour, continually resetting the space – rearranging the rig, attaching safety chains, focussing lights – recalls New Zealand's "do it yourself" mentality, and the pragmatism, influenced by our low pay industry, of practitioners taking on multiple roles, doing it all (performer, director, producer, designer etc.) to eke out a living. Croft's transformation into a tin-foiled astronaut, alone in the universe, is suggestive of the experience of isolation that a New Zealand artist can feel, at the "bottom of the world", removed from centres of theatrical activity. The work's transposition of the iconography of that great American myth, *The Wizard of Oz* (with Croft layering multiple copies of Dorothy's gingham dress onto herself), is highly significant and resonant within a New Zealand context (see Image C.1). Inviting an interrogation of home and travel in relation to the piece, Dorothy's Midwest yearning for "somewhere over the rainbow" registers with the New Zealand theatre makers' yearning for somewhere over *there*, somewhere bigger, a technicolour global market of opportunity. Within the performance we hear a sample of Dorothy's famous line, "there's no place like home", but *Working on My Night Moves* was not playing in Kansas anymore: it had successfully ventured over the rainbow and made it to the Emerald City – the Edinburgh Festival Fringe.

What I saw (or, at least, what thought I saw) in *Working on My Night Moves* is emblematic of the overseas experience of Aotearoa New Zealand theatre. Perceived isolation can be a powerful motivator for our theatre makers to seek communion with an international audience. Croft (2019) acknowledges that the isolation she feels acutely as a practitioner in Aotearoa is a part of the work. She travels because she has found that she can present her avant-garde productions only for so long in New Zealand before she begins to run out of audience; overseas touring can extend the life cycle of a work. Although New Zealand theatre makers may dream, like Dorothy's Oz, of an overseas paradise, the reality behind the Emerald City's curtain is more prosaic. Reaching the global marketplace can be financially and mentally challenging, and there can often be little difference in the monetary return compared to the domestic market (or, when the overseas dream becomes a nightmare, can result in a more substantial monetary loss). What is influential then is the validating and affirming power of international performance. Croft (2019) reported being

Image C.1 Julia Croft in *Working on My Night Moves*, Auckland, 2019. Credit: Andi Crown

"consistently delighted and surprised" about how well her work has been received by audiences in the UK. Bruce Mason (1963) expressed similar satisfaction that, "like some wines", his work travelled when he brought *The End of the Golden Weather* to the 1963 Edinburgh Fringe. The surprise and delight of finding that your little New Zealand piece travels (is mobile and portable) has echoed throughout the overseas experience of Aotearoa theatre. We might think of the stunned response of audiences in Brighton to *Waiora* in 1997, leading playwright Hone Kouka to "realise that we still haven't been completely accepted by New Zealanders" (Huria 1997: 6). It is overseas where you find yourself and find yourself found. In this frame, we can see entry into the global marketplace being motivated by the drive to have very human needs met: to be *seen*, to be *heard*, to be *understood*.

International performance shifts and denaturalises markers of national identity, potentially collapsing distance and difference. The cosmopolitan encounter with otherness is often made safe and comprehensible by emphasising the ways the other is like the self within the common space. This has led to a central contradiction in the performance of Aotearoa New Zealand theatre in the global marketplace: although Aotearoa New Zealand theatre has largely been concerned with establishing its own identity and legitimacy through overseas performance (the New Zealander says: "look how unique we are"), overseas performance destabilises the identity because audiences generally seek equivalence with their own contexts (the international audience says: "look how similar you are to me"). Consider the anecdotes from *Waiora* actor Rawiri Paratene sharing how a Jewish boy told him the play's Māori family reminded him of his own family (Sears 2016: 6), or Anya-Tate Manning reporting how audience members would tell her it felt like she was talking about their own town during her performance of *My Best Dead Friend* (Blake 2019), or Kila Kokonut Krew (2014) sharing a response to *The Factory* by an audience member in Australia who connected the play's story to their own family, moved to tears by the sacrifice their own father had made for them in working in a factory. These types of scenes repeat again and again in a series of three-act cyclical dramas staged in the global marketplace: Act One – Departure; Act Two – Arrival; Act Three – Return. The acts might take place over the duration of one night for an audience member, to potentially many months for a touring company. The departure by audience and performers into the unknown is weighed with expectation, a charged encounter takes place upon arrival, and hopefully, to borrow a lyric from another *Wizard of Oz* adaptation, both parties are "changed for the better" upon return.

A tension running through this study has been the oppositionality of locality and globality; the local attempts to become the global by entering international markets, inevitably displacing locality as work from one local is emplaced in another. In *Theatre and Globalization*, Dan Rebellato (2010: 10) puts forward the view that "the most significant thing about the theatre is that it is not global, but firmly, resistantly local", then immediately also offers the counter argument, that it is "the most globalised expression of human culture there is". Similarly, Pirkko Koski and Melissa Sihra (2010: x) argue that "theatre and performance events, because of their often inherent localism, have become globally more important than ever". One manifestation of the local versus global tension has been the desire to both embrace and reject distinct national and cultural identities in the theatre of Aotearoa New Zealand. Settler-invader society has an acute insecurity about its own lack of identity, so is especially anxious to fill this blank. The Pākehā/Anglo–New Zealander desires to demonstrate their belonging with their New Zealand home, thus attempts to establish a naturalised national identity through drama utilising self-referential markers of belonging. Repetition becomes a function of this identity formation through the repeated attempt to secure overseas performance to gain recognition and validation.

Over the past 30 years we can observe a significant shift towards transnational storytelling and a growing number of international touring works uninvolved with the need and motivation to construct and transmit a New Zealand identity to overseas markets. In the previous chapter I questioned whether such work, exemplified by *The Generation of Z: Apocalypse*, marks a maturing of New Zealand theatre makers in the global marketplace. There is some symmetry that *The Generation of Z* provided the case study in the final chapter of this book, and the Kiwi Concert Party provided the first case study in Chapter 1. They complement each other as products of popular entertainment in their periods, British-style concert parties versus Zombie media, the perfect travelling partners on their overseas experiences. Placing these cases together disrupts a progressive narrative where, after the battle for a national theatre has been won, artists are free to move past "national frontiers" (Graham 2013: 251). Anyone can tell global stories that homogenise culture to represent everywhere and nowhere. But choosing the global over the local in order to travel the global marketplace with national invisibility can be another means of avoiding a confrontation with the troubling aspects of the Pākehā identity and the politics of belonging in the imagined community of Aotearoa. The cultural labour of defining and representing markers of contemporary Aotearoa instead was largely carried by non-Pākehā theatre makers. Although locality can collapse due to homogenising globality, it can be consolidated and renewed as a resistance to this pressure. As a fluid fantasy, I am not convinced that a renewed emphasis on national identity is necessarily the answer, but it is my contention that a re-commitment to the specificities of the local, informed by intersections of globality and transnational influences, is a good *place* to begin.

As we enter the 2020s, theatre from Aotearoa continues to circulate widely throughout the global marketplace. We need only look at a snapshot of activity over recent months to appreciate both the range of New Zealand work and the range of markets being visited. Shortly after seeing *Working on My Night Moves* in Edinburgh, I was able to watch the European premiere of *Anahera* (2017) by Emma Kinane at the Finborough Theatre, London, as part of its month-long September season in 2019, performed true to label by a London company (which included two New Zealand actors living in the UK).[1] A drama in which Anahera, a young Māori social worker, supports a Pākehā family whose 11-year-old son has gone missing, Kinane interrogates cultural assumptions around parenting – the play's simmering bicultural tensions are directly relevant to the New Zealand context, but finds relevance in the UK as a "deft satire of class, race and family values" (Akbar 2019). Meanwhile, performer Julia Croft and producer Lydia Zanetti went from Edinburgh to Glasgow, Cambridge and Brighton with a tour of *Power Ballad* through September; Anya Tate-Manning and *My Best Dead Friend* went to Sydney to share her story of 1990s Dunedin at Riverside Paramatta alongside Trick of the Light's *Tröll* in October, and the Modern Māori Quartet embarked on an Asia tour to South Korea, Tokyo and China (October–November). Auckland Theatre Company's production of *Still Life with Chickens* (2018) by David Fa'auliuli Mamea also toured to China as part of Shanghai Grand Theatre's inaugural international theatre season in December. The Pop-Up Globe, a temporary scaffold replica of Shakespeare's Globe, first established in Auckland in 2016, announced that its 2019/2020 season of Shakespeare plays would be its last in New Zealand while the company pursues international touring. Having played to over 650,000 people in Auckland, Melbourne and

Sydney in the past four years, it already has a claim to be New Zealand's most commercially successful contemporary international theatrical venture (Elephant Publicity 2019).[2]

As I write this conclusion in January 2020, Tusiata Avia's *Wild Dogs under My Skirt* (2002) has just made history as the first Sāmoan female ensemble to perform at the off-Broadway SoHo Playhouse, New York (Wilson 2019).[3] The Modern Māori Quartet and *The Contours of Heaven* by Ana Chaya Scotney, Puti Lancaster, Marama Beamish and Owen McCarthy, a verbatim work about the experience of young people living in Te Matau a Māui (The Hawke's Bay, NZ) are also playing at the venue as part of a New Zealand showcase, initiated by SoHo Artistic Director Darren Lee Cole after viewing the works at the Performing Arts Network of New Zealand (PANNZ) Arts Market in March 2019 (Creative New Zealand 2019). Indian Ink continues the USA tour of *Mrs Krishnan's Party* from Virginia (January 25) to Maui, Hawai'i (March 6). In Australia, *Black Ties* by John Harvey and Tainui Tukiwaho, a cross-cultural rom-com created in collaboration between Indigenous companies Te Rēhia Theatre (Aotearoa) and ILBIJERRI Theatre Company (Australia), has debuted at the Sydney Town Hall as part of the Sydney Festival. At the Soho Theatre in London for the London International Mime Festival, Trygve Wakenshaw has opened *Only Bones v1.4*, created by fellow New Zealand artist Thomas Monckton. In February, *Working on My Night Moves* plays the Yard Theatre, London, as part of the NOW Festival. These theatrical activities are extending what Aotearoa New Zealand can mean to audiences in a global context.

These examples demonstrate the ready interest and demand for work from Aotearoa New Zealand in the global theatre marketplace, but there are challenges ahead in sustaining, let alone accelerating, this level of circulation. Our contemporary era is defined by the pressing climate crisis. While a reversal in course from the unprecedented and irrevocable global damage we are rapidly hurtling towards requires urgent multilateral mobilisation from political and corporate leaders, individuals are grappling with changes they can make to their own lifestyles to downsize personal carbon footprints. A slow travel movement eschewing air transport is gathering attention, with school strike climate activist Greta Thunberg's decision to sail to New York to address the United Nations in August 2019 gaining extensive publicity (Timperley 2019). This poses ethical questions for New Zealand theatre makers; as producer Lydia Zanetti (2019) put it, "touring overseas might help towards gaining a more sustainable career, but being sustainable for the planet is not touring overseas". Jo Randerson of Barbarian Productions is on record as saying that Barbarian do not "want to fly around the world to do stuff as a company" as the team does not "like that environmental footprint" (Joe 2019). This is a conversation that appears to still be in its infancy in Aotearoa's theatre community, but it is a conversation that is likely to grow in volume, as more theatre makers include climate sustainability as a crucial factor when weighing up whether to pursue international touring. Following the completion of this manuscript, the global theatrical economy as of June 2020 has collapsed as a result of the Covid-19 coronavirus pandemic, with the suite of public health containment measures including physical distancing, limits on public gatherings and border closures making live performance untenable. It may be that this study has taken on an unanticipated resonance, documenting a period of theatrical activity that has come to a close as we begin a new period marked by the global public health and economic crisis resulting from the pandemic.

What predictions then might we make for the future of Aotearoa New Zealand in the Global Marketplace? It may be that we see an increase in remote touring and digital collaboration, sending formats and scripts overseas instead of bodies. Instead of flying in and out to different markets, companies may attempt lengthier tours or more sustained seasons in a particular locale, potentially leading to a more meaningful communal relationship with overseas localities. Regardless, should international touring rebound post-pandemic, carbon offsetting needs to become a fundamental budget item for international tours subsidised by Creative New Zealand.[4] Lydia Zanetti (2019) reflects that "there's a certain expectation that we have to travel because we are a travelling nation and we are isolated already". Zanetti worries about the dangers of becoming siloed if Aotearoa's access to the global marketplace was affected by climate change, expressing the importance of "building actual connections, of crossing borders in an increasingly unengaged world". This vision of embodied performance as a connector seems an appropriate place to conclude this study, an act of resistance against the toxic nationalisms and dehumanising and dividing rhetoric that circulate across the contemporary globe. The performances archived in this book demonstrate the utopic potential of theatre to be a means for cross-cultural conversation and understanding – for audiences to see the lives of others onstage and find resonances within their own contexts, one performance at a time.

Notes

1 A small, unsubsidised theatre founded in 1980 above a pub, Finborough Theatre specialises in new writing, musicals and producing work that has not played in London in at least 25 years. The company has a track record of West End transfers.

2 I have previously criticised the Pop-Up Globe (on my website, *Theatre Scenes*) as colonially premised enterprise; the company's tours to Australia recall the 1949 Australian tour by Ngaio Marsh's student company of *Othello* (see Chapter 1).

3 Tusiata Avia toured *Wild Dogs under My Skirt* internationally as a solo performance in the 2000s. The 2020 SoHo Playhouse production was an ensemble cast version of the play that debuted at the Māngere Arts Centre, Auckland, in 2016 directed by Anapela Polata'ivao.

4 Creative New Zealand currently pays for carbon offsetting for the flights of international guests attending the Te Manu Ka Tau Flying Friends programme.

References

Akbar, Arifa. 2019. "Anahera Review". *The Guardian*. Last modified September 6, 2019. www.theguardian.com/stage/2019/sep/06/anahera-review-finborough-theatre-london-maori-social-worker-new-zealand-emma-kinane

Amkpa, Awam. 2004. *Theatre and Postcolonial Desires*. London; New York: Routledge.

Blake, Elissa. 2019. "My Best Dead Friend: Chalkin' about a Revolution". *Audrey Journal*. Last modified September 23, 2019. www.audreyjournal.com.au/arts/my-best-dead-friend-riverside-parramatta-preview/

Creative New Zealand. 2019. "NZ Theatre Picked by SoHo Playhouse for New York Showcase". *Scoop*. Last modified July 24, 2019. www.scoop.co.nz/stories/CU1907/S00250/nz-theatre-picked-by-soho-playhouse-for-new-york-showcase.htm

Croft, Julia. 2019. Interviewed by James Wenley. Edinburgh. August 21.

Elephant Publicity. 2019. "Last Chance to Experience Pop-Up Globe Before It Goes Global". *Scoop*. Last modified August 29, 2019. www.scoop.co.nz/stories/CU1908/S00293/last-chance-to-experience-pop-up-globe-before-it-goes-global.htm

Graham, Fiona. 2013. "Catalyst for Change: The Dramaturge and Performance Development in New Zealand". PhD Thesis. University of Auckland.

Huria, John. 1997. "Mā Te Rēhia e Kawē". *Playmarket News*, 16: 2–7.

Joe, Nathan. 2019. "Voice of an Intergeneration". *Theatre Scenes*. Last modified October 15, 2019. www.theatrescenes.co.nz/preview-sing-it-to-my-face-barbarian-productions/

Kila Kokonut Krew. 2014. Facebook update. June 27. www.facebook.com/92837192322/photos/a.10150095273117323.303062.92837192322/10152601783387323/?type=3&theater

Koski, Pirko and Melissa Sihra. 2010. *The Local Meets the Global in Performance*. Newcastle upon Tyne: Cambridge Scholars Publishing.

Mason, Bruce. 1963. "Edinburgh 1963". *NZ Listener*. November 1. (Edinburgh 1959–65 Scrapbook, Carton 5, Box 2, Bruce Mason Papers, J.C. Beaglehole Room, Victoria University, Wellington)

Rebellato, Dan. 2010. *Theatre & Globlalization*. Hampshire: Palgrave Macmillan.

Sears, Rachel. 2016. "Waiora Te Ū Kai Pō – The Homeland Education Pack". *The Court Theatre*. Last modified January 7, 2020. http://courteducation.org.nz/assets/Education-Packs/Waiora-Education-Resource-web.pdf

Timperley, Jocelyn. 2019. "Why 'Flight Shame' Is Making People Swap Planes for Trains". *BBC*. Last modified September 10, 2019. www.bbc.com/future/article/20190909-why-flight-shame-is-making-people-swap-planes-for-trains

Wilson, Kim Baker. 2019. "New Zealand–Based Play to Make History in US at New York Theatre". *One News*. December 29. www.tvnz.co.nz/one-news/entertainment/new-zealand-based-play-make-history-in-us-york-theatre

Zanetti, Lydia. 2019. Interviewed by James Wenley. Auckland. December 1.

Appendix: Aotearoa New Zealand theatre productions performed overseas

Note: Productions are listed by date of premiere under the name(s) of the playwright(s)/creator(s) or, in some cases, the company's name (listed alphabetically). This is not a complete list of Aotearoa New Zealand theatre produced internationally, but is intended as a reference for the productions mentioned within this book.

Amamus

Gallipoli: Premiered 1974 at Unity Theatre, Wellington, NZ (September). Dir. Paul Maunder.
———— Institute of Contemporary Arts, London, England, UK (October 7–11, 1975).
———— Poland Tour (1975): Fifth International Festival of the Open Theatre, Wrocław (October); subsequently Szczeczin, Gdańsk and Łódź (October–November).

Avia, Tusiata

Wild Dogs under My Skirt: Premiered 2002 at Otago Settlers Museum, Dunedin Fringe Festival, NZ (September 28–October 1). Performed by Tusiata Avia. [Also toured to Australia, Germany, Austria, Russia, Africa and Hawai'i, USA]
———— The SoHo Playhouse, NYC, USA (January 4–18, 2020). Dir. Anapela Polata'ivao, performed by an ensemble.

Balme, Tim

The Ballad of Jimmy Costello: Premiered 1997 at Taranaki Festival of the Arts, NZ (March).
———— Assembly Rooms, Edinburgh Festival Fringe, Scotland, UK (August, 1997). Dir. Simon Bennett, performed by Tim Balme, produced by Tasman Ray and Guy Masterson. [Also toured to Israel]

Bates, Jess Holly

Real Fake White Dirt: Premiered 2014 at Basement Theatre, Auckland, NZ (April 3–5). Dir. Geoff Pinfield, performed by Jess Holly Bates.
——— Sweet Grassmarket, Edinburgh Festival Fringe, Scotland, UK (August, 2014). [Also toured to London, UK; NYC, USA; and Melbourne, Australia]

Baxter, James K.

The Wide Open Cage: Premiered 1959 at Unity Theatre, Wellington, NZ (November). Dir. Richard Campion.
——— Washington Square Theatre, International Drama Council, NYC, USA (December, 1962). Dir. Robert Dahdah.

Belz, Abert

Astroman: Premiered 2018 at the Court Theatre, Christchurch (October 27–November 10). Dir. Nancy Brunning; simultaneously premiered at Fairfax Studio, Arts Centre Melbourne, Melbourne Theatre Company, Australia (October 27–December 8). Dir. Sarah Goodes.

Betts, Jean

Ophelia Thinks Harder: Premiered 1993 at Circa Theatre, Wellington, NZ (October 14–November 13). Dir. Jean Betts.
19 international productions licensed by Playmarket in USA, Australia and Singapore (as of 2018).

Binge Culture

Whales: Premiered 2013 at NZ Fringe, Wellington, NZ (February 16).
——— Assembly George Square, NZ at Edinburgh, Edinburgh Festival Fringe, Scotland, UK (August 5, 6, 12, 13, 19, 20, 2017).
Break Up (We Need to Talk): Premiered 2014 at Matchbox Studios, NZ Fringe, Wellington, NZ (February 8).
——— La MaMa, NYC, USA (March 21, 2015).
——— Basement, Summerhall, NZ at Edinburgh, Edinburgh Festival Fringe, Scotland, UK (August 7, 4, 21, 2017).
——— Australia Tour (2018): Trades Hall, Melbourne Fringe (August); Old 505 Theatre, Sydney Fringe (September).
Ancient Shrines and Half Truths: Premiered 2017 at Summerhall, NZ at Edinburgh, Edinburgh Festival Fringe, Scotland, UK (August 2–27).
——— Melbourne Fringe, Australia (September 18–22, 2019).

Bishop, Eleanor

Jane Doe: Premiered 2015 at Carnegie Mellon University School of Drama, Pittsburgh, USA (November 1). Dir. Eleanor Bishop. [Subsequently performed in various locations throughout USA in 2016]

—— Assembly George Square Studio Two, NZ at Edinburgh, Edinburgh Festival Fringe, Scotland, UK (August 3–28, 2017). Produced by Zanetti Productions.

—— Sydney Fringe, Australia (September 25–29, 2018).

Bright, Rochelle

Daffodils: Premiered 2014 at Q Theatre Loft, Auckland, NZ (March 14–29). Dir. Dena Kennedy, produced by Bullet Heart Collective.

—— Traverse Theatre, Edinburgh Festival Fringe, Scotland, UK (August 4–28, 2016). [Also toured to Australia in 2016 and the Salisbury International Arts Festival, UK, in 2016]

Broughton, John

Michael James Manaia: Premiered 1991 at Downstage, Wellington (February 15–March 9). Dir. Colin McColl, performed by Jim Moriarty.

—— Traverse Theatre, Edinburgh Festival Fringe, Scotland, UK (August 13–31, 1991).

—— Fortyfivedownstairs, Melbourne Arts Festival, Australia (October 10–28, 2012). Dir. Nathaniel Lees, performed by Te Kohe Tuhaka, produced by Taki Rua.

The Canterbury Student Players

Othello (1603) by William Shakespeare and *Six Characters in Search of an Author* (1921) by Luigi Pirandello, Australia Tour (1949): Sydney, Melbourne and Canberra. Dir. Ngaio Marsh.

Chapman, Kip

Apollo 13: Mission Control (with Brad Knewstubb). Premiered 2008 at BATS Theatre, Wellington (October 18–November 11). Dir. Kip Chapman.

—— Sydney Opera House, Australia (March, 2010).

—— Australia Tour (2011): Powerhouse, World Theatre Festival, Brisbane (February 9–20); Studio Underground, State Theatre Centre, Perth International Festival, Perth (February 19–March 7).

—— USA Tour (2012–2013): Tacoma Dome Exhibition Hall, Tacoma, Washington (December 21–30, 2012); Spokane Convention Center, Spokane, Washington (January 9–20, 2013); Milton Rhodes Center for the Arts, Winston-Salem, North Carolina (January 26–February 10, 2013).

The Conch

Vula: Premiered 2002 at BATS Theatre, Wellington, NZ (September 18–29). Dir. Nina Nawalowalo.
———— Festival of Pacific Arts, Palau (July, 2004).
———— The Charter Day Festival, Guam (2005).
———— Playhouse, Sydney Opera House, Australia (June 8–25, 2006).
———— The Vaka Vuku Conference, Suva, Fiji (July, 2006).
———— Australia Tour (2008): Brisbane Powerhouse, Brisbane; World Theatre Congress, Adelaide.
———— Holland Tour (2008): Rotterdam; Leiden; Amsterdam; The Hague; Utrecht.
———— The Pit Theatre, Barbican Centre, London, England, UK (April 23–May 3, 2008). *Masi*: Premiered 2012 at Soundings Theatre, Wellington, NZ (March 2–6). Dir. Nina Nawalowalo and Tom McCrory.
———— The Oceania Centre ITC Theatre, Suva, Fiji (2012).
———— Everest Theatre, Seymour Centre, Sydney Festival, Australia (January 20–25, 2013).
Stages of Change: Premiered 2014 at Solomon Islands (March). Dir. Nina Nawalowalo. [Subsequently performed Papua New Guinea, Sāmoa, and the European Parliament, Brussels]

Cosgrove, Johanna

Aunty: Premiered 2017 at Basement Theatre, Auckland, NZ (September 12–16). Performed by Johanna Cosgrove.
———— The Box, Assembly George Square, Edinburgh Festival Fringe, Scotland, UK (July 31–August 25, 2019). Produced by Zanetti Productions.

Croft, Julia

If There's Not Dancing at the Revolution, I'm Not Coming (with Virginia Frankovich): Premiered 2015 at Basement Theatre, Auckland, NZ (September 2–5). Dir. Virginia Frankovich, performed by Julia Croft.
———— Summerhall, Edinburgh Festival Fringe, Scotland, UK (August 4–28, 2016). [Also toured Australia in 2017 and Singapore and Ireland in 2018]
Power Ballad (with Nisha Madhan): Premiered 2017 at Basement Theatre, Auckland (March 7–11). Dir. Nisha Madhan, performed by Julia Croft, produced by Zanetti Productions.
———— Summerhall, NZ at Edinburgh, Edinburgh Festival Fringe, Scotland, UK (August 2–27, 2017). [Also toured to Australia in 2017 and 2018; UK 2018 and Canada 2019]
Working on My Night Moves (with Nisha Madhan): Premiered Basement Theatre, Auckland, NZ (March 6–23). Dir. Nisha Madhan, performed by Julia Croft, produced by Zanetti Productions.

———— Old Lab, Summerhall, Edinburgh Festival Fringe, Scotland, UK (July 31–August 25, 2019).

———— The Yard Theatre, NOW 20, London, England, UK (February 18–22, 2020).

Daniel, Laura

Two Hearts: The Comeback Tour (with Joseph Moore): Premiered 2019 at Q Theatre Loft, Auckland, NZ (July 17–19).

———— Cowgate, Big Belly, Underbelly, Edinburgh Festival Fringe, Scotland, UK (August 1–25, 2019).

Daniels, Erina

Party with the Aunties (devised with the cast): Premiered 2011 at the Garage, Wellington, NZ (April 9–15).

———— Festival of Pacific Arts, Guam (May to June, 2016).

Downes, Catherine

The Case of Katherine Mansfield: Premiered 1978 (See Heartache and Sorrow).

———— Southwark Playhouse, Air New Zealand Season of Kiwi Theatre, Festival of New Zealand Arts, London, England, UK (July 15–August 2, 1997). Performed by Catherine Downes.

Downstage

Hedda Gabler (1891) by Henrik Ibsen (adaptation by dir. Colin McColl): Premiered 1990 at Downstage, Wellington, NZ (February 16–March 31). Performers included Catherine Wilkin and Jim Moriarty.

———— St Bride's Theatre, Edinburgh International Festival, Scotland, UK (August 27–September 1, 1990).

———— Amfiscenen Amphi Theatre, Ibsen Festival, Oslo, Norway (September 4–5, 1990).

———— Jeannetta Cochrane Theatre, International Covent Garden Festival, London, England, UK (September 10–23, 1990).

———— Seymour Centre, Festival of Sydney, Australia (January 3–19, 1991). (For *Michael James Manaia* see Broughton, John)

Duncum, Ken

Cherish: Premiered 2003 at Circa Theatre, Wellington (October 18–November 15). Dir. Kathy McRae.

———— Northern Light Theatre, Edmonton, Canada (May 2–11, 2018). Dir. Trevor Schmidt.

Duncan, Barnie

Calypso Nights: Premiered 2013 at Basement Theatre (May 15–18). Performed by Barnie Duncan.
———— Assembly Roxy, Edinburgh Festival Fringe, Edinburgh, Scotland, UK (August 1–25, 2014).
Juan Vesuvius: I Am Your Deejay: Premiered 2017 at the Box, Assembly George Square, NZ at Edinburgh, Edinburgh Festival Fringe, Scotland, UK (August 3–27). Performed by Barnie Duncan. [Also toured to England and Australia in 2018]

Farrell, Fiona

Chook Chook: Premiered 1994 at Allen Hall, Lunchtime Theatre, University of Otago Theatre Studies, Dunedin. 18 Playmarket licensed international productions in the UK, Australia and Germany (as of 2018).

Flight of the Conchords (Jermaine Clement and Bret McKenzie)

Edinburgh Festival Fringe, Scotland, UK: The Cave (August, 2002 and 2003); The Gilded Balloon (August, 2004). [Extensive international touring]

Forster, Michelanne

Daughters of Heaven: Premiered 1991 at Court Theatre, Christchurch, NZ. 9 Playmarket licensed international productions in Australia, UK and USA (as of 2018).

Fraser, Toa

Bare: Premiered 1998 at Silo Theatre, Auckland, NZ (June 4–June 13). Dir. Michael Robinson, performed by Ian Hughes and Madeleine Sami.
———— Assembly Rooms, Edinburgh Festival Fringe, Scotland, UK (August 8–30, 1999). Produced by Guy Masterson & Real Productions.
[Subsequently performed in Sydney, Australia in 2000 and on a UK tour in 2001]
No. 2: Premiered 1999 at Silo Theatre, Auckland, NZ (June 16–26). Dir. Catherine Boniface, performed by Madeleine Sami, produced by Fenn Gordon (Compania Segundo).
———— Assembly Rooms, Edinburgh Festival Fringe, Scotland, UK (August 3–28, 2000) Produced by Guy Masterson & Companie Segundo.
———— Cervantino Festival, Guanajuato, Mexico (October 13–14, 2001). Produced by Companie Segundo.
———— Kings Head Theatre, London, England, UK (February 4–March 16, 2003).
———— USA and Canada Tour (January 20–February 11, 2012) [Also toured to Australia, the Netherlands and Israel]

Fuemana, Dianna

Mapaki: Premiered 1999 at BATS Theatre, Wellington, NZ (November 9–13). Dir. Hori Ahipene, performed by Dianna Fuemana.

———— International Women's Conference, Athens University, Greece (August, 2000).

———— Rooke Theatre, Mount Holyoke College, Pangea World Theatre, Massachusetts, USA (November 30–December 1, 2001). [Also toured to Hawai'i]

The Packer: Premiered 2003 at BATS Theatre, Wellington, NZ (August 26–30). Dir. Dianna Fuemana, performed by Jay Ryan (also known as Jay Bunyan).

———— Garage, Edinburgh Festival Fringe, Scotland, UK (August 8–28, 2004). Dir. Jeremy Lindsay Taylor [Also toured to Australia in 2003, 2004, 2008 and the Hollywood Fringe, USA, in 2010]

Falemalama: Premiered 2006 at Pangea World Theatre, Minneapolis, USA (November 16). Dir. Dipankar Mukherjee, performed by Dianna Fuemana.

————Festival of Pacific Arts, Utulei, Pago Pago, American Sāmoa (July, 2008).

———— Niue Arts Festival, Niue (2009).

———— Emwave Theatre, Planet Indigenous Festival, Toronto, Canada (August 21–22, 2009).

Birds: Premiered 2011 at Niue Culture & Arts Festival (April).

————11th Festival of Pacific Arts in the Solomon Islands (July, 2012).

George, Mīria

and what remains: Premiered 2005 at City Gallery, Wellington, NZ (November 16–19). Dir. Hone Kouka, produced by Tawata Productions.

————Playroom, Pasifika Styles Festival, University of Cambridge, England, UK (May 31–June 1, 2007).

Grace-Smith, Briar

Ngā Pou Wahine: Premiered 1995 at Taki Rua Theatre, Wellington, NZ (May 10–20). Dir. Nancy Brunning, performed by Rachel House.

———— The Festival of the Dreaming, Sydney Opera House, Australia (September 1997). [Also toured to Ireland in 1997]

———— Festival of Pacific Arts, Noumea, New Caledonia (October, 2000).

Purapurawhetū: Premiered 1997 at Downstage, Wellington, NZ (June 22– May 7). Dir. Catherine Downes, performers included Jim Moriarty, produced by Taki Rua.

———— International Women's Conference, Athens University, Athens, Greece (August, 2000). [Also toured to Canada]

Hall, Roger

Glide Time: Premiered 1976 at Circa Theatre, Wellington, NZ (August 11–September 11). Dir. Anthony Taylor.

——— *Flex-Time* [renamed]: The Playhouse, Canberra Theatre Trust, Australia (September 28–October 21, 1978). Dir. John Tasker.

——— *Flexi Time* [renamed]: Australia Tour (1979): Adelaide (July); South Australia (August); Victoria (September). Dir. Don Mackay. [Plus other Australian productions in 1995, 1997 and 2002]

——— *Middle Age Spread*: Premiered 1977 at Circa Theatre, Wellington, NZ (November). Dir. Michael Haigh.

——— Lyric Theatre, London, England, UK (September 17, 1979, to late 1980). Dir. Robert Kidd, performers included Richard Briers and Paul Eddington. [Preceded by a try-out season at Theatre Royal, Brighton in 1979 and followed by a tour of UK provinces in 1981]

——— Source Theatre Company, Washington D.C., USA (May, 1983).

——— Oz Duz NZ, Stables Theatre, Sydney, Australia (November 15–December 9, 1984). Dir. Aarne Neeme. [Subsequent Australia tour and other Australian productions in 1987, 1995 and 2005]

Footrot Flats: The Musical (with A.K. Grant and Phillip Norman): Premiered 1983 at Court Theatre, Christchurch, NZ (December 1983–February 1984). Dir. Elric Hooper.

——— Australia Tour (1984–1985): 32 venues across Western Australia, South Australia, Victoria, New South Wales, Queensland, Northern Territory and the Australian Capital Territory. Dir. Brian Debnam, produced by John Manford and Associates.

[Further Australian productions 1997, 1999, 2001, 2005, 2007, 2008, 2015, 2018]

C'mon Black: Premiered 1995 at Fortune Theatre, Dunedin, NZ (July 19–August 10). Dir. Campbell Thomas.

——— Southwark Playhouse, Air New Zealand Season of Kiwi Theatre, Festival of New Zealand Arts, London, England, UK (July 13–August 2, 1997). Dir. Danny Mulheron, performed by Grant Tilly. [Subsequently performed at the Edinburgh Festival Fringe, 1997]

[A number of Hall's plays have also been performed internationally including *Multiple Choice* (1984), *Love Off the Shelf* (1988), *Conjugal Rites* (1990), *Social Climbers* (1995), *The Book Club* (1999), *Take a Chance on Me* (2001), *Taking Off* (2003), *Four Flat Whites in Italy* (2009)]

Heartache and Sorrow

The Case of Katherine Mansfield (by Catherine Downes): Premiered 1978 at Theater De Kikker, Utrecht, Holland (October).

The Heartache and Sorrow Show: Premiered 1978 at Second International Women's Festival, Amsterdam, the Netherlands.

Heartache and Sorrow's Season at Netherbow Theatre, Edinburgh Festival Fringe, Scotland, UK (August, 1979). Presenting:

——— *Songs to Uncle Scrim* (1976) by Mervyn Thompson.

——— *Crossfire* (1975) by Jennifer Compton.

——— *The Case of Katherine Mansfield* (1978) by Catherine Downes.

——— *Sweetcorn* (1979) by Downes, Jane Waddell and Michael Houston.

——— *Hair of the Dog* (1979) by the company.

[*The Case of Katherine Mansfield* also toured to Australia in 1980 and 1983, and Holland and NYC in 1983. *Sweetcorn* was toured to Nimrod, New South Wales, Australia, in 1982]

Henderson, Gary

Skin Tight: Premiered 1994 at BATS Theatre, Wellington, NZ (March 10–19). Dir. Gary Henderson, performed by Jed Brophy and Larissa Mathesson.

——— Traverse Theatre, Edinburgh Festival Fringe, Scotland, UK (August, 1998). Produced by Guy Masterson & Skin Tight International. Additionally, 35 productions by international companies in USA, UK, Australia and South Africa (as of 2019), including:

——— South Africa Tour (1999): Richard Haines Theatre, Johannesburg; Theatre on the Bay, Cape Town. Dir. Moira Blumenthal.

——— Stables Theatre, Sydney, Australia (2000). Dir. Moira Blumenthal.

——— Perth Institute of Contemporary Art, Perth Theatre Company, Australia (March 20–April 12, 2003). Dir. Alan Becher.

——— Pleasance Theatre, Shaky Isles Theatre Company, London, England, UK (October 20–25, 2009). Dir. Stella Duffy.

——— Know Theatre, Cincinnati (October 9–November 6, 2010). Dir. Drew Fracher.

——— 45 Downstairs, Melbourne, Australia (2011). Dir. Justin Martin.

——— Cor Theatre, A Red Orchid Theatre, Chicago, USA (August 31–September 25, 2012). Dir. Victoria Delorio.

——— 59E59 Theatres, OYL Theatre Company, NYC, USA (November 6–December 1, 2012). Dir. Nick Flint.

——— Park Theatre, Epsilon Productions, London, UK (July 16–August 11, 2013). Dir. Jemma Gross.

——— Théâtre L'Instant/Théâtre Prospero, Montréal, Canada (2016), Dir. Andre-Marie Coudou, translated by Xavier Mailleux.

——— The New Theatre, Dublin, Ireland (August 6–17, 2019). Dir. Owen Lindsay.

Mo & Jess Kill Susie: Premiered 1996 at BATS Theatre, Wellington, NZ (September 12–28). Dir. Gary Henderson.

——— Third Space Theatre, Northern Light Theatre, Edmonton, Canada (September 11–21, 2008). Dir. Trevor Schmidt.

—— Trinity St. Paul's Church (Basement), Harley Dog Productions, Toronto Fringe Festival, Canada (July 3–13, 2013). Dir. Brenley Charkow.

[*Skin Tight* and *Mo & Jess Kill Susie* were also toured by Quartet Theatre Company to Belgium, Germany and Romania (October–November, 2010). Dir. Hilary Halba (*Skin Tight*) / Bronwyn Tweddle (*Mo & Jess*)]

Ihimaera, Witi

Woman Far Walking: Premiered 2000 at Soundings Theatre, Te Papa, NZ Festival of the Arts, Wellington, NZ (March 17–25). Dir. Catherine Downes, performed by Rachel House and Rima Te Wiata
—— Various venues, Hawai'i, USA (September 19–30, 2001).
—— Central Library, St Peters Square, Manchester, England, UK (June, 2002). [Also toured to Wales]
—— Festival of Pacific Arts, Palau (July, 2004).

Indian Ink Theatre Company

Krishnan's Dairy (by Jacob Rajan): Premiered 1997 at BATS Theatre, Wellington, NZ (August 20–September 13). Dir. Justin Lewis, performed as solo by Jacob Rajan.
—— Assembly Rooms, Edinburgh Festival Fringe, Scotland, UK (August, 1999). Co-produced by Guy Masterson.
—— Peacock Theatre, 10 Days on the Island Festival, Hobart, Tasmania, Australia (March 30–April 2, 2001). [Also toured to Australia in 2005, 2007, 2008 and 2012]
—— Singapore Repertory Theatre, Singapore (2004). [Also toured to Singapore in 2006]
—— India Tour (2016): Satyajit Ray Auditorium, Kolkota (November 11–12); Ranga Shankara, Bengaluru (November 16); Delhi International Arts Festival, New Delhi (November 18–19).
The Candlestickmaker (by Jacob Rajan and Justin Lewis): Premiered 2000 at Downstage, Wellington, NZ (March 15–25, 2003). Dir. Justin Lewis, performed by Jacob Rajan and Kate Parker.
—— DBS Arts Centre, Singapore (May, 2006).
—— Festival Theaterformen, Germany (2006). [Also toured to Australia in 2008 and 2009]
The Pickle King (by Jacob Rajan and Justin Lewis): Premiered 2002 at WEL Energy Trust Academy, Hamilton, NZ (July 4–13). Dir. Justin Lewis, performed by Jacob Rajan, Carl Bland, Ansuya Nathan.
—— Edinburgh Festival Fringe, Edinburgh, UK (August, 2003).
—— DBS Arts Centre, Singapore (January 30–February 16, 2007). [Also toured to Australia in 2008]
Guru of Chai (by Jacob Rajan and Justin Lewis): Premiered 2010 in various venues, NZ. Dir. Justin Lewis, performed by Jacob Rajan.

———— USA Tour (2011): Los Angeles (August); Virginia (September); St Louis (November).

———— Barrow Group Theatre, NYC, USA (January, 2013). [Also toured to Singapore in 2010 and Hawai'i in 2014. Toured mainland USA retitled *The Elephant Wrestler* in 2014–2015]

———— *The Elephant Wrestler* [Retitled]: Historic Theatre, The Cultch, Vancouver, Canada (November 1–5, 2016).

———— K.T. Muhammad Regional Theatre, Thrissur, Kerala, India (February 18, 2014).

———— Belvoir Street Downstairs Theatre, Sydney, Australia (May 16–June 14, 2017). [Also toured to Australia in 2018 and 2019]

———— ICT Center, Laucala Campus, University of the South Pacific, Suva, Fiji (November, 2019).

Kiss the Fish (by Jacob Rajan and Justin Lewis): Premiered 2013 at Q Theatre, Auckland, NZ (September). Dir. Justin Lewis, performed by Jacob Rajan, James Roque, Nisha Madhan, Julia Croft.

———— USA Tour (2015): Lied Center of Kansas (January 27–28); Gorecki Family Theater, College of Saint Benedict, Minnesota (January 30–31).

Mrs Krishnan's Party (by Jacob Rajan and Justin Lewis): Premiered 2017 at TAPAC Theatre, Auckland, NZ (December 6–14). Dir. Justin Lewis, performed by Kalyani Nagarajan and Justin Rogers.

———— Trust Arts Education Center, Pittsburgh Festival of Firsts, USA (October 17–21, 2018).

———— Culture Lab, Cultch, Vancouver, Canada (January 15–February 3, 2019).

———— Proctors, NY, USA (February 7–9, 2019).

———— USA Tour (2019/2020): Utah Presents, Utah (November 1–2, 2019); Green Music Center, Sonoma State University, California (November 6–7); Seattle Theatre Group, Seattle (November 15–24); Modlin Center, Richmond, Virginia (January 25–26, 2020); Moss Arts Center, Blacksburg, Virginia (January 30–February 1); Hampton Arts, Hampton, New Hampshire (February 7–8); Gallagher Bluedorn Performing Arts Center, Cedar Falls, Ioawa (February 11–12); Johnson County Arts and Heritage Center, Johnson County, Kansas (February 14–16); Quick Center, Fairfield, Connecticut (February 20–22); Kahilu Theatre, Kamuela, Hawai'i (March 1); Hilo Performing Arts Center, Hawai'i (March 4); Maui Arts and Cultural Center, Hawai'i (March 6).

Jones, Stella

The Tree: Premiered 1957 at Little Theatre, Rapier Players Ltd, Bristol, England, UK (April 8–20, 1957). Dir. Paul Smythe.

———— The Playhouse, Newcastle Repertory, England, UK (November, 1957).

Kinane, Emma

Anahera: Premiered 2017 at Circa Theatre, Wellington, NZ (September 9–October 7, 2019). Dir. Katie Wolfe.
────── Finborough Theatre, London, England, UK (September 3–28, 2019). Dir. Alice Kornitzer.

The Kiwi Concert Party/The Kiwis

The Kiwi Concert Party, the Entertainment Division of the Second New Zealand Expeditionary Force, performed during WWII throughout Crete, Syria, Malta, Italy and North Africa.
────── First Revue, Maadi, Egypt (May 1, 1941)
────── Final Revue, outside Siena, Italy (November 6, 1945). As the Kiwis, toured Australia and New Zealand (1946–1954), including:
────── Comedy Theatre, Melbourne, Australia (December 21, 1946–January 6, 1949).
────── Empire Theatre, Sydney (February 2, 1949–1950).

Kouka, Hone

Waiora Te Ū Kai Pō – The Homeland: Premiered 1996, Downstage, Wellington, NZ (March 15–24). Dir. Murray Lynch, performers included Rawiri Paratene, Rachel House and Nancy Brunning.
────── Corn Exchange Theatre, Brighton Festival, England, UK (May 20–24, 1997).
────── Hawaiian Islands Tour, USA (September, 1999): Kamehameha Schools; Leeward Community College; Kaua'i Community College; 'Iao Theatre, Wailuku; UH-Hilo Theater.
The Prophet: Premiered 2002 at Studio 77, Victoria University of Wellington, NZ (June)
────── Various venues, Hawai'i, USA (October 17–31, 2006). Dir. Nina Nawalowalo, produced by Taki Rua.

Last Tapes Theatre Company

Valerie (by Robin Kelly, Tom Broome and Cherie Moore): Premiered 2016 at Basement Theatre, Auckland (September 27–October 8). Dir. Benjamin Henson.
────── Summerhall, Edinburgh Festival Fringe, Scotland, UK (August 1–26, 2018).

Lees, Nathaniel

Fale Sa: Premiered 2016 at Padre Palemo Reserve, Festival of Pacific Arts, Guam (May). Dir. Nathaniel Lees.

Little Dog Barking

Paper Shaper (by Peter Wilson and Tim Denton): Premiered 2007 at Capital E, Wellington, NZ (June 30–July 14). Dir. Peter Wilson.
———— Asian Pacific Puppet Festival, Nanchong, China (June, 2014).
Duck, Death and the Tulip (by Peter Wilson): Premiered 2013 at Downstage, Wellington, NZ (March 18–23). Dir. Nina Nawalowalo.
———— Main Hall, Summerhall, NZ at Edinburgh, Edinburgh Festival Fringe, Scotland, UK (August 1–28, 2014). [Also toured to Brighton and Canterbury, UK]
———— Asian Pacific Puppet Festival, Quangzhou, China (November, 2015).
Guji Guji (by Peter Wilson): Premiered 2016 at BATS Theatre, Wellington, NZ (April 19–23). Dir. Peter Wilson.
———— Ricca Ricca Festival, Japan (July, 2016).
———— Nanchong International Puppet Festival (June 1–6, 2017).
———— Seoul ASSITEJ Korea Festival (July 19–20, 2017).

Lord, Robert

Meeting Place: Premiered 1972 at Star Boating Club, Wellington, NZ (October/November). Dir. Anthony Taylor.
———— The Playhouse, New Phoenix Repertory Company, NYC, USA (April, 1975). Dir. Michael Montel.
Well Hung: Premiered 1974 at Downstage, Wellington, NZ (January 21–March 2). Dir. Anthony Taylor.
———— Providence, Rhode Island, NY, USA (November, 1974). Dir. Adrian Hall. Produced by Trinity Square Repertory Company. [Also produced in Australia in 1974, 1976 and 1979]
———— *Country Cops* [Retitled, revised]: USA Summer Stock Circuit Tour (1986): Cape Playhouse, Dennis, Massachusetts (July 7–12); Ogunquit Playhouse, Ogunquit, Maine (July 14–19); Elitchs' Theatre Company, Denver, Colorado (July 21–August 2); Westport Country Playhouse, Wesport, Connecticut (August 4–9). Dir. Tony Tanner, performers included Conrad Bain.
———— Dorset Playhouse, Dorset Theatre Festival, Vermont, USA (August 4–20, 1988). Dir. John Morrison.
I'll Scream If I Want To: Premiered 1976 at Provincetown Playhouse, NYC, USA (August). Dir. Marshall Oglesby. [Subsequently renamed *High as a Kite*]
Bert and Maisy: Premiered 1983 (under the title *Unfamiliar Steps*) at Southern Ballet Theatre, Christchurch, NZ (July). Dir. Aarne Neeme, produced by Court Theatre.
———— Stables Theatre, Oz Duz NZ, Sydney, Australia (December 13, 1984 to January 6, 1985). Dir. Aarne Neeme.

———— Cassius Carter Centre Stage, Old Globe Theatre, San Diego, California, USA (November 30, 1985–January 12, 1986). Dir. Robert Berlinger.

The Travelling Squirrel: Premiered 1987 at Long Wharf Theatre, New Haven, Connecticut, USA (February 3–22). Dir. John Tillinger.

———— William Redfield Theater, Primary Stages, NYC, USA (February 23–March 9, 1990). Dir. Robert Lord.

China Wars: Premiered 1987 at Primary Stages, NYC, USA (March 2–9). Dir. Ethan Silverman.

Joyful and Triumphant: Premiered 1992 at Circa Theatre, Wellington, NZ (February/March). Dir. Susan Wilson.

———— Southwark Playhouse, Air New Zealand Season of Kiwi Theatre, Festival of New Zealand Arts, London, UK (July 8–31, 1997). [Also productions in Australia in 1993 and 1995]

Mamea, David Fa'auliuli

Still Life with Chickens: Premiered 2018 at Māngere Arts Centre, Auckland, NZ (March 8–14). Dir. Fasitua Amosa, performed by Goretti Chadwick, produced by Auckland Theatre Company.

———— Shanghai Grand Theatre, International Theatre Season, China (December 18–21, 2019).

Manusaute, Vela

The Factory: Premiered 2011 at Māngere Arts Centre, Auckland, NZ (August 13–September 10). Dir. Anapela Polata'ivao and Vela Manusaute, produced by Kila Kokonut Krew.

———— Australia Tour (2014): Adelaide Cabaret Festival, Adelaide (June 12–14); Riverside Theatre, Parramatta (June 18–21); Canberra Theatre Centre, Canberra (June 23–25); Merrigong Theatre, Wollongong (July 9–12); The Arts Centre, Gold Coast (July 15–16).

———— Assembly Hall, NZ at Edinburgh, Edinburgh Festival Fringe, Scotland, UK (July 31–August 25, 2014).

Massive Company

The Sons of Charlie Paora (by Lennie James): Premiered 2002 at Herald Theatre, Auckland, NZ (October). Dir. Sam Scott.

———— Royal Court Theatre Downstairs, London, England, UK (February 25–March 6, 2004).

The Brave (devised by the company): Premiered 2012 at Q Theatre, Auckland, NZ (April 17–22). Dir. Sam Scott.

———— Hawaiian Islands Tour, USA (March, 2015): Maui Arts and Cultural Centre; Leeward Community College Theatre, O'hau; Hilo Community College Theatre and Kahilu Theatre, Kamuela.

Mason, Bruce

Birds in the Wilderness: Premiered 1958 at Concert Chamber, Auckland Town Hall, Auckland Festival, NZ (May).
——— Lyric Theatre, London, England, UK (June 10, 1958).
The Pohutukawa Tree: Premiered 1957 at New Zealand Players Theatre Workshop, Wellington (August). Dir. Richard Campion and Bruce Mason.
——— Theatr Fach, Llangefni, Wales, UK (October 11–13, 1960).
The End of the Golden Weather: Premiered 1959 at New Zealand Players Theatre Workshop, Wellington, NZ (August). Performed by Bruce Mason.
——— Regent Hall, Abbeymount, Edinburgh Festival Fringe, Edinburgh, Scotland, UK (August, 1963). [Subsequently performed in London, USA, Australia]
Blood of the Lamb: Premiered 1980 at Court Theatre, Christchurch, NZ (March). Dir. Elric Hooper.
——— Australia Tour (1981): Phillip Street Theatre, Sydney (October); Newcastle (October). [Also produced in Adelaide, Australia, in 1989]

MAU

I Am: Premiered 2014 at Festival d'Avignon, France (April 18–23). Dir. Lemi Panifasio.
——— Edinburgh Playhouse, Edinburgh International Festival, Scotland, UK (August 16–17, 2004) [MAU's work has also performed at Théâtre de la Ville in Paris, Prague Quadrennial, Venice Biennale, Holland Festival, Adelaide Festival, Lincoln Centre in NYC and the Santiago a Mil International Festival in Chile]

McArthur, Jen

Echolalia: Premiered 2011 at BATS Theatre, Wellington, NZ (June 30–July 9).
——— Gilded Balloon, Edinburgh Festival Fringe, Scotland, UK (August 2014).

McGee, Greg

Foreskin's Lament: Premiered 1980 at Theatre Corporate, Auckland, NZ (October/November). Dir. Roger McGill.
——— Stables Theatre, Oz Duz NZ, Sydney, Australia (October 18–November 11, 1984). Dir. Aarne Neeme. [Also produced in Australia 1987, 1994, 2008]
——— Judi Dench Theatre, London, England, UK (February 9–12, 2000).

────── Baby Grand, Pleasance Courtyard, Edinburgh Festival Fringe, Scotland, UK (August, 2008). Dir. Lindsey Brown. [Also Hackney Empire Studio, London, 2008]

Meek, Arthur

On the Upside Down of the World: Premiered 2011 at Concert Chamber, Town Hall, Auckland, NZ (July 1–16). Dir. Colin McColl, performed by Laurel Devenie, produced by Auckland Theatre Company.

────── United Solo Festival, NYC, USA (October, 2013).

────── Upstairs at the Roxy, NZ at Edinburgh, Edinburgh Festival Fringe, Scotland, UK (July 30–August 25, 2014).

On the Conditions and Possibilities of Hillary Clinton Taking Me as Her Young Lover: Premiered 2015 at First Floor Theatre, La MaMa, New Zealand Performance Festival New York, NYC, USA (March 12–15). Dir. Geoff Pinfield, performed by Meek. [Subsequently performed at Joe's Pub at the Public Theatre, NYC]

────── Summerhall, Edinburgh Festival Fringe, Scotland, UK (August 7–28, 2016).

Erewhon: Premiered 2017 (as *Erewhon Revisited*) at Great Hall, the Arts Centre, Christchurch Arts Festival, NZ (September 12–16). Dir. Nicholas Bone and Geoff Pinfield.

────── Cairns Lecture Theatre, Summerhall, Edinburgh Festival Fringe, Scotland, UK (August 1–26, 2018)

Mika

Mika and the Uhuras: Premiered 1995 at Promenade Café & Bar, Auckland, NZ (January 1995)

────── Assembly Theatre, Edinburgh Festival Fringe, Scotland, UK (August 3–September 1, 1997).

Salon Mika on Bare Feet Street: Premiered 2018 at Dance Base, Edinburgh Festival Fringe, Scotland, UK (August 4–24). [As of 2018 Mika has performed at 10 Edinburgh Festival Fringes since 1992]

Modern Māori Quartet

That's Us: Premiered 2017 at Assembly George Square Studios Three, NZ at Edinburgh, Edinburgh Festival Fringe, Scotland, UK (August 3–28). Produced by SquareSums&Co.

Two Worlds: Premiered 2018 at Assembly George Square Studios Three, Edinburgh Festival Fringe, Scotland, UK (August 2–27). Produced by SquareSums&Co.

────── Assembly George Square Studios Three, Edinburgh Festival Fringe, Scotland, UK (July 31–August 26, 2019). [Also toured to Korea, Tokyo and China]

——— SoHo Playhouse, NYC, USA (January 14–18, 2020).

Garage Party: Premiered 2019 at Ermintrude, Bristo Square, Underbelly, Edinburgh Festival Fringe, Scotland, UK (July 31–August 25). [Modern Māori Quartet has also toured to London, Brighton, Cardiff, in the UK, Uzbekistan, Australia, Hawai'i, Singapore, Malaysia, Rarotonga]

Mokaraka, Rob

Strange Resting Places (with Paolo Rotondo): Premiered 2007 at BATS Theatre, Wellington, NZ (July 3–21). Dir. Leo Gene Peters, produced by Taki Rua.
——— Dreaming Festival, Brisbane, Australia (June, 2008).
——— Festival of Pacific Arts, Pago Pago, American Sāmoa (July, 2008). [Taki Rua production also toured to London and Singapore]
——— Assembly George Square Studios, NZ at Edinburgh, Edinburgh Festival Fringe, Scotland, UK (July 31–August 25, 2014). Produced by Cuba Creative.

Monckton, Thomas

The Pianist: Premiered 2013 at Hämeenlinna Theater, Finland (September 2013). Dir. Sanna Silvenoinen.
——— Assembly Roxy, Edinburgh Festival Fringe, Scotland, UK (August, 2014).
Only Bones (with Gemma Tweedie): Premiered 2015 at Bandoliers Hall, Wellington, NZ (February 26–27). Performed by Thomas Monckton.
——— *Only Bones 1.0* [Revised]: Summerhall, Edinburgh Festival Fringe, Scotland, UK (August 7–28, 2016). Produced by Kallo Collective. [Also presented at Avignon Fringe in 2016 and again at the Edinburgh Festival Fringe in 2019]
——— *Only Bones v1.4* [Revised]: Soho Theatre, London International Mime Festival, England, UK (January 7–25, 2020). Performed by Trygve Wakenshaw.

The Naked Samoans

Naked Samoans: The Trilogy: Premiered 2001 at Herald Theatre, Auckland (June 19–30).
——— Edinburgh Festival Fringe (August, 2002)

Ngākau Toa

Toroihi rāua ko Kāhira (The Māori Troilus and Cressida) (translated by Te Haumihiata Mason): Premiered 2012 at Te Papa, Wellington (March 9–10). Dir. Rachel House.
——— Globe Theatre, Globe to Globe Festival, World Shakespeare Festival, Cultural Olympiad, London, England, UK (April 14–23, 2012).

O'Brien, Richard

The Rocky Horror Show: Premiered 1973 at Royal Court, London, England, UK (June 19–July 20). [Numerous subsequent productions worldwide.]

O'Reilly, Morgana

The Height of the Eiffel Tower: Premiered 2009 at Basement Theatre, Auckland, NZ (March 10–13). Dir. Abigail Greenwood.
—— New York Fringe Festival, NYC, USA (August, 2010).
—— Assembly Hall, Edinburgh Festival Fringe, Scotland, UK (July 31–August 25, 2014).

Pacific Underground

Fresh Off the Boat (by Oscar Kightley and Simon Small): Premiered 1993 at Arts Centre, Christchurch, NZ (November 17–December 4). Dir. Nathaniel Lees.
—— Apia, Sāmoa (1994). [Also toured to Brisbane, Australia in 1995]
Tatau: Rites of Passage (co-created with Zeal): Premiered 1996 at Herald Theatre, Auckland, NZ (February 1–29). Dir. Oscar Kightley and Stefo Nantsou.
—— Zeal Theatre, Bondi Pavilion, Pacific Wave Festival, Sydney, Australia (November 1996).

Papps, Stephen

Blowing It (with Stephen Sinclair): Premiered 1999 at Silo Theatre, Auckland, NZ (September 11–October 9). Performed by Stephen Papps.
—— Assembly Wildman Room, Edinburgh Festival Fringe, Edinburgh, Scotland, UK (August 1–25, 2003). Produced by Company Gavin Robertson and Guy Masterson. [Subsequently toured Australia and Europe]

Red Leap Theatre

The Arrival (by Kate Parker, Julie Nolan and original cast): Premiered 2009 at the Civic, Auckland, NZ (March 12–15). Dir. Julie Nolan.
—— Carriageworks Bay 17, Sydney International Arts Festival, Australia (January 10–17, 2010).
—— City Hall Theatre, Hong Kong Arts Festival (February, 2010).
—— South Korea Tour (2012): LG Arts Centre, Seoul (May 3–6); Busan International Performing Arts Festival, Busan (May 11–13).
—— Macau Cultural Centre, Macau (March, 2013).
—— Kaohsiung Spring Arts Festival, Taiwan (March, 2013).

——— Out of the Box Festival, Brisbane Powerhouse, Australia (June 26–
July 7, 2018).

Red Mole Enterprises

Goin' to Djibouti: Premiered 1979 at Westbeth Theatre, NYC, USA
(January 4–21).

The Last Days of Mankind: Premiered 1979 at the Theatre for the New City,
NYC, USA (April 5–22).

——— England, UK Tour (July, 1979): at Crucible Theatre, the Commonwealth
Youth Festival, Sheffield (July 9, 11, 14); Oval House, London (July 19–
25); Surrey Free Arts Festival, Guildford (July).

Blood in the Cracks: Premiered 1979 at Theatre Space, London, England, UK
(August 9–11 and 16–18, 1979).

Dead Fingers Walk: Premiered at NZ House, London, England, UK
(1979).

——— Theatre for the New City, NYC, USA (September 13–23, 1979).
[Subsequently performed on Red Mole Enterprises' "An American Tour"
to various USA locations.]

Numbered Days in Paradise: Premiered on "An American Tour" (October,
1979 to January, 1980): Labour Theatre, NY (October); Rikers Island
Prison, NY (October); 10 Bleeker St, NY (October); Laurel Theatre,
Knoxville, Tennessee (November 5); Mexican American Unity Council,
San Antonio, Texas (November 10–11); Esther's Pool, Austin, Texas
(November 15); Kimo Theatre, Albuquerque, New Mexico (November
22–December 2); The Performing Space, Santa Fe, New Mexico
(December 7–15); Wayfarer's Inn, Taos, New Mexico (December 11–
December 31); Odyssey Theatre, Los Angeles, California (January 7–19,
1980).

The Early Show and *The Late Show*: Premiered 1981 at Pyramid Theatre,
NYC, USA.

Playtime: Premiered 1986 at Caravan of Dreams, Fort Worth, Texas, USA
(1986). [Subsequently performed in Austin, Texas and Sante Fe, New
Mexico]

——— English Speaking Theatre of Amsterdam, De Stalhouderij,
Amsterdam (1987).

Hour of Justice: Premiered at English Speaking Theatre of Amsterdam, De
Stalhouderi, Amsterdam (January 15–31, 1988).

[Other productions premiered in the USA included *The Excursion* (1982),
Childhood of a Saint (1982), *2 Quacks on Io* (1983), *Dreamings End* (1984),
Circu Sfumato (1985), *Lost Chants for the Living* (1986). For further
details see NZEPC, "Red Mole: A Chronology of Works 1974–2002",
Last modified December 15, 2003. www.nzepc.auckland.ac.nz/authors/
brunton/brief/mole_chron.asp]

Reid, Stella

The Basement Tapes (with Jane Yonge): Premiered 2017 at Chaffers Apartments, Wellington, NZ (February 10–14). Dir. Jane Yonge, performed by Stella Reid.

———— Arts House Warehouse, Melbourne Fringe, Australia (September 23–30, 2017).

———— Basement, Summerhall, Edinburgh Festival Fringe, Scotland, UK (July 31–August 26, 2018).

———— Blue Room Theatre, Fringe World, Perth, Australia (January 29–February 2, 2019).

———— UK Tour (2019): Home Manchester; New Diorama London; Tobacco Factory Bristol; Phoenix Arts Bordon; The Maltings Wells-next-the-Sea; Stantonbury Theatre Milton Keynes; Arts at the Old Fire Station Oxford; Greenwhich Theatre, Woodville Gravesend; Ashcroft Arts Centre Fareham, Forrest Arts Centre New Milton (June 25–July 11).

Rodger, Victor

Black Faggot: Premiered 2013 at Basement Theatre, Auckland, NZ (February 16–20). Dir Roy Ward.

———— North Melbourne Town Hall, Melbourne Fringe, Australia (September 28–29, 2013).

———— Visy Theatre, Brisbane Powerhouse Arts, Australia (February 19–23, 2014).

———— Assembly Roxy Upstairs, NZ at Edinburgh, Edinburgh Festival Fringe, Scotland, UK (July 31–August 25, 2014).

———— Grasworks Arts Park, Midsumma Festival, Melbourne, Australia (February 3–7, 2015).

My Name is Gary Cooper: Premiered 2007 at Maidment Theatre, Auckland, NZ (September 20–October 13). Dir. Roy Ward.

———— Kumu Kahua Theatre, Honolulu, Hawai'i (January 22–February 21, 2015). Dir. David O'Donnell.

Sarkies, Duncan

Lovepuke: Premiered 1994 at BATS Theatre, Wellington, NZ. 10 Playmarket licensed international productions in Australia and UK (as of 2018).

Scotney, Ana Chaya

The Contours of Heaven (with Puti Lancaster, Marama Beamish and Owen McCarthy): Premiered 2017 at Hawke's Bay Arts Festival, NZ (October 4–8).

———— SoHo Playhouse, NYC, USA (January 11–13, 2020).

Sinclair, Stephen

Ladies Night (with Anthony McCarten): Premiered 1987 at Mercury Theatre, Auckland, NZ. Numerous productions by international companies in the UK, France, Germany, Austria, Italy, Russia, Greece, Scandinavia, Iceland, Poland, Ukraine, Belarus, Spain, Brazil, Argentina, Canada, USA, Australia. Including:
——— Mermaid Theatre, London, UK (1989).
——— Paris, France (2001). [Received the Meilleure Pièce Comique Molière Prize]
——— Jagsthausen, Germany (July 2020)
Ladies Night 2: Raging On: Premiered 1993 at Court Theatre, Christchurch, NZ. [Various international productions in Australia, UK and Germany] (For *Blowing It* see Papps, Stephen.)

A Slightly Isolated Dog

Don Juan: Premiered 2015 at Circa Two, Wellington, NZ (April 25–May 23). Dir. Leo Gene Peters.
——— The Bubble, Assembly George Square, Edinburgh Festival Fringe, Scotland, UK (August 2–26, 2018)
——— England, UK Tour (2019): The Other Palace, London (July 15–20); Greenwhich Theatre, London (July 24); Holmfirth Civic Hall, Holmfirth (July 26).
Jekyll and Hyde: Premiered 2016 at Circa Two, Wellington, NZ (March 19–April 16). Dir. Leo Gene Peters.
——— Piccolo Tent, Assembly George Square Gardens, Edinburgh Festival Fringe, Scotland, UK (August 1–26, 2019).

Spooner, Rutene

Super Hugh-Man: Premiered 2017 at Basement Theatre, Auckland International Cabaret Festival, NZ (September 20–23). Dir. Jennifer Ward-Lealand, performed by Rutene Spooner.
——— Assembly George Square Studios Three, Edinburgh Festival Fringe, Scotland, UK (July 31–August 26). Produced by SquareSums&Co.

Sproull, Hayley

Miss Fletcher Sings the Blues: Premiered 2012 at BATS Theatre, Wellington, NZ (May 15–19). Performed by Hayley Sproull.
——— The Caves, Edinburgh Festival Fringe, Scotland, UK (July 31–August 24, 2014).

Tate-Manning, Anya

My Best Dead Friend (with Isobel Mackinnon): Premiered 2016 at Blue Room Theatre, Fringe World, Perth (February 10–13). Dir. Isobel Mackinnon, performed by Anya Tate-Manning.
——— Arts House, Melbourne, Australia (September 14–21, 2018).
——— Old Lab, Summerhall, Edinburgh Festival Fringe, Scotland, UK (July 31–August 25, 2019).
——— Riverside Paramatta, Sydney, Australia (October 10–12, 2019).

Te Rēhia Theatre

Black Ties (by John Harvey and Tainui Tukiwaho): Premiered 2020 at Sydney Town Hall, Sydney Festival, Australia (January 10–18). Dir. Rachel Maza and Tainui Tukiwaho, co-production with ILBIJERRI Theatre Company.

Theatre Action

Once Upon a Planet: Premiered 1972 at Downstage, Wellington, NZ (June 6–17). Dir. Francis Batten.
——— NZ Trade Week, Suva, Fiji (1972).

Tikapa Productions

Not in Our Neighbourhood (by Jamie McCaskill): Premiered 2004 at Studio 77, Putahi Festival, Victoria University of Wellington, NZ (March 1). Dir. McCaskil, performed by Kali Kopae
——— Gilded Balloon Rose Theatre, Edinburgh Festival Fringe, Scotland, UK (August 1–26, 2018).
The Moa Show (by Jamie McCaskill): Premiered 2016 at BATS Theatre, NZ International Comedy Festival, Wellington, NZ (April 26-30). Dir. Craig Geenty, performed by McCaskill.
——— Gilded Balloon Teviot, Edinburgh Festival Fringe, Scotland, UK (August 1–27, 2018).

Trick of the Light Theatre

The Road that Wasn't There (by Ralph McCubbin Howell): Premiered 2012 at Free Sisters, Edinburgh Festival Fringe, Edinburgh, Scotland, UK (August). Dir. Hannah Smith.
——— Zanetti Productions, Assembly Roxy Upstairs, NZ at Edinburgh, Edinburgh Festival Fringe, Edinburgh, UK (August 3–27, 2017). [Also toured to Adelaide and Perth, Australia, 2016 and London, UK, 2018]

The Bookbinder (by Ralph McCubbin Howell): Premiered 2014 at Arty Bees Bookshop, NZ Fringe, Wellington, NZ (February 19–March 1, 2014). Dir. Hannah Smith.

—— Assembly Roxy Downstairs, Edinburgh Festival Fringe, Scotland, UK (August 6–31, 2015).

—— The Cellar, Pleasance Courtyard, Edinburgh Festival Fringe, Scotland, UK (August 3–28, 2016). [Also toured to Australia, England, USA, Canada, South Africa]

Beards! Beards! Beards! (by Ralph McCubbin Howell): Premiered 2015 at Circa Theatre, Wellington, NZ (March 16–21, 2015). Dir. Hannah Smith.

—— Assembly Roxy Upstairs, Edinburgh Festival Fringe, Scotland, UK (August 4–28, 2016) [Also toured to Salisbury and Brighton, 2016]

Tröll: Premiered 2018 at BATS Theatre, Wellington, NZ (April 3–7). Dir. Charlotte Bradley.

—— Demonstration Room, Summerhall, Edinburgh Festival Fringe, Scotland, UK (July 31–August 11, 2019).

—— Riverside Theatre, Spot on Children's Festival, Paramatta, Australia (October 3–4, 2019). [Also toured to Perth, 2019]

Trouble

Bleach (with Boilerhouse): Premiered 1999 at Shed 6, Queen's Wharf (March 4–20). Dir. Andrew Foster, Paul Pinson, Jo Randerson.

—— Edinburgh Festival Fringe, Scotland, UK (August, 1999). [Also presented at Tramway Festival of Site Specific Theatre, Glasgow, September, 1999]

Urale, Makerita

Frangipani Perfume: Premiered 1997 at BATS Theatre, Wellington, NZ (December 16–23). Dir. Erolia Ifopa.

—— Playroom, Pasifika Styles Festival, University of Cambridge, England, UK (May 29–30, 2007). Dir. Rachel House. [Also toured to Canada in 2006 and Australia in 2007]

—— Laboratory Theatre, Leeward Theatre, Leeward Community College, Ala Ike, Pearl City, Hawai'i, USA (September 17–26, 2015). Dir. Ashley DeMoville.

Van Horn, David

Apocalypse Z (with Simon London): Premiered 2013 at Aotea Square, Auckland, NZ (April 12–17). Dir. Andrew Foster, produced by Royale Productions. [Subsequently titled *Zombie: Red Zone* in Christchurch, NZ, 2014]

———— *The Generation of Z: Edinburgh* [retitled] (with Simon London and Benjamin Farry): Assembly George Square, NZ at Edinburgh, Edinburgh Festival Fringe, Scotland, UK (July 31–August 25, 2014).

———— *The Generation of Z: Apocalypse* [retitled]: Dept. W, Whitechapel, London, England, UK (April 4–July 19, 2015).

Wendt, Albert

The Songmaker's Chair: Premiered 2003 at Maidment Theatre, Auckland, NZ (September 13–27). Dir. Nathaniel Lees.

———— Kumu Kahua Theatre, Honolulu, Hawai'i (March 16–April 15, 2006). Dir. Dennis Carroll.

White Face Crew

La Vie Dans Une Marionette (by Jarod Rawiri, Justin Haiu and Tama Jarman): Premiered 2013 at Basement Theatre, Auckland Fringe, NZ (February 28–March 3).

———— Gilded Balloon at the Museum, NZ at Edinburgh, Edinburgh Festival Fringe, Scotland, UK (August 2–28, 2017).

Index

Taylor & Francis Group
an **informa** business

Taylor & Francis eBooks

www.taylorfrancis.com

A single destination for eBooks from Taylor & Francis
with increased functionality and an improved user
experience to meet the needs of our customers.

90,000+ eBooks of award-winning academic content in
Humanities, Social Science, Science, Technology, Engineering,
and Medical written by a global network of editors and authors.

TAYLOR & FRANCIS EBOOKS OFFERS:

A streamlined
experience for
our library
customers

A single point
of discovery
for all of our
eBook content

Improved
search and
discovery of
content at both
book and
chapter level

REQUEST A FREE TRIAL
support@taylorfrancis.com

 Routledge
Taylor & Francis Group

 CRC Press
Taylor & Francis Group